Mind-Forg'd Manacles

Mind-Forg'd Manacles

Slavery and the English Romantic Poets

Joan Baum

ARCHON BOOKS

1994

First published 1994 as an Archon Book,
an imprint of The Shoe String Press, Inc.,
North Haven, Connecticut 06473

Baum, Joan, 1937–
Mind-forg'd manacles: slavery and
the English romantic poets/Joan Baum.
p.   cm.
Includes bibliographical references (p.) and index.
ISBN 0-208-02187-6
1. English poetry—19th century—History and criticism.
2. Slavery and slaves in literature.
3. Romanticism—Great Britain.
I. Title.
PR575.S53B38   1994
821'.709353—dc20   93-45722
                                    CIP

The paper used in this publication
meets the minimum requirements of
American National Standard for Information Science—
Permanence of Paper for Printed Library Materials,
ANSI Z39.48-1984. ∞

Book design by Abigail Johnston

Printed in the United States of America

To Jim

Contents

Preface		*ix*
Acknowledgments		*xiii*
1	Bristol 1795	1
2	The West Country 1798	28
3	Grasmere 1807	57
4	Barbary 1816	80
5	Hampstead 1819	102
6	Exile 1822	136
7	Rydal 1833	162
	Notes	181
	List of Works Cited	235
	Index	247

Preface

Although I didn't know it at the time, this book began a number of years ago when I handed out a syllabus to my students, most of them juniors and seniors at an open admissions college of The City University of New York. A handful had elected to take the course because it was required of them as English majors, but the majority were nonmajors who needed to complete their area requirements in the humanities. "The English Romantic Poets" fit into their schedules.

It became apparent when we went over titles and names, that many of the students were seeing "Byron" and "Shelley" for the first time. Some knew that "Wordsworth" was a poet but no more than that. Surprising to me then (though perhaps it should not have been in a university where Caribbean students constitute a significant portion of a growing nonwhite population) the name "Toussaint L'Ouverture" elicited ready response. The students seemed curious: why did Wordsworth write a poem about Toussaint? Later in the semester when I gave a "guest lecture" at the college on the 1802 sonnets to Toussaint and a Negro passenger Wordsworth met on the Dover ferry coming back from France, the room was full. Students from the Haitian Club were in attendance, and several came up to me afterward, friends and relatives in tow, wanting to know more about this "old-fashioned

English man" who had taken an interest in the blacks of St. Domingue. A colleague from Morocco, new to the English department and somewhat aloof, began talking to me about the poets and what they knew of colonial slavery and the slave trade. One day, after a discussion on the spread of the Haitian revolution from the northern provinces, he extended a gracious invitation to attend a voodoo ceremony in Brooklyn (I respectfully declined).

In preparation for another chance to teach the poets, I carefully vetted the reading list. The temptation was, in the buzzword of subsequent years, to make the poets "politically correct," to suggest that the sympathies and compassion they felt for the outcast and the oppressed were anticipations of Marxism, feminism, and various movements for emancipation; to show, in effect, that these "dead white males" should remain big guns in the literary canon because they were "correct" and "relevant."

Coleridge's little-known essay "On the Slave Trade" (1795) would replace chapters on poetic subject matter and style in *Biographia Literaria*; Shelley and Blake would get more representation than Byron and Keats. The times were symbolically momentous for blacks and for Britain—The passage of the Abolition Act in 1807 and in 1833 legislation outlawing slavery in the British colonies helped shape the future world. What did the poets think of the antislavery movement? Why with their poetic effusions to Liberty, Equality, and Fraternity did they not speak out more against slavery and the slave trade, abominations Shelley called "the deepest stain upon civilized man"? The questions were provocative. They were also misguided to the extent that I was asking defensively why the poets had not been abolitionists and more active participants in the literary drive to end slavery.

It was C. L. R. James's fierce narrative of Toussaint and the Haitian Revolution in *The Black Jacobins* that set my narrative direction, for James goes beyond political and military events to examine motives, culture, newspaper accounts, economic conditions. The result is a passionate story of international politics and a cool analysis of the seductions of power, a diatribe against totalitarianism and racism to be sure, but also a subtle inducement to keep an eye on revolutionaries and reformers as well. In his preface, James alludes to Wordsworth without identifying him. The reference is natural, inevitable, for James is part of the Romantic tradition. His Toussaint could have easily been the subject of a Romantic drama or epic about a noble savage who wrests freedom for his enslaved countrymen only to become enslaved by his own "mind-forg'd manacles." James, who loved English and American literature, appreciated the difference between ideas and ideology, between poetry and propaganda. His own life bore witness to the poets' observations that political revolution alone could not lead to an evolution in consciousness or humanity. Only imagination—not legislation—could make and keep people free.

It was a difficult moral, intellectual, and aesthetic struggle the poets initiated, because it was so thoroughly radical; and in the end they were unwilling to take satisfaction in the comfort of false or even partially true solutions. Their separate but similar responses, I came to think, had implications that were both important and cautionary.

Acknowledgments

I am deeply grateful to those whom I know only through their writings but who graciously answered my letters, and more than once. I would also like to thank colleagues—Alan Cooper of the department of English, York College CUNY, for advising me to rethink early stirrings; Stanley Engerman of the department of history and economics at the University of Rochester, who generously commented on an early draft, and Donald H. Reiman, editor of *Shelley and His Circle*, who read the completed manuscript with his usual meticulous care. What errors remain are mine alone. Although it is impossible to name all the librarians and archivists, here and in England, who helped me sort out problems or who sent me material, their assistance is reflected in the bibliography. I am also appreciative of patient family and friends, but most of all I would like to express indebtedness to my publisher and editor James Thorpe III whose quirky, quarrelsome, uproarious, unsentimentally honest and affectionately encouraging letters during the years this work was in progress were truly inspirational.

I wander thro' each charter'd street,
Near where the charter'd Thames does flow
And mark in every face I meet
Marks of weakness, marks of woe.

In every cry of every Man,
In every Infant's cry of fear,
In every voice; in every ban,
The mind-forg'd manacles I hear

How the Chimney-sweeper's cry
Every blackning Church appals,
And the hapless Soldier's sigh
Runs in blood down Palace walls

But most thro' midnight streets I hear
How the youthful Harlot's curse
Blasts the new-born Infant's tear
And blights with plagues the Marriage hearse.

William Blake, "*London*"
SONGS OF EXPERIENCE

CHAPTER I

Bristol

1795

THE NORTHWESTERLIES BLEW IN across the channel with the June rain, whipping clean wind into the holds.[1] At rest, their massive hulls herded into port, the ships dominated the landscape. A few days earlier, sails thin and sere, they had glided listlessly up river from the sea, lumbering with the current, coming home from their perilous night journey.[2] The carpenters had long since rearranged the storage areas for rum, tobacco, sugar, spices, coffee, cacao—the usual stuff that replaced the human cargo, once it was unloaded in the West Indies. But the smell was still there, dyed into the wood—the odor of men, women, and children jammed together in sweat and blood, the heat and stench of diseased bodies rotting the very planks of the ship, though the suffocated and dead had been weeded out from the living every morning, and the decks washed down.[3]

Berthed now where the Avon snaked its way into the heart of the city as the River Froom, the ships also attracted the attention of the curious who wanted to see where the "black ivory" had been stowed, the slaves stashed "heel and point, like logs" as the ships made their way westward across the Atlantic. By the time the tourists arrived, however, most of the crew would have already left for the taverns, perhaps the Black Boy inn. The return of a slaver to its port city signaled hard-drinking time. A certain young poet on his way to give a lecture against the slave trade would have passed such sailors warily.

Though they might deny it, the wealthy sons of commerce sauntering by, "Bristowa's citizens," well understood the reach of "the beneficial system," as it was sometimes called. The "thirst of idle gold" which had driven their fathers and grandfathers to Africa and the West Indies had made Bristol in the early eighteenth century the leading slave-trading port in the country, indeed in the world.[4] So pervasive was the business of "Guinea Cargo," so natural a part of the life of the city, that it was not surprising to find even opponents of the slave trade involved in it in some way. The emancipationist James Stephen, for example (brother-in-law of the famous abolitionist and Member of Parliament William Wilberforce), was an associate of one Thomas Leyland, the most important slave-ship owner and merchant in Liverpool, and Leyland was a friend of William Roscoe (1753–1831), an "intrepid enemy of the slave trade," as Herman Melville would admiringly refer to him.[5] So immediate were the associations of West Indian trade with the Traffick, that Thomas De Quincey would declare in his *Autobiographic Sketches* that for the very reason his father was known to have been in "foreign" trade as a "West India merchant," serving in Jamaica and St. Kitts, it was necessary to "acquit his memory of any connection with the slave trade, by which so many fortunes were made at that era in Liverpool. . . ."[6] "Far from lending himself even by a *passive* concurrence to this most memorable abomination," De Quincey insisted, his father had been a conscientious protester and "strictly abstained from the use of sugar in his own family." Of course, De Quincey was looking back to the days before Abolition, when it would have been unusual to find a West India merchant *not* involved in the slave trade. As the docks of Bristol or Liverpool could testify, such was the promise of African commerce that even pleasure sloops were sometimes fitted out as "slavers." To be sure, telltales fluttered in the wind, signaling change, but Abolition was still twelve years away, Emancipation thirty-eight. In 1795 the breeze of freedom was still offshore, and then rippling only on the surface of the sea.

"Mr. Slave-Trade Clarkson," as De Quincey would later designate the indefatigable abolitionist, visited the slave ports regularly, stalking the "sickly," "ulcerated" seamen to their pubs to question them. Particularly when a slaver had just returned from its hellish journey, there would be dreadful tales to recount about the Middle Passage. In Liverpool, where every seventh house sold liquor, Thomas Clarkson sensed a "more hardened" crew than in Bristol, but the threat of speaking out against the slave trade in any slave-port town was formidable.[7] The former slave ship officer turned abolitionist and poet, Edward Rushton (1756–1814), adding his voice to the growing number of confessional narratives of the day, remembered that "to speak irreverently of the King, or even to deny the existence of a God" in the years leading up to Abolition were "in the town of Liverpool, venial offences," compared with the "atrocity of condemning the sale and purchase of human flesh."[8] Whether owing to smaller size or longer intellectual tradition, however, Bristol was also home to inquiring minds and crusading spirits.

It was in Bristol, in fact, that Clarkson had begun his abolition work, looking into the grisly return of the slave ship *Brothers*, with thirty-two dead mariners and a mutilated black on board.[9] "Similar barbarities" were reported for other slave ships, but in spite of such horrors, "the common talk of the city," slave-ship captains usually kept their commands, and business went on as usual. A decade later to the month, *Felix Farley's Bristol Journal* quietly announced under "Shipping News" the arrival of the *Brothers*. Back on land, seamen conveniently forgot the nightmare of the Middle Passage, which could include throwing live men overboard and cannibalism as a way of managing dwindling supplies.[10] But because they needed money, and most often when they were drunk, the sailors would succumb and sign on again for another journey. At the inns where he would stay, and in the taverns where he went to interview, Clarkson would listen to such men defend the slave trade "with great warmth," toast its success, and accuse him of trying to destroy the city "and all its glory"—not to mention the nation and empire. "Horrible facts" were in "everybody's mouth," Clarkson recorded in his diary, but still, merchants and captains were reluctant to testify for fear of having "their houses pulled down" and being shamed as "public instruments in the annihilation of the trade" and their city.[11] Clarkson was well aware that some who knew about his midnight crusades along Marsh Street might lay waiting for him, but he persevered. To advance the cause of abolition in Bristol in the late eighteenth century might not be as threatening as it was in Liverpool, but there was peril. Particularly for a poet pledged to speak truth "at all times, but more especially at those times, when to speak Truth is dangerous," it took some courage to walk along the darkening quay, but by June 16, 1795, Samuel Taylor Coleridge had already set a course of dead reckoning against the slave trade.[12]

Twenty-three, dreamy, round-faced, with long, pendulous hair broadstroking his forehead, Coleridge was said to be a spellbinding speaker.[13] In a poem that fall he would recreate the "summer's evening hour" in Bristol, air misty and "loaded with vapours," the spars and shrouds of nearby ships angled against the sky.[14] The week had been relatively quiet in the harbor, the papers noted, many ships having "entered out," and of the several still in port, most were not slavers but merchantmen and coasters, watched over by "many a dozing Tar / Rude cradled on the mast." It was a balmy scene, but appearances could be deceiving. Bristol streets were treacherous in many ways. "Worse paved than those of any other city in England" and never cleaned, they could also be traps after midnight, when the feeble oil lamps ran out and warehouse watchmen looked the other way—decrepit, inefficient members of the Bristol Corporation, "suspected of conniving at nocturnal offences."[15] It had been such a hazy June evening in Liverpool eight years earlier when Clarkson, picking his "melancholy" way on horseback to the Seven Stars inn, bells pealing, fog rolling in, had trembled at the mission before him— "to subvert one of the branches of the commerce of the great place." The "slave-merchants of Liverpool fly over the heads of the slave merchants of Bristol, as vultures over carrion crows," Coleridge wrote to his friend Tom Poole, but Coleridge also knew, from the days of the French Revolution, that mobs anywhere could be volatile, especially if they contained knots of women—a sure sign of impending political violence.[16] A lecture against the slave trade could easily spark trouble.

There had been difficulty earlier in the year, when he had "endeavored to disseminate Truth" in "A Moral and Political Lecture On the Present War."[17] Though exasperation appears to have triumphed over fear, at least in his recounting of the incident years afterward, Coleridge had already begun questioning the wisdom of speaking out against repressive government policies. In 1794, to his friend George Dyer, he had written how he had been greeted at some of his lectures: "Mobs and Mayors, Blockheads and Brickbats, Placards and Press gangs" had leagued in horrible conspiracy against him, and two or three "uncouth and unbrained Automata," full of fury and determination, had even threatened his life. "*Genus infirmum*," he joked, the lower orders scarcely restrained from attacking the house in which the "damned Jacobine was sawing away," but the experience made him momentarily doubt his purpose.[18] Was the good he was intending with his lectures "proportionate to the Evil" he seemed to be engendering? The owners of the Assembly coffee house that June night might well have been asking themselves a similar question. Increasingly nervous, tavern and assembly-room proprietors were growing reluctant to lease their premises to potential troublemakers.

Second now to Liverpool, but still a powerful slave port, Bristol had become a favorite retirement area for West Indian merchants and ex-slave traders. Jane Austen subtly drew on this fact in her fiction. In *Emma* (1816), Mrs. Elton, whose brother-in-law Mr. Suckling made his money in Bristol, protests too much when Jane Fairfax, sniffing out slave-trade connections, rejects the supercilious offer of help. She is confident of getting her own position, she says. The exchange is telling. There are places in town, "[o]ffices for the sale—not quite of human flesh—but of human intellect," Jane declares. Mrs. Elton is taken aback: "Oh! my dear, human flesh! You quite shock me; if you mean a fling at the slave-trade, I assure you Mr. Suckling was always rather a friend to the abolition." Jane carefully replies that she "did not mean, she was not thinking of the slave trade," but of the "governess" trade, "widely different certainly as to the guilt of those who carry it on; but as to the greater misery of the victims, I do not know where it lies."[19] Then, as later, the dictates of class required a certain distance from the vulgarity of financial transactions. The Traffick was, after all, still trade. And business was business. Even Josiah Wedgwood (d. 1795), the famous potter who designed the official antislavery medallion, did not at first inscribe his name on his work, for fear, it was said, of antagonizing wealthy patrons. Wedgwood had been in the pottery business for nineteen years with one Thomas Bentley (d. 1780), a "Liverpool merchant."[20] Inspired by Cowper's "The Negro's Complaint" (1781), the most popular abolition song of the period, the Wedgwood medallions showed a black figure in chains and contained the motto, "Am I Not a Man and a Brother?" The poets in 1795 unhesitatingly thought they knew the answer to the question.[21]

Between dry goods and human cargo, West African commerce was profitable business, and Bristol merchants made out well enough to earn a reputation for sharp dealing. "The people of Bristol seem to sell everything that can be sold," including their cross, eagle, and now the cliffs over the river, Southey noted, and even the pious and philanthropic Hannah More (1745–1833), running schools for the indigent in town with her sister, was well aware of the "true spirit" of the local businessman. Once, excusing a thin and tardy response to an eloquent letter from Horace Walpole, she compared herself to the Bristol trader who sends "worthless beads, and bits of glass" in exchange for "ivory and gold dust." Of course, the abolitionist author of the 1788 poem "Slavery" knew that slaves were traded in Bristol. In an earlier note to Walpole, she wrote how unnerved she had been recently, seeing a black woman forcibly recaptured and put on board a slave ship bound for the West Indies.[22] It was not that Bristol was unusual in tolerating such activities, but that slave trading was so pervasive a business there. In truth, however, given the city's theaters, schools, and knots of young literary intellectuals, it could also be said that Bristol was a growing center of radicalism and reform. Just four years earlier, when a motion to end the slave trade had been defeated in Parliament, the city had celebrated with a half-day closing. Yet it was in Bristol that a cadre of support had developed for the American Revolution, and that abolition found ready voice.

Coleridge had friends in town, including the bookseller and publisher Joseph Cottle (1770–1853), whose shop at High and Corn Streets had become a gathering place for young poets— "unemployed intellectuals," a descendant of Cottle would affectionately call them.[23] A second shop, at No. 5 Wine Street, had darker associations. Slaves were concealed there underground, it was whispered, along with Jacobin spies—rumors that showed the ease with which abolition was linked to revolution, talk of moral mandates interpreted as undermining the economy. The situation would reverse itself a few years later when Napoleon's orders to restore slavery in the West Indies would free the English abolition movement from the "taint of Jacobinism" and give it new life as a patriotic force.[24] In 1795, however, Bristol merchants, insisting on their "Birth right" to do business, not on the universal rights of man, declared they were not so much in favor of the repugnant slave trade as against the international disadvantage of immediately ending it. Everyone, it would seem, had a rationalization for continuing the Traffick, though there was no compelling reason to offer one, since it was legal. Clergy who held shares in slave-related enterprises pointed to the need to stand against "foreign," meaning French, policies of heretical republicanism and religious dissent. Dissenters, known to be minor partners in the trade, defended their role in preventing bad conditions from being worse. And there were the rich and powerful shipowners whose business managers, they said, never told them how much their companies were involved.

Of course, some anomalies were deliberately left unexplained: The Society of Friends disowned the Bristol Quaker Samuel Galton for "fabricating and selling instruments of war," but Galton continued to attend Society meetings anyway, and the Birmingham firm of Farmer & Galton went on providing guns to slave traders on the Gold Coast and their African accomplices, who were eager enough to sell their own people. "For what were simple bow and savage spear / Against the arms which must be wielded here?" as Byron would sarcastically comment.[25] Although shipowners could be counted on to oppose abolition out of fear of personal loss, merchants sensed they might still do business, even if prohibited by legislation. And indeed, the various measures passed by Parliament in 1811 and 1818 to enforce the 1807 Abolition Act would only prove the shrewdness of their intuition. By then, however, concerns other than "getting and spending" would begin to make themselves felt in the antislavery movement, and the very poets who had spoken out for abolition in 1795 would become advocates for going slow on emancipation. Eyewitness accounts by repentant slave-ship captains might wring heartfelt sympathy in Parliament and London drawing rooms, but the hearts of the compassionate could also beat with fear of giving advantage to the satanic enemy across the sea, or bleed only for poor Christians held as slaves on the Barbary Coast. That the two slaveries, black and white, might be related and arise from similar impulses generally escaped notice. Abolitionists were intent on petition drives, abolition poets with crafting diatribes against oppression at a distance. At least two years before Coleridge's Lecture on the Slave Trade, Blake made the essential connection, but not many were reading him: "In every cry of every Man, / In every Infant's cry of fear, / In every voice, in every ban, / The mind-forg'd manacles I hear."[26] That many of the children were black would have come as unwelcome or indifferent news to most of Coleridge's Bristol audience that June. Outside London, blacks in Britain were a shadowy presence in the late eighteenth century. Inside, despite their numbers, they were in effect invisible.

By 1795, thousands of Negroes crowded the streets and back alleys of the great city—beggars, criminals, children who had not had the smallpox and were therefore unsuitable as domestics or playthings for the upper class. Docile, a world unto themselves, unseen by government ministers and even by most abolitionist Members of Parliament, the Negroes of England were far removed in the public mind from the surly blacks and mulattoes of Jamaica and Dominica, whose rebellions were increasingly being reported in the press. Public, Parliament, newspapers, all were alarmed. Though abolition would steadily continue to attract support, it would advance slowly, as fears of war and domestic unrest incited opposition and muted the effect of the petition drives whose numbers seemed to indicate imminent success: 50 in the early 1780s, 102 by 1788, the year of Byron's birth, 519 in 1792, the year Shelley was born. By 1795, abolition bills were continually stalled or defeated on amendment. Coleridge perceptively sought cause beyond the obvious. It was a "falling off of zeal in the friends of Abolition" that concerned him, he wrote Clarkson a few years later, the cooling of moral passion among the sympathizers that prompted his Lecture On the Slave Trade. And so it had been his hope that fiery words might counter the specious arguments in favor of the Traffick, expose the true causes of opposition, and reawaken the public to a full sense of the trade's "fervor and the horror." A speech to rouse the troops, though he knew he would have to tread the boards carefully. The curious who were poking around the slave ships at the Bristol docks were not necessarily the converted, the politically powerful in the movement not always the politically consistent. Abolition was still twelve years down the road.

The topic that June night was in fact not a new one for Coleridge. Abolition as a literary subject had attracted him as early as 1792, when he was a "Cantab" well versed in Greek and Latin. That year, his first at Cambridge, he won the Browne gold medal for a hundred-line poem in Greek, an "Ode Against the Slave

Trade," which he regarded for a while as his "chef d'oeuvre in poetical composition." The topic had been set by the university—"Sors Misera Servorum in Insulis Indiae Occidentalis [On the Unfortunate Lot of Slaves in the West Indian Islands]," but Coleridge brought to the exercise more than might have been required by a theme of dying slaves redeemed in heaven.[27] "O Death," the Ode begins, "welcome respite for a race yoked to misery, passport out of hell; to die is to be set free." Ironically, the very year the topic was set, drums were carrying a similar message along the voodoo routes of revolution in the northern hills of St. Domingue, unnerving the white planters at Le Cap and the functionaries in Paris. A university competition on the slave trade might therefore have suggested a moderate, temporizing tone, but what Coleridge delivered in his Ode was in some ways strikingly incautious and provocatively extravagant: images of burning heat and plague set in poetic lines that groan with evocations of despair. Released from life at last, "saved" from their misery, slaves tell of "Islands, full of murderous excess, abounding in evils ill to look upon, where Hunger is sick and a bloody blow roars." Overdone, repetitive, numbing at times with rhetorical insistence, the Ode overcomes stereotype where it turns from suffering victims and addresses those who "revel" in the evil they perpetuate and, by extension, those who bear silent witness and do nothing. The emphasis is on punishment, not crime. Repent or suffer certain revenge and everlasting hellfire, a speaker warns. The radical political leader John Thelwall saw truly into the heart of things when he noted that Coleridge in his early poetic years could be violent, sanguinary, a "downright zealous leveller and indeed in one of the worst senses of the word . . . a Jacobin, a man of blood."[28]

Some years later Coleridge conceded syntactical weaknesses in the Ode—his own mentor claimed to have detected 134 errors—and in a letter to Cottle referred to the poem as stylistically "contemptible." But he never repudiated its antislavery sentiment. That was his "first public Effort" in the cause of abolition, he would proudly write to Clarkson in 1808, though Clarkson may have wondered about the effectiveness of a public effort in the form of a Sapphic Ode in Greek.[29] The lines, nonetheless, clearly showed Coleridge's position on the slave trade at a politically risky time. On July 4, 1792, the day after the Senate House walls reverberated with his Attic diatribe, the *Times* was gleefully reporting the triumph of government "patriots" over pro-French "incendiaries," also known as "reformers."[30] Cleverly, Coleridge has a narrator near the end of the Ode invoke the name of Wilberforce, staid "herald of Pity," rather than that of Clarkson, radical worker in the field. Wilberforce, conservative M.P. for Yorkshire, was the establishment's man, and by May 1794 the establishment consisted of both Whigs and Tories fueled by fear and patriotism, who supported suspension of the writ of habeas corpus and called for state trials and imprisonment. By 1795, the country had grown even more jittery.

The Assembly coffee house, not far from the docks, was only a short walk from Britain's oldest public library, on King Street. Here, along with Robert Southey (1774–1843), Coleridge borrowed narratives and tracts on the slave trade. Records show that volumes checked out by the one poet were often returned by the other, with annotations in both hands.[31] Those who knew both poets would therefore not have been surprised that Southey's ballad "The Sailor Who Had Served in the Slave Trade" (October 1798) would call to mind "The Rime of the Ancient Mariner," written a few months earlier, or that Coleridge's ballad would bear traces of Southey's popular *Poems Concerning the Slave Trade*. Coleridge and Southey moved in the same literary and political atmosphere. Both had written for the *Cambridge Intelligencer*, both were associated with the *Morning Post*, newspapers with a decided anti-government stance, and both saw themselves as necessary advocates for abolition—though not as abolitionists. Years later, defending Southey from the charge of having written a seditious play (*Wat Tyler*) during the heady days of the French Revolution, Coleridge would comment, "Who in the Devil's Name ever thought of reading Poetry for political or practical purposes till these Devil's Times that *we* live in?" The pronoun emphasis was more telling than might have seemed. Coleridge and Southey were political poets, not versifying propagandists. Still, journalism would serve long after poetic impulse would fail. Though years later Coleridge would write Clarkson that his claim as an author was "feeble" in comparison with Southey's, "whose twelve Sonnets on the Slave Trade were not only among his best, but likewise among his most popular productions," it was more a confession of his own indolence than a comparative literary judgment. Perhaps by 1808 it was also an apology that his poetry had not sold well or been admired.[32] Southey, of course, would steer a literary and political course unencumbered by guilt or "holy dread" and sail into the laureateship.

The easy discourse between the two poets had begun in 1794, when they met at Oxford and joined forces to establish Pantisocracy, a utopian scheme for "friends of liberty" destined for the banks of the Susquehanna—and for abandonment. They had also joined families, an even less promising enterprise, when Southey became joyously engaged to Edith Fricker, an intended pantisocratic bride, and Coleridge the reluctant suitor of Sara Fricker, a sister. Eventually they would see their intellectual partnership through "Chill'd Friendship's dark disliking eye," but the summer of 1795 they were of one mind, if not soul, on the subject of abolition.[33] They had recently discussed Anthony Benezet (1713–1784), for example, the Philadelphia Quaker, merchant, philanthropist, and author of *A Caution and Warning to Britain and Her Colonies on the Calamitous State of Enslaved Negroes* (1766) and *A Historical Account of Guinea* (1771). And they both knew well Clarkson's essay *On the Impolicy of the African Slave Trade* (1788) and C. B. Wadström's *Observations on the Slave Trade* (1789), an account of an authentic voyage to the Guinea coast, although Wadström needlessly worried in his preface about divulging information that might better be "buried in silence."[34] *Observations* was a confessional slave trade narrative, a genre much in vogue in the late eighteenth century due in part to an appetite for travel literature prompted by commercial journeys to the East. In truth, what Wadström "divulged" was rather typical—descriptions of the horrors of the Middle Passage and slave colonies. It is doubtful that his familiar litany of man's inhumanity to man struck a moving blow among authorities, though it might indeed have created the impression of having done so in Parliament.

In addition to such firsthand accounts Coleridge may also have seen the manuscript version of Captain John Gabriel Stedman's *Narrative of a Five Years' Expedition Against the Revolted Negroes of Surinam, in Guiana, on the Wild Coast of South America,* 1796, a remarkable compendium of facts about the slave trade and native lore and an acknowledgment of Stedman's love affair with Joanna, a slave girl. Since 1790 the book had been in the hands of the radical London bookseller Joseph Johnson, and sixteen of its remarkable engravings were executed by Blake, who had contributed £10 to the London Abolition Society and was Stedman's only illustrator to subscribe to the *Narrative*.[35] The pale-colored plates are brutally disarming: "A Negro Hung Alive by the Ribs to a Gallows," "The Execution of Breaking on the Rack," "Flagellation of a Female Samboe Slave." In some cases, Blake went further than Stedman, turning the author's implicit plea for all nations to support one another into satiric commentary. The plate "Europe Supported by Africa and America" depicts the darker sisters, Africa and America [Indian], wearing gold slave bracelets, while Europe is shown sporting a string of pearls. The published version of the *Narrative*, less forthcoming about Joanna, could still shock in the amount of detail Stedman unflinchingly offered about life on a slave plantation. Ironically, though hardly unexpected to those who read him carefully, Stedman adamantly refused the label of abolitionist, and his thoughtless gift of thanks to Blake for the illustrations probably occasioned no surprise—a goose and . . . sugar. It was the English appetite for that "nefarious ingredient" sugar, along with demon rum, of course, that was held mainly responsible for the continuation of the slave trade.[36]

Several years after the passage of the Abolition Bill the London *Morning Chronicle* snidely (and safely removed in time) would remind readers of the days when the "mercenary habit [of the Traffick] forced the production of sugar beyond the limits of consumption and sale." Thank God that time was past, and that Parliament and the people had "yielded" something "to the reclamations of humanity," albeit with "bad grace"; thank God they interdicted "the further robbery of the people of Africa" while only "continuing the slavery of those they possessed."[37] The observation would have been enough to drive Blake back to the engraving board, were it not that he had already taken on the friends of Satan in his poetic Prophecies, even if few read them and fewer still understood. By contrast, Coleridge's Lecture on the Slave Trade could not have been more "sugar-crystal" clear, so to speak.

The Lecture had been scheduled for 8 o'clock in the evening, but some in the audience might have wondered if the speaker, already notorious for a confusion of "time imaginary and time imaginary," as he would later entitle a poem, would even show up.[38] Years later, writing about his first acquaintance with the poet, Hazlitt would recall that once out strolling with him and asking about the subject of a lecture scheduled for the following day, Coleridge replied that "he had not even thought of the text, but should as soon as we parted."[39] Was this Coleridgean tendency to pass from subject to subject related to his inability "to keep on a strait line" when walking? mused Hazlitt. Not many in an audience, however, complained when time or topic went astray, for S.T.C. in fine frenzy was in fine form. A plain man at first glance, with wide mouth, thick lips, and "longish loose-growing half curling rough black hair," Coleridge "on the wing" was memorable. His stare then, almost vacant, was soon forgot: "you hear him speak for five minutes" and the plainness is gone, Dorothy Wordsworth wrote admiringly, though some could indeed be put off by his "slovenly appearance."[40] Need those who would liberate the mind look so libertine, the sympathetic Bristol *Observer* wondered, some time after the talk. Dedicated to taking account of young Bristoleans for purposes of recommending them "Worthy of Imitation, or otherwise," the *Observer* judged "Mr. C—" "Worthy," though it advised him to "appear with cleaner stockings in public" and comb his hair.[41] On matters intellectual, however, there was no equivocation: "Undaunted by the storms of popular prejudice, unswayed by magisterial influence, [Coleridge] spoke in public what none had the courage in this City to do before." The reference was to the Lecture on the Slave Trade.

Bristol itself had helped shape Coleridge's thoughts on the slave trade and deepen his feelings about abolition. From the dormer window of his rented room he would have seen "masts of ships—slavers, merchantmen, and men-of-war, lying in the pools and at the wharves. . . ." In town, the reality of the "inhuman Traffic" was evident everywhere as slave ships prepared themselves for their journeys, or when they returned, skeleton ribs backlit "suddenly against the sun."[42] Signs of the trade could also be found in notices of slave auctions, advertisements for runaways, announcements of the return of ship captains, mates, and surgeons with their "privilege" Negroes—the young blacks they got to keep, sell, or smuggle north to work in the mines or the homes of the wealthy. Other evidence was more grim, including shops that blatantly displayed slave-restraining mechanisms such as thumbscrews with torture keys and "African pacifiers," muzzles three feet long for the neck. Lest stalwart citizens deny the existence of such instruments, Stedman published illustrations of them, and Clarkson, who bought several in Liverpool, depicted them in his *History of the Slave Trade*, which Coleridge would enthusiastically review. There were also medical devices to force mouths open so owners would not lose their uninsured "property" to starvation. As Southey's own penitent mariner would tell it, "some were sulky of the slaves / And would not touch their meat, / So therefore we were forced by threats / And blows to make them eat" (stanza xvii of "The Sailor who had served in the Slave Trade," 1798).

It was not just that many people did not want to hear about the "enormities" of the slave trade, horrors which even the gloomy imagination of Dante would "scarcely have dared attribute to the Inhabitants of Hell," as Coleridge lectured. It was that they did not want to hear how they themselves were responsible, the good people of England, driven by "imaginary wants" for luxuries and prevented by lack of imagination from seeing that their pleasure was connected to others' pain. The Lecture on the Slave Trade revisited the idea of "The Aeolian Harp" (1794) that there is "one life within us and abroad." An expression there of Pantisocracy, the one life is now benevolence or "Natural Sympathy made permanent by an acquired Conviction, that the Interests of each and of all are one and the same." But its new interpretation that June night must have made many in the audience uncomfortable, for Coleridge boomed at them that it was not just slave captains and slaveholders, men of "darkened minds, and brutalized hearts," who were responsible for the slave trade, but they themselves—"you [who] profess yourselves Christians." The speaker's challenge was to awaken empathy: "Would *you* choose, that a slave merchant should incite an intoxicated Chieftain to make war on your Country, and murder your Wife and Children before your face, or drag them with yourself to the Market? Would you choose to be sold? to have the hot iron hiss upon your breasts, after having been crammed into the hold of a Ship with so many fellow-victims?"

Coleridge tacked a lot but did not sail beyond the general understanding. When he intoned sarcastically against the inane literary taste of the day for what seemed to him failed moral judgment, he drove points home with memorable, accessible imagery: "the citizen at the crowded feast is not nauseated by the stench and filth of the slave-vessel—the fine lady's nerves are not shattered by the shrieks! She sips a beverage sweetened with human blood, even while she is weeping over the refined sorrows of Werter."[43] The imagery may have come by way of the Welsh bard Morgannwg (Edward Williams), whose Cambridge bookshop was advertising East India sweets "uncontaminated with human gore," but its use to differentiate imagination from mere "imaginary wants" was distinctively Coleridgean.[44] In "Reflections on Having Left a Place of Retirement," composed a few months after the Lecture on the Slave Trade, Coleridge would return to the theme, indicting those who "sigh for Wretchedness, yet shun the Wretched" (l. 57). In the Lecture, the distinction is between sentimentality, which merely and temporarily excites the senses, and benevolence which "impels to action and is accompanied by self-denial." The lady crying over Goethe has merely the illusion of suffering, but the will to do good, true benevolence, comes from a deeper source. Coleridge sees benevolence as a motive force in poetry, related to imagination, sentimentality as related to immediate wants and superficial emotions. As he had written a year earlier (and somewhat pretentiously) to his brother George, a clergyman, "Slavery was an Abomination to every feeling of the Head and the Heart" but better than trying to get rid of the offense was placing attention on those "principles," the "necessary effect" of which would be to get rid of all slavery. Jesus did not advocate "Abolition," Coleridge lectured the Reverend Coleridge, but taught instead how man must prepare his mind to make slavery impossible.[45] In these early days of confident mood, before his genial spirits failed, Coleridge believed that imagination might be the power to effect such change.

The Lecture on the Slave Trade certainly suited Coleridge's sense of himself as sentinel of his country's soul. He dwells "anxiously" on the subject of abolition, he says, because he knows it has "insinuated in the minds of many, uneasy doubts respecting the existence of a beneficent Deity." It had been rumored that the Lecture would be Coleridge's last in a series of historical, theological, and political essays that he and Southey had agreed to give in Bristol. It was far from true. The Lecture would not even be Coleridge's last public statement on the slave trade. By June he had already determined to publish the Lecture in a periodical of his own devising to be called, appropriately enough, *The Watchman*. The decision had been made at the Rummer tavern on High Street, a point not lost, perhaps, on those who remembered his abolitionist urging of a boycott of sugar and rum, "the one useless and the other pernicious." Indeed, the essay "On the Slave Trade" was the Lecture slightly changed, but showing stronger connection between poet and journalist and conveying more the sense of an argument.

An opening passage quotes from the manuscript version of "Religious Musings," a "desultory poem written on the Christmas Eve of 1794." Hardly musings, the poem is more a denunciation of man as an acquisitive being wanting more than he needs, and thus inviting the "Miseries" and "Vices" that befall him. In 1796, "Religious Musings" would become one of the most important *Poems on Various Subjects* in Coleridge's first published collection of poetry. That year, in Birmingham to canvass subscriptions for *The Watchman*, Coleridge even button-holed a poor tallow-chandler and made him listen to a "spirited recitation" of the poem.[46] It haunted him. In the fall, writing "Reflections On Leaving a Place of Retirement," it was "Religious Musings" that seems to have been most on his mind as he lay dreaming away on a rose-leaf bed at Clevedon Cottage, while his "unnumbered brethren toil'd and bled" abroad (l.45). The image recalls the "unnumbered tribes" in "Religious Musings" who "toil and groan and bleed, hungry and blind" (ll. 241–42); men dragged across "A sea of blood bestrewed with wrecks, where mad / Embattling Interests on each other rush / With unhelmed rage!" (ll. 124–26). The Lecture on the Slave Trade echoes the plea of "Religious Musings" to the "Holy One" to rain wrath upon those who allow "Trade / Loud-laughing" to pack his bales with "human anguish."[47] Manuscript fed essay, essay fed poem. In the published version of "Religious Musings" (1796), the slave trade becomes even "more hideous" than war (l.140), and "[M]id groans and shrieks," packs bales with "living" anguish—a more stifling image than the earlier reference. Against syntax, convoluted and snarled, almost defying sense, a subject "I" strains after its verb, "would raise up," five lines away, as Biblical exhortation and abolitionist sentiment merge to create the fury of outrage. In "calmer moments," apparent in his "conversation" poems, where wild-working imagination is subdued by introductory and con-

cluding passages of domesticity, Coleridge would declare that
though redemption would be a "long and dark process," he had
the "firmest Faith that all things work together for the Good."
   It was Good Friday, in fact, March 25, 1796, when "On the
Slave Trade" appeared in *The Watchman*.[48] It was not a good day
for the forces of antislavery, the *Times* reporting another defeat
for an abolition bill. A motion in Parliament, just denied, had
called for the apprehension and trial of anyone in Africa or on
the high seas "carrying, transporting, exporting, or lading on
board any ship, boat, or other vessel . . . any negro or negroes,
slave or slaves." The motion had also demanded a complete ac-
counting "of all the vessels in the African Slave Trade, cleared
out from the Port of London [and Liverpool, Bristol, and Lan-
caster], from the year 1788," a move that would have flushed out
the slave traders from behind their desks in London. Naturally,
the Standing Committee of West India Planters and Merchants
was delighted with the turn-back vote, and the *Times*, not about
to bite the ministerial hand that fed it subsidies, hardly disap-
proved. If the editors had not intended to prejudice opinion that
day, the placement of news and advertisements was nonetheless
suggestive. An account of the defeated Wilberforce bill was run
alongside a report on continuing unrest in France, and on the
front page of the newspaper, where the ads appeared, an announcement for the sale of the 1796 Parliamentary Register,
"containing a very full and exact account of the [abolition] Debates," was placed near an advertisement for the *English Review*,
containing an account of Godwin's *Political Justice* (second edition)
and a summary of a recent treason trial. These, in turn, were
boxed up directly above an advertisement for a new book on "ve-
nereal complaints"—the "French" disease, as the English liked to
call it. The Watchman's beacon light in the essay "On the Slave
Trade" could not have beamed out across stormier seas.

Coleridge's essay opens with a restatement of objections to abolition, namely, that ending the slave trade would put England at a disadvantage with France. In response, Coleridge notes that French planters take the same point of view, thus ensuring that no one will make the first move. The standoff provokes an analogy: The inevitability of robbery in general does not mean that one man should therefore not be prevented by law from robbing. The tone then shifts, cool reasoning giving way to open contempt. A second objection to abolition, that slaves are happier in their West Indian confinement than back in Africa, is dismissed with sarcasm. Appropriating Wadström's mocking sentimental vision of "innocent and happy" natives untouched by corrupt Europeans, Coleridge acknowledges the "tyranny" of African chiefs seduced by greed into selling their own people. But in a consideration highly unusual for the day, he also points to the variety of skills and chores engaged in by the typical African, discerning therein an "acuteness of intellect" which the "[English] Mechanic whom the division of labor condemns to one simple operation is precluded from attaining." Though not positing a humanity common to the West Indian Negro and the English poor, Coleridge does take issue with the anti-abolition position that plantation slaves are at least as well off as the peasantry of England. That, Coleridge contends (prematurely), is the same as saying that the peasantry of England are as badly off as the Negro slaves, and were that so, the peasants would rebel (which, of course, they would soon do). As to the charge that abolition would mean loss of revenue, the Watchman is particularly incensed: What revenue! The spoils of war, which are then used for the improvement of mankind, to prevent the poor from drinking, the higher ranks from enjoying luxury, and all men from the infection of bribery? What about the financial losses due to the slave trade itself? he counters. Again, the answers came in mocking form: what about the ships and men lost at sea, lost to pirate raids, to disease, to the rigors of life on a slave ship? He was not even talking about black lives but white, reportedly one in ten, excluding the even greater number of officers and crew who remained in Africa and died. No, Coleridge feels certain, financial loss is not to be feared from abolition. Besides, he argues, following Adam Smith, men work harder if they are not coerced—the very point he would speak against years later during the debates over immediate emancipation. The essay "On the Slave Trade" strives to be effective rhetoric, though the Watchman knew that logic was no way to move against the Traffick. More forceful arguments, he recognized, were those directed at the pocketbook.

What kind of "injury" would planters sustain to their "property" the Watchman challenges, if abolition left estates and everything on them untouched, and only prevented owners from forcing Negroes to work? Coleridge was also well aware that though emancipation had not been the object of Wilberforce's recent bill, the very mention of men living like slaves "in a climate so unwholesome or beneath a usage so unnatural" that it was against the "universal law of life" would likely put the distasteful eventuality of emancipation in mind. Even the Mansfield Decision, in 1772, had pointed up the difference between slave trade and slavery, between abolition and emancipation. In denying the claim of an owner of an escaped slave who had jumped ship, Lord Mansfield had pointed out that the ruling did not mean that all slaves were thus automatically free. The decision, eloquent and compassionate, gave no comfort to the friends of the Negro. Besides, Lord Mansfield noted, emancipating 14,000 or 15,000 men at once by solemn opinion was setting the court to do Parliament's job, and such a prospect struck him as "much disagreeable in the effect it threatens."[49] The Watchman was undeterred: If not now, when? he asks, conflating the issues of slavery and the trade. We send officers to preach to Negroes about the rights of man and give them guns to assert those rights. Are planters worried about insurrections? They should be, he hints darkly, for slave "intrigues" will not be prevented by guns but only by "active humanity." On that note, the logician gave way to the moral philosopher.

In the final section of "On the Slave Trade," Coleridge rails against the "cosmetics with which our parliamentary orators have endeavoured to conceal the deformities of a commerce which is blotted all over with one leprosy of evil." Abolition bills already passed by the House of Commons lie "mangled and mutilated" by amendments, waiting for the House of Lords to kill them off altogether. But it is not just the planters' men in Parliament who cover up. Coleridge's indictment is clearly extended to the good Christian citizens in the coffee house, probably a more various and curious assembly that June night than readers of *The Watchman*, several months later. Coleridge's use of the first-person plural is calculated: Everyone is indicted: Misled by sentimentalism, a false sensibility that feeds paternalism, *we* fail to exercise "Natural Sympathy," and "to this grievous failing *we* must attribute the frequency of wars, and the continuance of the Slave-trade."[50] "Gracious God," he declaims, the slave trade authorizes enormities "at which a Caligula might have turned pale." The historical reference is deliberately deceiving, for Coleridge knows that slavery has been a convention of history and that Roman slaves of war, though slaves, were not therefore deprived of their humanity. But rhetoric may do what deduction may not. What if such "Fiends," slave traders, slave owners, are just the tyrants of the moment? What if man by nature is a "sordid solitary thing," as "Religious Musings" dared imagine, a "vicious and discontented *Animal*," as the essay speculates, not just God's creature capable of noble deeds? If so, government can go only so far in preventing evils like the slave trade. The "Watchman" was coming perilously close to denying his own logic, for if man was so full of sin, then petitioning Parliament to right moral wrongs would be "superfluous." A dangerous dialogue had begun between poet and journalist. Almost lost in the advocacy of the essay, the theme would persist and deepen in Coleridge's poetry. The blank-verse lyric, "Fears in Solitude" (1798) would conclude in sobering tones: what futility for those who, "groaning with restless enmity . . . expect / All change from change of constituted power; / As if a Government had been a robe / On which our vice and wretchedness were tagged / Like fancy-points and fringes. . . ." (ll. 161–65). Years later, a conservative Wordsworth, on the defensive for not supporting immediate emancipation, would inadvertently echo his old friend: "The world is running mad with the notion that all its evils are to be relieved by political changes, political remedies, political nostrums. . . ."[51]

Despite a sardonic comment some years later that the articles in his "obscure and short-lived periodical" at least found use as "winding sheets for herrings and pilchards," Coleridge thought enough of the concluding passage of the essay "On the Slave Trade" to reprint it later on in *Omniana*, and enough of abolition to continue the subject in the next issue of *The Watchman*.[52] On April 2, *Watchman* no. 5 contained a letter from one T.P., a "beloved friend" of the editor, who gives an account of a "dream" about the end of slavery. The editor thinks the letter particularly fine. He probably even solicited it, for the beloved friend was Tom Poole, Coleridge's landlord at the time at Nether Stowey and one who strongly shared his views on abolition. Poole, not incidentally, would have been another source of information about Bristol and the slave trade. The year T.P's "dream" appeared in *The Watchman*, Poole's sister Sarah, a frequent Coleridge correspondent, married a Mr. King of Acton, "a Bristol merchant in African goods," who most certainly would have been privy to details about the Traffick and trading on the Guinea coast. Indeed, the word "Guinea" itself, standing for both coin and territory, was suggestive of the broad commerce borne of Moneta (goddess of memory and money), queen of the mother lode of African trade, whose reign Keats would invoke several years later in *The Fall of Hyperion*. In any case, T.P.'s dream was an appropriate sequel to "On the Slave Trade," for it sought to allay fears being whipped up by the London papers that black "savages," once emancipated, would retaliate against their oppressors.[53] Recent reports of violence in St. Domingue dwelled on the torture and mutilation blacks were inflicting on whites and mulattoes. T.P. provided another picture. Even though he has "longed for the abolition of the slave-trade" since he has been "capable of reasoning," he writes, he "trembles" at the thought (who wouldn't?) that freed Negroes might turn vengeful. But what triumphs in the letter-dream is love. In a vision in the dream (the very nesting technique Coleridge would use in "Kubla Khan," employed here perhaps for protective political purposes), former slaves take T.P. to see a statue of their revolutionary hero, their Hampden, their Tell, their Washington. The references are sufficient for *Watchman* readers to rest assured that Toussaint L'Ouverture, the self-styled Napoleon of the West Indies, would prove humane. In T.P.'s dream, the revolution is over, freedom has been won, people sing, humanity prevails.[54] But what about that "vicious and discontented animal" Coleridge had coaxed out of its lair in the essay "On the Slave Trade"?

Despite T.P.'s promise of a better world, Coleridge heard in his inner ear ancestral voices prophesying war. By May 1796 he would declare dejectedly, "O Watchman! thou hast watched in vain!"—a cry of more than frustration at having been unable to sustain *The Watchman* beyond ten issues.[55] On December 31,

New Year's Eve, Coleridge followed poetic tradition by publishing an end-of-the-year reflection, but it was a far from comforting tribute to the old or new year. "Ode on the Departing Year" stands in dark contrast to the inane "Christmas Pyes" that the Poet Laureate, Henry Pye, and others had been offering.[56] In the "Ode on the Departing Year," Coleridge scorches his country with hellfire for the havoc of the last few years—for war, tyranny, conspiracy, and, "chief" among the perversions, multiplying merchants above the stars of heaven, for "Afric's wrongs, / Strange, horrible, and foul!" (ll.88–89). A note on the lines—as though the ferocious diction of the poem itself were not sufficient—calls attention to the "putrified fields of La Vendée" and the "unnumbered victims of [the] detestable Slave-Trade."[57] The ending is dire but ambiguous. The poet hurries away from the bleak vision—"In vain, in vain the Birds of warning sing—" but he holds out the slight possibility of change: England is "[n]ot yet enslaved, not wholly vile." Hope lies in removing not the chains of the slaves but the chains of the enslavers.

An internal drama had begun. Soon another "bird of warning" would make an appearance, following mariners on a wide, wide sea. Although Coleridge himself would not become the obsessive conscience he would create in "The Rime of the Ancient Mariner," his ballad would portray the inner force that lay behind the slave trade. There the bird of warning would cry in vain, and it would seem to Coleridge, as to Keats after him, that it might be, after all, a frighteningly seductive world without love, without compassion, a world in which "no birds sing."[58]

CHAPTER 2

The West Country
1798

THE WEST COUNTRY, south of the Bristol Channel, was not the most hospitable place for radicals in the late eighteenth century, but since New Year's Eve 1796, Coleridge had been living in Poole's cottage on Lime Street, Nether Stowey, three miles from Wordsworth at Alfoxden, a place "to make a man forget there is any necessity for treason."[1] Their neighbors, however, were not likely to forget the likes of them. What with Wordsworth striding the Quantock hills "like a partridge," Dorothy wandering gypsy-like around the countryside, and Coleridge visiting constantly, in moody flight from his own cottage, the Tory families and rustics who had been in the area for generations looked on the lot of them with suspicion. Just months after being introduced to Wordsworth in Bristol, late in the summer of 1795, Coleridge was already declaring that they had known each other long and well. Visiting William and Dorothy was certainly preferable to "lolling in his shirt-sleeves" at home, Sara nearby, "garrulous at the washing tub."[2] Still an ardent advocate of reform in the spring of 1796, when Coleridge came bounding over the gate at Racedown in Dorset to meet him, Wordsworth was a great talker, Coleridge would recall, though adding that Wordsworth did not talk much about politics. But of course the great "whirl-brain" was looking back twenty years.[3] In their West Country days, Coleridge was well aware that though he was the more publicly outspoken of the two, Wordsworth had been the more radical, the more Jacobin.[4]

No longer the rhetorical firebrand of 1793 who had proclaimed "rather than restrain the liberty of the press I would suffer the most atrocious doctrines to be recommended," Wordsworth in 1796 remained a believer in the "Great Upheaval," as he would refer to the Revolution. Its principles had formed his "creed" even through the days of the Terror and England's alliance with the tyrant states, Prussia and Austria. Indeed, as he would declare in *The Prelude*, the fullness and intensity of his commitment to the revolution had made a separate embrace of abolition unnecessary. Returning to England from France in 1792, he found the air busy with the stir of "contention which had been raised up / Against the traffickers in Negro blood."[5] Though the whole nation was crying out against the slave trade "with one voice," his own was muted, he acknowledged, but for this reason: Such was his "belief" that there was one and "only one, solicitude for all," that he trusted to the revolution to secure universal liberty. If France prospered, "good men would not long / Pay fruitless worship to humanity." There may have been other reasons, however, for Wordsworth's reluctance to speak out.

In 1796, living quietly at Racedown Lodge, forty-five miles south of Bristol, Wordsworth was as eager as ever for news about the political world. Always the trusty messenger, Azariah Pinney, whose father had a house in Great George Street in Bristol, would run copies of Coleridge's *Watchman* down to Racedown, another Pinney residence. Azariah hoped to get "the People that sell the Watchman" to take as well a few copies of Wordsworth's poem, "Guilt and Sorrow," which Coleridge particularly admired.[6] A few years younger than Wordsworth and an admirer, Azariah Pinney and his elder brother John Frederick, had given over their three-story Georgian house in Dorset, Racedown Lodge, to William and Dorothy to live in rent-free. As much to be with Wordsworth as to hunt, the Pinneys would spend days, sometimes a week, at Racedown to hear Wordsworth recite poetry. The time was idyllic. With Dorothy in their first real home after long years of separation, Wordsworth wrote and read poetry (he particularly admired "Religious Musings"), grew vegetables, took care of little Basil Montagu, the child of a friend, and rambled around the countryside with Coleridge, Southey, Poole, and other frequent visitors. When he and Dorothy left Racedown Lodge in July 1797, Pinney Sr. had their potatoes dug up and put in his own cellar, but by then, Wordsworth had already moved on to plant something of far more lasting value with Coleridge.

"Gaunt and Don Quixote-like," as Hazlitt would describe him in 1798, looking older than his years, Wordsworth in the West Country was a man of consuming passions, physical and intellectual, who could devour at one sitting half a Cheshire cheese and heated ale with cider, not to mention the occasional hare the Pinney boys would bring in from hunting. If the world was not too much with him, neither was it banished. He kept up with the latest periodicals and corresponded with his brother Richard, a London lawyer, and friends in the city. He was never far from news of the day. Coming down from Bristol, Azariah would have confirmed the caution with which critics of the government should proceed, given the recent failure of a petition campaign to repeal the 1794 treason and sedition acts. Living atop a hill, the Dorset countryside gloriously spread out before him, Wordsworth might have had some misgivings about his lodgings, for Azariah's father, John Pretor Pinney (1740–1818), a wealthy investor from Bristol, was a West Indian plantation owner who controlled most of the fifty-square-mile sugar island of Nevis, an active outpost of the slave trade. In September 1795, Dorothy had innocently written her good friend Jane Pollard that "a very rich Merchant of Bristol" with whom Wordsworth was "particularly" delighted, had sanctioned their stay at Racedown Lodge.[7] In fact, the deal was negotiated with the sons, and Pinney Sr. was not pleased when he discovered that his house had been given to "a friend" of John Frederick, a reference that suggests something of Wordsworth's reputation at the time. Certainly by May 1797 Pinney Sr. would have been most unhappy at having anyone living at Racedown at no cost, for he was writing to his London banker, anxiously inquiring after his stocks after hearing rumors of French invasion plans for the West channel coast.

Azariah (who would die in a few years) and John Frederick (a "nervous peevish nonentity") had been in England almost all their young lives, and were not much interested in their father's business, but they surely knew about it, especially Azariah, who had been groomed to take it over. It would be another brother, however, Charles, born in 1793 (a "surprise"), who would reinvigorate the Pinney slave-holding tradition as merchant, slave owner, advocate of slavery, and finally, in the contentious years leading up to passage of the Emancipation Bill in 1833, mayor of Bristol.[8] Pinney Sr.'s "rapid acceleration" of fortune in the West Indies had been owing to his shrewd business sense, it was said, which meant, of course, having had something to do with the slave trade. A successful plantation owner in the late eighteenth century, Pinney was five times more wealthy as a Bristol merchant and financier. Though resident in England since 1784, when he returned from Nevis with a small entourage of Negroes, Pinney Sr., like Sir Thomas Bertram in Jane Austen's *Mansfield Park*, would make periodic trips to the West Indies to check on his investments, though unlike Austen's heroine, Fanny Price, who asks Sir Thomas about the slave trade, Wordsworth seems never to have inquired about Pinney's wealth or management policies, at least not publicly. Sir Thomas, the son of a highly prosperous plantation owner, visits his estates in Antigua shortly before Abolition but only because a "crisis" in business affairs threatens Mansfield Park. He will not talk about the Traffick, however, and Fanny's questions to him about it go unanswered. The virtuous Edmund, Sir Thomas's son and Fanny's favorite, who has heard her questions, hoped they might have been followed by others. His father would have been most "pleased to have been inquired of it farther." Fanny replies that she "longed" to ask more but kept quiet because of the "dead silence!" that ensued. The stillness that reverberates throughout the Bertram household, and the book, leaves the reader to wonder not only about Sir Thomas's silence, but Edmund's too.[9]

Financially dependent on the Pinneys indirectly, and sensitive to their dependency on Nevis for income, Wordsworth surely knew, as did Coleridge, from their reading alone, how life was typically conducted on a West Indian slave plantation. Twenty years after Abolition, Coleridge's own nephew, Henry Nelson Coleridge would inadvertently counteract owners' claims of being humane by noting in his travel diary that "the planters of Nevis and Monserrat ought to be more attentive to the clothing of their slaves than for the most part they appear to be." Nevis, the coldest of the islands, was particularly hard on African men and women who were used to a warm climate, Henry pointed out, but on Nevis they had no shoes, were not well fed, and were dressed improperly. Here are no "savages of the forest," he would comment ominously; they know they're naked, but treat them like savages, and they will behave like savages.[10]

Though account books would seem to show that Pinney's

plantations were run with a comparatively light hand, the records also contain detailed instructions to managers not to discipline slaves in front of visitors.[11] It is interesting to speculate how discerning Coleridge might have been about conditions in 1801, had he not survived his fears that year that he would cease to be and pursued his application to stay at Pinney's "comfortable house" on Nevis.[12] In a note to Southey that July, and in a similar, more restrained, one to Poole in September, Coleridge describes how he was thinking of asking Pinney for the use of his "very large mansion" and, if it could be arranged, alleviation "as much as possible" of the "expences" of food and "necessary conveniences." The letter to Southey is full of childlike enthusiasm: Pinney has many advantages on Nevis "in a family way" and might even "appoint us sinecure negro-drivers, at a hundred a year each, or some other snug and reputable office, and perhaps, too, we might get some office in which there is quite nothing to do under the Governor." The "we" suggests a recurrent fantasy of Pantisocracy, a vision that he—a "Gentleman-poet and Philosopher in a mist"—and Southey and Southey's wife Edith, and Wordsworth and Dorothy would constitute an intellectual community on Nevis and make the island "more illustrious than Cos or Lesbos!"[13] Wordsworth would assuredly go, Coleridge feels certain, but Southey is to say nothing about the plan, "on account of old Pinney." Perhaps with thoughts of Wordworth and Racedown Lodge in mind, Coleridge counted on the Pinney sons to ease the way, suggesting that in 1801 Pinney Sr. would have been no more on his estates than he was in 1796, which was not much indeed. This fact alone would have constituted proof against claims of humane treatment, for if Nevis was indeed being managed most of the time in absentia (which seems to have been the case, and not at all untypical of plantation management throughout the West Indies), then the consequences for Pinney's blacks, free or enslaved, were not auspicious. There was also the evidence of Pinney Sr.'s less than humanitarian attitudes, recorded in his account books. Negroes, he wrote, were "the greatest single item of the capital investment" and the "sinews of a plantation." Thus, they had to be well treated, rendered "clean from ticks," and kept healthy for the sake of the enterprise. Had not the Negro been "ordained" by God for "use and benefit"? Did Divine Will ever vouchsafe by "particular sign or token" anything to the contrary? Racist beliefs lay relatively restrained in the more strident arguments against ending the slave trade, but they would be unleashed with greater frequency as the nation moved with more divided mind toward immediate emancipation.

Meanwhile, Clarkson and others would continue to confirm in numerous documents how absentee owners invited the abuse meted out to their Negroes. Matthew Gregory "Monk" Lewis, the Gothic novelist and playwright, would confess that he should have been aware of the cruelties on his own estates but too infrequent a visitor, he did not even know that his deputed authority, a kind and proper man, had given over management of the estate to a ruthless overseer and a negligent attorney. In *Journal of a West India Proprietor*, kept during his residence on Jamaica (1815–16), Lewis would write how "fully persuaded" he was that "instances of tyranny to negroes are now very rare," at least in Jamaica, but he emphasized how essential it was for proprietors to visit their plantations often.[14] Such a point was hardly lost on the West Indian lobby in Parliament. Reluctantly acknowledging "irregularities" on their plantations due to absenteeism, the planters offered in place of immediate emancipation intentions of ameliorating harsh conditions and making more frequent visits. But in truth, they argued, did not slave insurrections prove that the Negroes, despite already softened working conditions, were simply wild and ungovernable? On Jamaica alone, the wealthiest of the British islands, blacks showed themselves to be nothing but "indubitably alienated" and totally devoid of the affectionate feelings that seemed to govern the reciprocal master-slave relationship in the American South.[15]

In spite of his own snide comments in *The Watchman* about well intentioned plantation owners, Coleridge referred to Pinney as a "humane" merchant-planter who had denounced the Traffick. This was no doubt a sincere belief, though also a convenient one. In 1795, Coleridge might well have seen Pinney as a likely benefactor, but he knew that Pinney was first and foremost a businessman, who had freed his older slaves not from promptings of the heart but from pressures of the purse. Older slaves, especially females, were useless goods, unfit for heavy work or reproduction, though, to judge from slave prices at the time, not completely useless. Indeed, though the Pinney boys did not seem to know about it, soon after Abolition, on the instructions of a new owner, Azariah's childhood nurse, an aged black woman, was turned out to work in the fields, a fate that meant certain death. There was also the matter of some of Pinney Sr.'s early Bristol associates—Thomas Lucas of Narrow Wine Street, for one, listed in ships' records as part owner of the slaver *Africa*. Another business partner, James Tobin, a prominent adversary of abolition, testified in 1789 in favor of the slave trade with what can only be surmised as Pinney's blessing.[16] Tobin's son, however, James Webbe Tobin (1767–1814), was no stranger to Wordsworth and Coleridge. A friend of John Frederick and Azariah Pinney and of Tom Wedgwood, another of the poets' benefactors, J.W.T. was a constant caller at Racedown Lodge, afterward at Alfoxden, and the "dear brother Jem" in the opening line of Wordsworth's "We Are Seven."[17] Not only dear, young Tobin was also helpful. Like the Pinneys, he supplied Wordsworth with literature on request, including one item that particularly interested Wordsworth at the time—a banned verse tragedy about Gustavus Vasa, a sixteenth-century Swedish revolutionary and one of a small group of "high-souled men" Wordsworth was considering as a subject for a poem. Ironically, the name of "Gustavus Vasa" would not have been unknown in late-eighteenth-century England, for it was also identified with a celebrated, educated African whose autobiography, *An Interesting Narrative* (1787), was well into an eighth edition by 1794.[18] Black Vasa, with his affected cognomen and assimilated English ways, was a prince of sorts, exotic enough to carry the myth of noble savage while also bearing witness to the opposing myth of the superior Englishman. The Vasa stereotype was an influential staple not only of the English stage but of travel narratives and slave-trade diaries—an exception to popular images of blacks as either murderous or lazy. It was this kind of domesticated "noble" savage who would move racism forward.

Pity did not necessarily translate into advocacy. For all his stated opposition to the cart whip, "Monk" Lewis believed that Negroes were generally "perverse" and got their just punishment. Even Stedman, in love with Joanna and thoroughly against "the most unjust and execrable barbarity" of the slave trade and its "shocking cruelties," was no supporter for ending it, and he was decidedly against emancipation, despite Blake's sly engravings. Stedman knew his profession and the temper of the times. A Dutch army captain sent to suppress slave rebellion, his *Narrative of a Five Years' Expedition Against the Revolted Negroes of Surinam* helped fuel British fears that blacks, once freed, would turn on their former masters and kill them. The specter of 1791, when 40,000 soldiers were sent to help quell Negro rioting on St. Domingue haunted the British, while the violence that ensued between blacks and mulattoes and between both groups and whites only proved the necessity for inculcating Christian values and

English ways.[19] Most abolitionists tended to expound an arrogant, at times chauvinistic, benevolence, seeing Britain as the bearer of "the Standard of humanity," by virtue of being the first European nation to propose ending the slave trade. There were obvious ironies and contraditions in the claim: Many abolitionists, members of the upper class, separated by thousands of miles from the objects of their compassion, were not eager to enlighten those they would protect or save. The wilderness, after all, with its strange and untamed beauty, was the natural habitat of wild creatures, and education, even minor instruction by evangelical missionaries, might only teach the natives how to manage rebellions more effectively.[20] In any case, it was not the best of times to insist on liberty for blacks.

It was also not the best of times to offer "experiments" in verse that would subvert current taste in literature and politics, as the Advertisement to *Lyrical Ballads* by Wordsworth and Coleridge proclaimed. In 1798 Coleridge assessed their reputations accurately: Worthworth's name "is nothing and mine stinks."[21] Those acting to end the slave trade as well as those opposing Prime Minister Pitt's policies toward France, were still being lumped together, charged with weaving similar conspiratorial designs from the same tricolor cloth. Wordsworth's North Country accent and oddity of dress alone would have fed the kind of anti-French hysteria that caused government agents once to report them as suspicious émigrés, "violent democrats," in league with one "Spy Nozy" (Spinoza) and foreign agents based in Bristol. Seizing Bristol, "the second city in England for riches and commerce," would certainly ease the way to Liverpool and London, as a French communiqué put it. And indeed, all through the summer of 1797, it was related that the Somerset coast was under surveillance by the "enemy," while friends of the enemy, including that "mischievous gang of disaffected Englishmen" at Alfoxden, two miles inland, were being watched for their weird ways. Indeed, what else but spying or smuggling could have been meant by all that "tramping away" toward the sea? "Would any man in his senses take all that trouble to look at a parcel of water" and not be "on the look-out for some *wet* cargo"?[22]

By April, the level of anxiety in the country could be gauged by the subtitle Coleridge gave to "Fears in Solitude": "written . . . during the alarms of an invasion." But Coleridge's fears were more than an expression of apprehension over the prospect of war. They were also fears that liberal governments would not or could not promote liberating change. Though he had already concluded in the essay "On the Slave Trade" that it was impossible to enact laws for the heart, Coleridge was still attracted to the possibilities of political reform, though less so than in the heady days of his Bristol radicalism. On a personal level, there were also "viper fears," sinful thoughts that coiled round his brain and made him doubt his resolution and purpose. Insecurity masked as guilt and sorrow, marital discord, literary frustration, the beginnings of opium dependence, feelings of inadequacy around Wordsworth—Coleridge felt occasions begin to inform against him. Hazlitt, sensing something odd in a sermon Coleridge delivered at Shrewsbury in January 1798, noted how two words in particular, pronounced "loud, deep, and distinct," seemed to echo "from the bottom of the human heart": *HIMSELF* and *ALONE*.[23]

Uneasily domesticated in the countryside and nursing wounds real and imagined, Coleridge yielded in "Fears in Solitude" to a darker muse. He dismisses preachy, "vain, speech-mouthing" hypocrites, abolitionists among them, who play "tricks with conscience" and dare not look at their own vices; he proclaims himself now a willing servant of "filial" fears, a word with humanitarian and religious connotations. He calls on victors in war to return not in "drunken triumph" but in "fear," repenting of the wrongs that made their foes so frenzied in the first place (ll. 151–53). He alludes dishearteningly to earlier violence in France, to what *Biographia Literaria* would refer to as the "storms" succeeding the "morning rainbow" of revolutionary promise. "Fears in Solitude" takes a bleak view of the human condition, suggesting that mankind may be irrevocably enslaved to willful passion and guilt, and that the best there is moves only in cycles. Seduced by power or indifferent to its abuse, we succumb to what we say we abhor and turn from evidence of tyranny and carry on, with business and pleasure as usual. The Reign of Terror already showed how liberty could lead to license, how a call for brotherhood could degenerate into a cry for blood. Political self-determination meant little if free men could not govern their own anarchic and savage impulses. "The Sensual and the Dark rebel in vain, / Slaves by their own compulsion!" Coleridge wrote earlier in the year, in "France, An Ode" (stanza v). Though his poetry, more than Wordsworth's, only hints, there were somber lessons lurking here for zealous advocates of abolition that went beyond mistrust of legislative reform. It would remain for the younger poets— particularly Keats, ironically the least political among them—to fasten on reform itself as a source of tyranny. But Coleridge knew, Wordsworth saw, how bloodless virtue in place of wanton excess could excite violence. These were fears to muse on in solitude. The nation meanwhile, uneasily alert to France consorting with tyrant allies, was nervously eyeing the West Indies, scene of recent rioting. Coleridge would come increasingly to appreciate Burke's eloquent argument in *Reflections on the Revolution in France* (1790) that change should be advanced slowly, radicalism be slowed by custom and tradition, if culture and civilization were to prevail. In doing away with utopian fantasies, however, Coleridge, unlike Wordsworth striding determinedly toward

Christian resolution, had nothing more powerful to offer as motive for opposing tyranny—other than guilt.

"We have offended, we have offended very grievously, / And been most tyrannous," he intones in "Fears in Solitude" (ll.41–43). The voice is Old Testament prophet. His readers—"O my countrymen," he calls them—were probably limited to those who might have read the essay "On the Slave Trade," sympathizers and those disposed to be sympathizers. Were they put off now by the breast-beating exhortation of the poetry? Religious fervor, so much a staple of abolitionist verse, pulses through the poems of 1798. From east to west (the direction of the Middle Passage), "A groan of accusation pierces Heaven! / The wretched plead against us; multitudes / Countless and vehement, the sons of God, / Our brethren!" (ll. 43–47). The bard implores, the bard threatens: ". . . what if all avenging Providence, / Strong and retributive," should make us know the "meaning of our words, force us to feel / The desolation and the agony / Of our fierce doings?" (ll. 127–29). Just such a doomsday warning had been issued by Wilberforce's brother-in-law, James Stephen, who charged that the nation's social and political problems were the result of God's wrath on the British people because of the slave trade.[24] Coleridge's main targets are not, however, the slave traders off the Guinea coast, but the defenders of the faith at home, the so-called good people who, "playing tricks with conscience," overthrow tyrants only to embrace new ones ("Fears in Solitude," l. 158). "Courts, Committees, Institutions, / Associations, Societies," all were "One Benefit-Club for mutual flattery" (ll. 55–57). Such as "they"—he disdains even to name them in "France, An Ode"—they "burst their manacles" in vain and wear the name of Freedom "graven on a heavier chain!" (stanza v). Coleridge's deprecating irony anticipates Byron's in *Don Juan*. In a provocative (but canceled) last stanza to "France, An Ode," Coleridge

sneers, "Shall I with *these* my patriot zeal combine?" Shall the
moral man stand alongside those who protest the invasion of
Switzerland and at the same time countenance the slave trade?
"No, Afric, no!" (stanza vi).[25] The hypocrites are fixed in the
Ode's image of African carnivores—"Hyaenas" in a murky den
who whine over their prey and "mangle as they whine." The vicious diction suggests Coleridge's keen awareness (his "loathing,"
in fact) of ministers of zeal who pick and choose their cause, then
pursue it to the death in the name of freedom. Such dark truths,
which stood before his "ken," were, however, obviously not
pressing upon the conscience of the "present Ministry" (stanza vi).

The very day Coleridge was composing "Fears in Solitude"
the *Times* was urging the government to strengthen the militia
because of "threats of an immediate invasion." Just fourteen
months earlier, in February 1797, twelve hundred Frenchmen
had managed to slip into Fishguard on the western coast of Wales,
a bungled affair whose audacity nonetheless shocked the area's
inhabitants and the Home Office.[26] Intrigues, detected everywhere, were traceable mainly to the "machinations of domestic
traitors." Recent arrests in some northern districts revealed the
existence of conspiracy plans to set fire to London, cut off water
pipes in Manchester, and feed the flames of rebellion all over the
country. The *Times* was alarmed: The more it heard about radical
corresponding societies, the greater it saw an "urgency for every
good Citizen to arm in the defence of his country." The Watchman of 1796 was by 1798 in danger of becoming one of his own
"tired preachers," mocked in "Fears in Solitude." He whips up
rhetoric now on behalf of his "fellow brethren" (l. 154), but he
also whispers blessings for a green and quiet place away from
"bodings" that would undo him (l. 211). Fiery outbursts are
cooled alongside paeans to domestic tranquility. The poet clearly
wants to have it both ways: to indulge in, and apologize for, se-

clusion fantasies—"My God!" to think that in the solitude of a "green and silent dell" one must fear for the country in its bloody madness.

The choice was not, as Keats would declare it, whether to vex the world or soothe it, but whether to vex the world or soothe oneself. Coleridge would "fain preserve / His soul in calmness," for solitude protects against the wearying world. Yet such are the times that he cannot but speak out. Indeed, fears in solitude are also "fears *of* solitude" (the title, in fact, when the poem was published a few years later in *The Friend*), fears of yielding to retreat and nature, of running away from the world's "uproar" and "strife."[27] In the fall of 1799, anticipating the seduction, Coleridge would urge Wordsworth to write a blank verse poem (a continuation of *The Recluse*) "addressed to those, who, in consequence of the complete failure of the French Revolution, have thrown up all hopes of the amelioration of mankind, and are sinking into an almost epicurean selfishness, disguising the same under the soft titles of domestic attachment and contempt for visionary *philosophes*."[28] For Coleridge in 1798, cradled in the Somerset hills, the night journey of the Ancient Mariner had revealed something disturbing about the human condition that no amount of vexing the world could counteract. Statesmen, however, preoccupied with power, were in no mood to reflect on man's inhumanity to man, let alone encourage legislation against it. And Wordsworth, quite convinced that it was "The Rime of the Ancient Mariner" that did in *Lyrical Ballads*, was in no hurry to explain or reprint it.

That spring, Daniel Stuart, the editor of the *Morning Post*, uneasy about the last stanza, published "France, An Ode" without the lines alluding "to the slave trade as conducted by this country." In a headnote to the poem, however, Stuart acknowledged Coleridge as a "zealous and steady" advocate of freedom,

much admired for "his sentiments, and public censure of the un-
principled and atrocious conduct of France." But the practical
matter was not to antagonize the ministry by printing the verse
of a poet known for having held Jacobin sympathies who was now
linking abominations in France to British trading interests in the
West Indies. It was one thing for a somewhat eccentric poet/phi-
losopher to rail against the government in a local weekly like *The
Watchman*, destined to run out of funds; another for a major London daily, at the height of a war scare, to risk condemnation and
retribution. A few days after the publication of "France, an Ode,"
the *Times* accused the *Morning Post* of coloring reports on Parliament with "revolutionary jargon." Coincidentally, that same day,
the *Times* ran a prominent front-page notice for a ballet panto-
mime, "The Merchant and the Slave," keeping before the London public an image of slaves as exotica. But as the Watchman
of 1796 well knew, the business of the Traffick had already become politics in the North and Midlands.

In Birmingham—the devil's "nursery garden" Southey would
call it—Coleridge had met stiff resistance when he had gone can-
vassing for *The Watchman*, for the city was not only an integral
part of the triangle trade, through its cotton industry, but also
the center of gun manufacturing for Africa.[29] As narratives such
as Stedman's pointed out, native headsmen or African chieftains
("caboceers") learned quickly from their European masters how
to exploit and enchain. "I have received so many abusive letters—
postpaid," Coleridge wrote Cottle, "many from the North country," from "literati," not at all "trivial or simply about business,
imperiously demand[ing] immediate answers."[30] That some of
the abuse was for the Watchman's stand against the slave trade
can be inferred from Coleridge's *Notebook* jottings at the time. An
entry for March 19 (1796) followed an angry *Watchman* blast two
days earlier at those who "harangue against the Slave-Trade,"

mutter about scarcities of food during war, then "wear powder, and eat pies and sugar!"[31] "'Tis the times' plague when Madmen lead the blind," he scribbled, echoing *Lear*. Sparking his fury then had been an anti-abolition speech in the House of Commons on March 19 protesting a foreclosure bill against West Indian planters, main beneficiaries of the trade. A speaker had objected to the bill, claiming that errant "Gentlemen" might then be shipped to Botany Bay for fourteen years, where they would have to mingle with the lowest orders of society. Coleridge was outraged: *"Gentlemen*!!" In other words, "those who contemning the laws of their country & of human nature, had been buying, (or kidnapping) *enslaving*, and (in the consequences) *murdering* some hundreds of their fellow-creatures,"—that such "Gentlemen!!" would not want to mingle with the "poor wretches, who, ignorant and half-famished, had stolen a few paltry guineas!"—that such could ever be considered *Gentlemen* was like calling "The Prince of darkness" a *Gentleman*.[32] As Coleridge well knew, gentlemen could and did break laws with impunity. Though the Mansfield Decision of 1772 had determined that escaped slaves were not to be forced back on board slave ships in English ports, advertisements after that date for the return of runaways were evidence enough, as Hannah More had observed to Horace Walpole, that slaves continued to be "found" in England and shipped to plantations in the West Indies and America. "Gentlemen" in fact engineered more than kidnapping. There was a difference between what African tribal leaders greedy for guns and misled by trinkets perpetrated on their own people, and what was coolly executed in the countinghouses of Bristol, Liverpool, and London. Two years after comparing "Gentlemen" and "The Prince of Darkness," Coleridge extended his indictment in "Fears in Solitude" by implicating everyone.

Far deadlier than the "slavery and pangs" borne to "distant

tribes" by the slave traders and their banking accomplices were the vices that accompanied the traders—"our" vices, whose "deep taint / With slow perdition murders the whole man, / His body and his soul" ("Fears in Solitude," ll. 50–53). And what if political power would tend always to corrupt? What if Blake's "mind-forg'd manacles" were lodged permanently in the brain, coded into the human condition?[33] Certainly the revolution in France showed that idealistic beliefs could rouse—and rationalize—destructive behavior. Wordsworth had just completed a play dramatizing such considerations. In *The Borderers*, composed the previous fall (Coleridge much admired it for its sharp delineation of the making of a recluse), Wordsworth, in a gloomy post-Godwinian mood, had demonstrated how "sin and crime are apt to start from their very opposite qualities."[34] Though neither Wordsworth nor Coleridge at this time had traveled far from the days when it was bliss to be alive and to be young very heaven, they did sense that "the hiding places of man's power," as Wordsworth would call them in *The Prelude*, might contain dark, destructive energies. If so, then malevolence was as much a birthright as benevolence, and it was not the world without that needed revolution so much as the world within. Such thoughts drew the poets to fasten increasingly on what Wordsworth in the "Preface" to *Lyrical Ballads* would speak of as the "fluxes and refluxes" of the mind, rather than on changing governments, and the "mind" that was meant was not the victim's but the (potential) oppressor's.

For Wordsworth, Coleridge, and Blake, as for Byron, Shelley, and Keats a generation after them, slavery was not only morally wrong and politically despotic—the typical and trite observation of abolitionist verse since the middle of the eighteenth century—but psychologically destructive to the enslaver as well as to the enslaved, conditioning both to tyranny, the one because of indifference, the other because of revenge. As Wordsworth would write to the indefatigable advocate of abolition in the House of Commons, Charles James Fox (1749–1806), in January 1801, it was his hope and Coleridge's at this time when sympathetic energies were being "sapped in so many ways" (the "Preface" would describe the "evil" as a "craving for extraordinary incident," a passion for the gaudy and lawless[35]), that poems such as his own "The Brothers" or "Michael" would enlarge "feelings of reverence for [the] species," and contribute to the "illustrious effort" Fox was making "to stem this [the slave trade] and other evils with which the country is labouring."[36] In fact, as the poets soon discovered when *Lyrical Ballads* came out in October, the critics easily and mischievously mistook their intentions, seeing in their simple verse simplistic thinking. *Lyrical Ballads and Other Poems*, however, were not first-person sermons but dramatic tales meant to rouse not sympathy but empathy. Somehow—he does not explain—Wordsworth says he hopes that the poems he is sending to Fox might help arrest the "rapid decay of the domestic affections," which he attributes to the growth of manufactures, the loss of small farms, "the increasing accumulation of men in cities," and most of all—he widens the arc—to "the great national events which are daily taking place."

It was not change but the speed of change that alarmed Wordsworth, not specific events that made him uneasy but their number and variety. As he would put it in the "Preface," "A multitude of causes, unknown to former times are now acting with a combined force to blunt the discriminating powers of the mind, and, unfitting it for all voluntary exertion, to reduce it to a state of almost savage torpor." Why else did Leonard stay away so long, or Luke leave Michael, or the Ancient Mariner succumb so readily to promptings of motiveless malignity? Unlike abolitionists, who would move agenda by awakening pity and outrage for victims of the slave trade, Wordsworth and Coleridge subtly promoted identification with those who would go astray, yield to cynicism or bitterness, or remain indifferent. Where abolitionist poems and tales tended to focus exclusively on the horrors of the Guinea coast and the cruelties of the Middle Passage, Wordsworth and Coleridge (and Blake before and after them) would seek inner cause beyond particular time and place. *Lyrical Ballads* would be nothing less than poetry "well adapted to interest mankind permanently." This was not abolitionist poetry, nor was it meant to be.

Despite the voluminous amount of abolitionist poetry and song rolling from well intentioned pens for years, there was still widespread ignorance about many aspects of the slave trade and plantation slavery. As late as 1805, Southey would be writing to his sailor brother Tom, stationed in the Caribbean, "Little is known here of the W. Indies except commercially" and next to nothing about "the state of the slaves." A letter giving the "moral and physical picture" would have "all the effect of novelty" and bear "considerable weight before the House of Lords, now that the question of abolition is again coming on," he pointed out. The request was not for another heart-wrenching description of how slaves lived but for a factual account that would constitute a "moral" picture of the white planter, a "history of his day"—his meals, the hours he takes them, his dress, amusement, employments, pleasures, the education of his children and family—in short, a "picture" that might, by comparison, indict.[37] Southey's own sympathies were unequivocally behind legislation for full and immediate cessation of the Traffick. He had written sonnets on the slave trade, many for newspapers, but nothing spoke more effectively for the abolition movement at the moment than the grisly poetic tale he composed in the fall, keeping his eye on "The Rime of the Ancient Mariner."

Southey's "The Sailor Who Had Served in the Slave Trade" was based on a true-life incident related to him by Cottle, who had heard it from a friend. Firmly rooted in the tradition of slave-trade confessions, the ballad is clearly superior as protest literature to the enigmatic "Rime," written a few months earlier. Southey found "The Rime" obscure and said he could not analyze it, which did not prevent him, however, from absorbing some of its influence.[38] In fact, the opening lines of "The Sailor Who Had Served in the Slave Trade"—"He stopt it surely was a groan / That from the hovel came"—echo the opening lines of "The Ancient Mariner"—"It is an Ancient Mariner / And he stoppeth one of three," and both tales begin under sunny skies before descending into a world of violence from which only a narrator escapes. In Southey's ballad, a ship "merrily" sets out from the African coast with a cargo of 300 slaves; the Ancient Mariner's ship drops "merrily" from harbor view in England, moving south. Southey's ballad begins somewhere "near Bristol's ancient towers," and though the port from which the Mariner embarks is not named, West Country readers may well have surmised it was Watchet on the Channel coast. Hazlitt thought so, for on a jaunt once with Coleridge down the Bristol Channel, his feet in synch to the rhythm of the poet's incessant talk, he would point out the "bare masts of a vessel on the very edge of the horizon and within the red-orbed disk of the setting sun"—very much like the "Spectre-ship in the Ancient Mariner."[39] In any case, anyone who had spent time in Bristol in the late eighteenth century would have known that "[f]our times fifty living men," the number on board the Mariner's vessel, was the average for a slave ship at the time. In *An Authentic Narrative* (1764), an account of his years in the slave trade (which Wordsworth would draw on almost verbatim for his shipwreck scene in *The Prelude*), Captain, then the Reverend, John Newton, native of Liverpool, notes that his ship the

African carried 250 black souls.[40] Speculation, of course, is not fact: Nowhere in "The Rime of the Ancient Mariner" does Coleridge provide certain hints that the Mariner's harrowing experience had taken place on board a slave ship. Nonetheless, in its distinct echo of "The Rime of the Ancient Mariner" Southey's ballad suggests in retrospect that the milieu of slave trading may have strongly influenced the earlier poem's theme.

Though both ballads rely on a stranger to relate the tale of a ghastly incident at sea, in "The Sailor Who Had Served in the Slave Trade" the device is irrelevant to the brutal facts of the story, which is told as narration within narration, a familiar mode of English ballads. Devoid of the dramatic interventions that characterize many Wordsworth and Coleridge ballads, Southey's poem recalls Coleridge's in its opening lines of an unidentified narrator who happens along and hears strange sounds. Tracing these to a stone cave, he enters and finds a half-crazed, "conscience haunted" wretch in prayer. It is a Sailor, intent on purging his "miserable" self from "deepest guilt." With no prompting or resistance, the Sailor launches into his tale, and the narration within the narration begins. It is a tale about a "wicked thing," a "sin" he has committed, and his confession constitutes the heart of the poem, though clearly, for Southey, the crime is more important than the punishment. The Sailor has flogged a female slave to death. In words that would take on ominous meaning for later generations, the Sailor says he was just following orders: The captain "made me tie her up / And flog while he stood by, / And then he curs'd me if I stai'd / My hand to hear her cry." Because the woman refused to eat, the Sailor had been ordered to beat her into submission. (Obviously his ship had not been equipped with the torture devices described by Newton and Clarkson.) He overdid his part, however; the woman died and her mangled body was tossed overboard. Ah, the Sailor moans, looking back, if only the sea had swallowed him then, when he was still "innocent." The word is not crucial for Southey, but it would have given Blake and Coleridge serious pause. Southey's Sailor looks upon his life before his act as one of innocence. It does not occur to him that he may have been already guilty in knowingly setting sail from Bristol "on board a Guinea-man" destined for "the slave coast." By contrast, the Mariner's moral descent may be said to begin the moment, if not earlier, his ship leaves harbor and mysteriously drops "Below the Kirk, below the Hill / Below the Light-house top." For the very reason that "The Sailor Who Had Served in the Slave Trade" leaves nothing to mystery, it was an effective abolitionist poem, with recognizable scene and purpose: Its time is close to the date of composition; the scene of the murder, the deck of a British slaver as it journeyed west on the Middle Passage; the crime, an act against Christian values.

By contrast, the action in "The Ancient Mariner" moves along strange seas of thought and seems symbolic of something ancestral in the soul. It is in this sense that the Mariner is "ancient." Years later, criticizing the "enormous blunder" in an artist's rendering of the Mariner as an old man, Coleridge would declare that the Mariner was "the everlasting wandering Jew" who had told his story "ten thousand times since the voyage, which was in his early youth and 50 years before."[41] By focusing attention not only on his narrator but also on the wedding guest, Coleridge suggests that the difference between innocence and sin is not overt action. If Southey's Sailor would diminish his crime by blaming his captain—a man "far worse than me"—then, by extension, Bristol businessmen, far removed from the Middle Passage and the African coast, could ease their conscience even more easily, which of course they did. "So familiarized to the process of that abominable traffic" was the average Liverpool citizen, writes the abolitionist poet Edward Rushton, that "people of the greatest respectability, and even of the most amiable character, felt no more remorse at the idea of buying and selling thousands of their fellow man, than the butcher experiences at the idea of slaughtering his cattle."[42] Rushton was, of course, condemning indifference or willful ignorance in the face of evil, and implicitly calling for greater support for the abolition petition campaign.

Southey's ballad holds out forgiveness to those who sin by commission. Though the Sailor who serves in the slave trade says he is haunted "night & day" by the image of his deed, he does not feel compelled to tell about it or intuit who must hear, and by the end of the ballad, which marks the end of his confession, the reader senses that the Sailor will be absolved if he continues to pray. The Ancient Mariner, on the other hand, is a damaged soul, forever beyond redemption. Saved for a state of life-in-death, his condition recalls the psychological torture Rivers experiences as a political prisoner in *The Borderers* (1796), eternal punishment in a "slavery, compared to which the dungeon / And clanking chain are perfect liberty."[43] But more to Coleridge's point in "The Rime of the Ancient Mariner" is the suggestion that everyone who hears his tale is somehow tainted—wedding guest, author, reader. The theme of "The Ancient Mariner" is not its moral, as Coleridge would gently point out to his friend Mrs. Barbauld, who was worried that she could not readily identify one. Indeed, Coleridge replied, the "fault" of the poem was that moral sentiment was "too apparent."[44] The point was probably lost on Mrs. Barbauld, however, as it was lost on many readers who were confused by the poem or, like Wordsworth, annoyed by it. But at least certain parts of "The Rime" must have been clear enough for Southey.

Although Southey's Sailor vows he'll "never more go to the

Negro shore" to commit the sin of hiring out on a slaver, Clarkson knew from his talks in the taverns how easily such vows were broken, how simple it was to overlook an unpleasant but still legal business or confuse commerce in flesh with the maritime enslaving and piracy that had always flourished during the European wars. To have served on any ship plying the Atlantic, South Seas, or Caribbean in the Napoleonic period was to know about African slave trading and slavery. In *Mansfield Park*, Midshipman William Price, after seven years "in the Mediterranean and the West Indies," remarks that he's seen "every variety of danger, which sea and war together could offer," some of it no doubt putting down slave rebellions on Antigua. Just about everyone in the late eighteenth and early nineteenth century had a relative or friend at sea who had terrible accounts to give of the slave trade. Did the poets and pantisocrats gathered in the West Country not hear such horror stories from Henry Hutchinson, Mary's brother, who was a visitor at Racedown? Hear him relate the story of a merchant on the slave ship *Betsey* who had nailed the ears of two young blacks to a table for having brought him a dirty plate?[45] And what of the "interesting tales" Wordsworth heard on his endless chance encounters around the countryside, such as the ghastly events recounted by the "faint and pale" sailor he meets on the road one day who tells about a voyage to the Guinea coast on board a slaver, on which a man was killed, "a boy put to lodge with the pigs" and "half eaten," and another "set to watch in the hot sun till he dropped down dead"? Dorothy, who "trembled" to hear such atrocity tales, nonetheless recorded them in her *Journal*, this one, perhaps with special care, since the poor but well-dressed sailor, who was on his way to Whitehaven to testify against the slave-ship captain, was "excessively like" their sailor brother John, as Wordsworth would observe.[46] In short, Tom Southey, who was sent a copy of "The Sailor Who Had Served in the Slave Trade," was far less "innocent" than the Sailor who served in the slave trade before his "sin."

Innocence aside, which is where most abolitionist versifiers tended to put it in their concentrations on remorse and redemption, the miserable Sailor in Southey's ballad does gain forgiveness, no small inducement for those still involved in the slave trade who might be urged to repent. By contrast, what does the "The Rime of the Ancient Mariner" promise? Nothing but everlasting hell. Southey confessed he did not "sufficiently understand" the poem to analyze it, but though Wordsworth regretted its placement as the first poem in *Lyrical Ballads*, it is of a piece with the blank-verse lyrics and ballads Coleridge and Wordsworth were composing at the time that show preoccupation with the wretched and poor, many of them women left behind by men who went to serve in the slave trade, wars, or in the West Indies. Is Wordsworth's Mad Mother from over the Main with her coal-black hair, brown cheek and English speech, a mulatto from Jamaica or Dominica? What destiny lay ahead for those on board a ship with the Female Vagrant, as it sets sail for the "equinoctial deep" and a western land full of pain, plague, disease, famine, agony, and fear? In Wordsworth's "The Discharged Soldier" the region is clear: The "uncouth shape" the poet meets on the road one evening—a tall, bony creature from whose lips there issued "murmuring sounds, as if of pain / Of uneasy thought"—has recently returned from the Caribbean.[47] He has a soldier's tale to tell, though he does not really tell it, other than indicate that he had been serving in the "tropic islands" when he grew ill and was let go. Now, back in his own country, sick and distracted, he speaks with a "strange half-absence" as though dead inside but remembering "too well" his experience. Wordsworth, so recently under Godwin's spell, might have recalled Godwin's definition of a soldier: "a man whose business is to kill those who never offended him & who are the innocent martyrs of other men's iniquities. Whatever may become of the abstract question of the justifiableness of war, it seems impossible that the soldier should not be a depraved & unnatural being."⁴⁸ Though Wordsworth does not explain, the soldier's groans "scarcely audible," make him uneasy. The soldier does not appear to be hurt and though no doubt hungry, his groans, the passage suggests, seem to come from other cause, for what has been seen, for what has been done. The soldier has been, after all, in the West Indies. He appears now on the landscape of the poet's imagination much like the Ancient Mariner before the wedding guest, a wraith-like solitary thing invoked to challenge the poet and the reader's sense of humanity. The poet's response to the discharged soldier is at first like the wedding guest's—one of hostility, an instinct to retreat, "specious cowardise," Wordsworth calls it. In listening to the soldier, however, the poet is chastened. Like the Sailor who served in the slave trade, the discharged soldier trusts to God to get by, but like the Ancient Mariner, he also counts on the "eye" of a passing stranger to know to whom he should tell his tale.

The incident of The Discharged Soldier (though not in *Lyrical Ballads*) and "The Rime of the Ancient Mariner" both exemplify the ambitious intention of *Lyrical Ballads* which was "above all" to trace, "though not ostentaciously, the primary laws of our nature." "The Rime of the Ancient Mariner," with its deceptively simple language and flat tone (made even more impersonal by the added marginal gloss in 1816), suggests that one of those primary laws may be an instinct for savagery, an impulse to destroy. It dramatizes the suspicion of "Religious Musings" that man may be a "vicious and discontented *Animal*," and realizes Wordsworth's great fear, expressed briefly in *The Recluse*—that neither "Chaos" not the "darkest pit of lowest Erebus," not even worst nightmares could "breed such fear and awe / As fall upon us often when we look / Into our Minds," the mind of Man.[49] "The Rime of the Ancient Mariner" yields particularly harsh truth, impossible to deny, impossible to sustain. Though the Mariner insists at the end that he is "free," he admits that the release is only temporary. At an "uncertain hour" his "agony" returns, and he is driven to find someone new to whom to confess. It is significant that the Mariner is "ancient," not old. Like Ahasuerus, much on Coleridge's mind when he was putting out *The Watchman*, the Mariner can never rest. A *Notebook* entry at the time reads, "Wandering Jew / a romance," but directly under it appears another entry: "Just like a slave, who happens to enjoy imaginary freedom in sleep, as soon as he begins to suspect that he is sleeping, and afraid of waking from his fond illusions, contrives to slip into a deep pool where he can neither touch bottom nor swim to the surface."[50] Both entries describe a purgatorial condition, between the devil and the deep blue sea. There was no turning back from such visions, but there was no acting on them either, and eventually Wordsworth and Coleridge would glance away from such harsh truths, preferring the comforts of Christianity.

One year after completing "The Rime of the Ancient Mariner," Coleridge would confidently conclude that the effect of abolition in the West Indies would be the elimination of slavery in a generation or two. Without the slave trade, slave masters would take better care of their slaves who would evolve in future generations into a working class of free men. Abolition would thus do for the slave-trading nations what the end of conquest did for the Roman Empire, Coleridge incredibly analogized: create a system of "vassalage" out of the system of the Traffick, and make indentured servants from enslaved forebears, and then working men who would buy their freedom. But he also opened a Pandora's box that would not close: the steps toward freedom would have to be gradual, for West Indian slaves lived in "a state of Dependence more suited to a wild people."[51]

In *The Borderers* Mortimer tells Rivers, "I have loved / To be the friend and father of the helpless ["oppressed" in the later version], / A comforter of sorrow," but, he adds, "there is something / Which looks like a transition in my soul / And yet it is not."[52] Rivers, Wordsworth, Coleridge, they were hardly alone in intuiting the conservatism that naturally comes with age and reflection, but the poets would have been horrified to see the direction it would take later on in the century.

1. *The official medallion of the British Anti-Slavery Society, "Am I Not a Man and a Brother?" was designed by the famous potter Josiah Wedgwood (d. 1795), who declined at first to sign the work for fear (it was said) of antagonizing wealthy patrons whose businesses included trafficking in Africans. Courtesy of the Moorland-Spingarn Research Center, Howard University, Washington, D.C.*

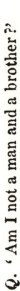

Q. 'Am I not a man and a brother?'

A. 'No!—you are a poor weaver!'

2. *As the Industrial Revolution flourished, reformers and radicals alike focused on oppression of the growing proletariat by what came to be called "wage slavery." The Peterloo Massacre of August 15, 1819, in which cavalry and militia attacked an assembly of Manchester workers, was satirized by the Peterloo Medallion, an obvious appropriation of Wedgwood's design. "Am I Not a Man and a Brother?" was answered "No! You are a poor weaver." The plight of West Indian slaves was increasingly seen as a distraction from or evasion of "real" reform—a shift accompanied by overt racism directed against "violent" and "immoral" Negroes. Courtesy of The Newberry Library, Chicago.*

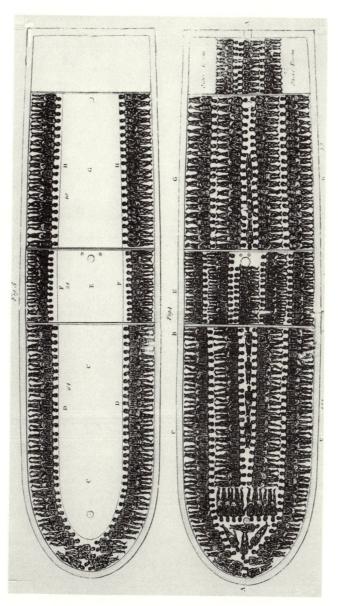

3. *Thomas Clarkson's* History of the Rise, Progress, and Accomplishment of the
Abolition of the African Slave Trade *(two vols.,* 1808*) was widely influential; Coleridge
reviewed the book. The illustration of slaves packed in a ship for the Middle Passage from Africa
to the New World is both classic and accurate. If the ship suffered storms, disease, or shortages,
the cargo was commonly thrown overboard, since it could be cheaply replaced and paid for in rum
on a subsequent voyage. The ship itself, however, was valuable, and a captain risked it at his
peril. Courtesy of The New York Public Library.*

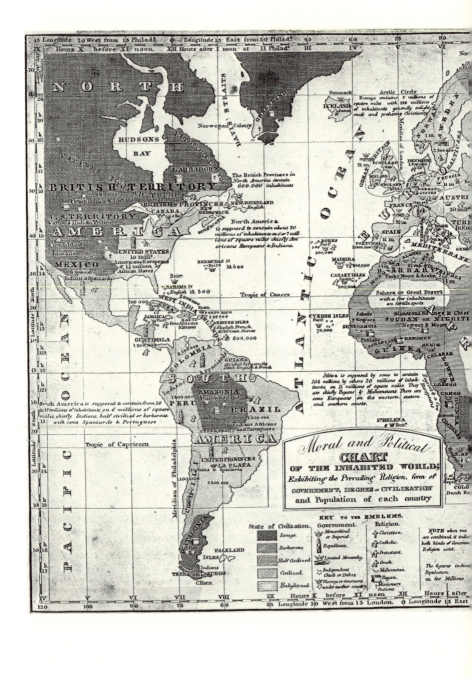

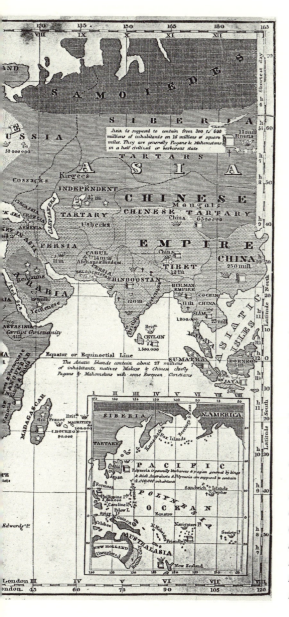

4. *"Moral and Political Chart of the Inhabited World; Exhibiting the Prevailing Religion, Form of Government, Degree of Civilization and Population of Each Country" (1821). As in most world pictures of the time, "Negroes" and "Indians" are designated "unsubdued," "savage," "barbarian," and "pagan," as can be seen in the key to the "state of civilization" here. Only Christians of European origin are "civilized" and "enlightened." Courtesy of the Map Room, The New York Public Library, Astor, Lenox and Tilden Foundations.*

Flagellation of a Female Samboe Slave.

5. *William Blake, "Flagellation of a Female Samboe Slave," from John G. Stedman,* Narrative of a Five Years' Expedition Against the Revolted Negroes of Surinam, in Guinea, on the Wild Coast of South America, *Vol. I (1796), opp. p. 339. "The first object that attracted my compassion while visiting on a neighboring estate was a truly beautiful Samboe girl of about eighteen, tied up with both arms to a tree, as naked as she came to the world, lacerated in such shocking condition by the whips of two Negro drivers that she was, from her neck to her ankles, literally dyed over with blood" (chapter 13). Courtesy of The Rare Book Room of The New York Public Library and The Schomburg Center for Research in Black Culture, NYPL.*

The Execution of Breaking on the Rack.

6. William Blake, "The Execution of Breaking on the Rack," from Stedman, Narrative, Vol. II, opp. p. 308. The Narrative *is a remarkable first-person account of the slave trade, and the author's love affair with Joanna, a fifteen-year-old slave girl. It shocked many who held naive views about life on a slave plantation. Blake, who contributed £10 to the London Abolition Society, was the only illustrator who subscribed to the* Narrative, *and received in payment for his brutally disarming engravings a goose . . . and sugar, the "nefarious ingredient" mainly responsible for the flourishing slave trade. Courtesy of The Rare Book Room of The New York Public Library and The Schomburg Center for Research in Black Culture, NYPL.*

A Negro hung alive by the Ribs to a Gallows.

7. *William Blake,* "A Negro Hung Alive by the Ribs to a Gallows," *from Stedman,*
Narrative, *Vol. I, opp. p. 116. Coleridge may have read a manuscript version of Stedman's*
Narrative, *which had been in the hands of the radical London bookseller Joseph Johnson since
1790. Blake's sixteen remarkable engravings in the published version (1796) illustrated the text
faithfully, but with a subtly shocking effect that goes well beyond Stedman's plea for mere
humanitarian reform. Courtesy of The Rare Book Room of The New York Public Library and
The Schomburg Center for Research in Black Culture, NYPL.*

CHAPTER 3

Grasmere
1807

To JUDGE FROM PARISH RECORDS and household accounts in the early nineteenth century, Negroes would seem to have been virtually nonexistent in the North Country, even though the pronunciation of "necromancy," as "nigromancy" in Westmorland and Cumberland suggested otherwise. Some were children, taken outright from West Indian estates and smuggled into the country by naval officers in league with powerful landowners; others were the natural sons of planters and sea captains who brought them home, without acknowledging them, to be instructed (though not too much) in Christian ways.[1] Those lucky enough to work as domestics and pages in country homes were too young to divine what would happen to them when they got older or became disabled. Fetishes for the wealthy, they peep out of late-eighteenth and early-nineteenth-century prints and etchings, elaborately dressed, smiling blandly, signs their owners have arrived.[2] The unlucky ones, like Blake's little "Black Boy"— "black, as if bereav'd of light"—drifted to the slums and black ghettos, while the slightly older boys were usually sent to the marble quarries, or to London to become valets and coachmen.

Mulattoes and their descendants born in England enjoyed—

if that could be the word for it—a more ambiguous status. More favored still were the quadroons, such as Miss Lambe from Barbados in Jane Austen's unfinished novel, *Sanditon* (1817), though Miss Lambe pays for her good fortune by being made a sickly character.[3] When later generations were to wonder if the "dark-skinned" Byronic figure in *Wuthering Heights* was mulatto, the answer was never as important as the persistence of the question. To Emily Brontë's neighbors, the query would have been understandable: Old Mr. Earnshaw had gone to Liverpool one day and returned with Heathcliff, whom he found in the street—a "dirty, ragged, black-haired" gypsy child, a "little dark thing" (chap. 34) with "sharp cannibal teeth," whom the Lintons refer to as the "little Lascar, or an American [Indian] or Spanish castaway" (chap. 17). Indeed, the housekeeper Mrs. Dean, tells Heathcliff that he might be helped to a bonny face, were he "a regular black" (chap. 7). She toys with his anxieties about his origins, insinuating that he might have been taken by "wicked sailors and brought to England"; later on it is suggested that he prays to "his own black father!" (chap. 17). Significantly, his outcast state as a possible mixed blood seems to matter less than his status as a servant. Such children were not unique, but it was best not to ask questions. Heathcliffs could be found in villages all across the northern face of England, from the Irish Sea to the Yorkshire moors, living in families that formed "the hinterland of Liverpool and Lancaster slave trading."[4]

Whitehaven, twenty miles west of Keswick, an active trading port for Jamaica since the 1750s and the most prosperous coal port in England, sent out an average of four slave ships a year. Cumbria, Lancashire, Merseyside—all had strong slave-trading districts. Lancaster itself, just five miles east of Morecambe Bay on the southern boundary of the Lake District, harbored families like the Lowthers, well known for their involvement in the slave trade, whose interests until 1832 were consistently represented in Parliament and whose plantations in Dominica and Barbados "earned for these islands the nickname," "little Cumberland in the West Indies."[5] The tight-fisted first earl of Lonsdale (d. 1802), whom Wordsworth's father had served as agent at Cockermouth, seat of strong candidacies against emancipation, was certainly familiar to the Wordsworth children, who spent their childhood suing him for their inheritance.[6] Around John Bolton (1756–1837), one of the most powerful men in the Lake District, there had been a whole network of slave traders from the Furness area, with Lancaster and Liverpool connections going back a century.[7] Tales about Bolton's smuggling operations were hardly a secret in the North Country. Spotting young blacks on his ships at Liverpool, Bolton would quietly arrange to have them put on small boats destined for Morecombe Bay, where a local operative would slip them into Windermere.[8] The young boys would then be sold to local gentry or businessmen, who might display the fact by having black boy figurines carved into their staircases or black boy faces painted on tavern signs. Whether or not Wordsworth knew about such murky goings-on he never said, not even on that summer's day in August 1825, nine years before Emancipation, when he would sit with Sir Walter Scott, George Canning (soon to be prime minister), and "other celebrities" in John Bolton's comfortable Windermere home, watching a regatta. There was indeed a "Negro Trail in the North of England," and a growing black population in villages and seaports all over the country.[9]

By the turn of the century, many of the estimated 20,000 Negroes living in London could trace their roots back generations. They had been runaways, sailors, and cooks on merchant ships, army and navy men who served the British in various wars. Others, concentrated in city districts such as the "blackbirds" of

St. Giles, flitted in and out of the city's demimonde: criminals, prostitutes, beggars, sweeps, street musicians—all part of the "mighty concourse" Wordsworth saw when he came visiting with Lamb and Dorothy in September 1802. In Book 7 of *The Prelude*, Wordsworth notes a "silver-collared Negro" with his timbrel (l. 677), part of the motley of misfits and outcasts thronging St. Bartholemew's Fair along with Malays, Lascars, Tartars, Chinese, Hunter-Indians, albinos, Moors, Negroes with spotted skin—all colors of the sun on parade, a "parliament of monsters." The image is hardly comforting, though it verifies the existence of a squalid underclass not yet classified by race. In *Letters from England*, caustically commenting on things English from his assumed "Spanish point of view," Southey would describe how "rogues" on the south bank of the Thames hawked so-called wild Indian women from cannabalistic America, displaying them under conditions "worse than even the slave trade."[10] Of course, the grotesque was no more typical of blacks in Britain than the noble savage. *The Prelude* notes the "silver-collared Negro" but also the majestic "Negro Ladies in white muslin gowns" who glide by in cool procession (l. 243). Their stately presence closes the London section of *The Prelude*, a verse paragraph pulsing with ethnic nouns that catalog the "perverted" things of the city, but the image is formal, as on a classical frieze, lifeless and unreal. Weeks earlier, in a sonnet to be published in the *Morning Post*, Wordsworth had expressed himself quite differently.

In late August 1802, returning from France, where he and Dorothy had been visiting his daughter and Annette Vallon, Wordsworth met a female passenger on the Channel crossing, a "Negro woman like a lady gay." The woman is only "like" a lady gay, however; she is neither aristocratic nor happy, though she assumes a dignity as best she can. Her "downcast state" moves the poet to talk to her and then commemorate the meeting in a sonnet called "September 1, 1802." Just days before, he had completed a sonnet to Toussaint L'Ouverture. Together, the poems about the Negro woman and the black liberation leader constitute a small record of Wordsworth's sympathetic response to the plight of West Indian blacks in the years directly preceding Abolition.

The Wordsworths had been following political events closely. In her reverential obsession to treasure everything that belonged to her brother, Dorothy noted in her Grasmere *Journal* on March 4 how she had been setting William's room in order, cherishing his half-bitten apple and carefully filing away a "two months" supply of newspapers for him.[11] The news, often woefully behind the times, sometimes bearing datelines from America, told of heightened political tension and stepped-up bloodletting in the West Indies, of infighting on St. Domingue between blacks and blacks, blacks and mulattoes, and of blacks and mulattoes against the remaining whites. The stories were full of gory detail: Of limbs hacked off, people burned alive, orgies of vengeance. Though Jefferson's shrewd negotiations for the Louisiana Territory depended on Toussaint's drawing off Napoleon, and leaving France and Spain to drain each other's energies, the American president was no admirer of the wily black commander-in-chief, who had taken to calling himself the black Napoleon. Jefferson hoped that Toussaint would soon die, a wish that was granted on Wordsworth's birthday the following spring. To Jefferson, the West Indies were Nature's "recepticle" for blacks transported into the Western hemisphere, and St. Domingue, its most promising dumping ground. Jefferson foresaw a collision of liberty and equality; Wordsworth saw only the human heart.

For Wordsworth that late summer of 1802, the "desolation" that was France had much to do with the First Consul's betrayal of the hopes for freedom for the West Indian blacks. In April

Napoleon had ordered his brother-in-law, Gen. Charles Leclerc to restore slavery on Guadaloupe, the very design he had been trying to effect secretly for St. Domingue. Certainly by midsummer 1802 it was clear to planters and radicals alike, French and English, that Napoleon had moved contrary to his declaration of November 22, 1801, that "At St. Domingue and at Guadaloupe there are no more slaves. All is free there; all will there remain free."[12] Wordsworth's "fellow passenger" on the Channel crossing may therefore have been one of those who fled the West Indies for France, then found herself a victim of an edict to expel all Negroes and mulattoes not in military service and round up those arriving at French seaports.[13] Although there may have been other reasons why a "dejected" black was on board the Dover ferry that August, Wordsworth thought such an edict responsible, and reflected the belief in the title he gave the sonnet when it was first printed a few months later: Generalizing from the single instance to the race, he changed "September 1, 1802" to "The Banished Negroes."

In the years before Abolition, Daniel Stuart's liberal *Morning Post*, not yet the "Fawning Post" Hazlitt would tag it later on, had a daily circulation of 4500, thus guaranteeing Wordsworth a readership appreciably larger than what he had for *Lyrical Ballads*.[14] To be published in a newspaper was, of course, to make a political statement. There, and in the other politically biased periodicals of the day, was where the abolition and emancipation debates were colorfully fought out, alongside reprints of speeches in Parliament. Although Stuart wanted the *Morning Post* to be "cheerfully entertaining" and "not entirely filled with ferocious politics," he trumpeted Wordsworth's sonnets with an editorial, promising readers "little political essays" on recent proceedings by "one of the first Poets of the age." If a bit hyperbolic, at least the comment suggested that Wordsworth's name was no longer the "nothing" Coleridge had protectively assigned it in 1798 (it may even have been Coleridge himself who wrote Stuart's editorial). In any case, publication in a major London daily was taking the high road for poetry as politics.

In toto, Wordsworth's "little political essays" in 1802 sent out some powerful ideas about freedom. As he declared in another sonnet composed that year, "England! the time is come." Any phrase might have followed, but the common theme was that the country must be roused. It was "emasculating" itself with a "freight" of "trespasses," and heavy "offences," and temporizing in "Greece, Egypt, India, Africa."[15] Although Napoleon's forays in the Middle East had been contained by the time the sonnets appeared in the spring of 1803, the west coast of Africa remained a Napoleonic killing field. In 1805, looking back and across the sea from Malta, Coleridge would reflect that had the First Consul for Life succeeded in Africa, nothing would have stopped his drive toward a second Rome.[16] Significant for what they show of Wordsworth's sympathies toward blacks in 1802, the sonnets on Toussaint and the banished Negroes also show why abolition, though imminent, would take four more years to be enacted. Tame, even maddeningly subdued from an abolitionist perspective, the sonnets gain respect in the context of contemporary events, and as poems set against the usual inane or incendiary versifying of most abolition verse of the period.

Though Wordsworth changed "The Banished Negroes" back to "September 1, 1802" for the first collected edition of his poetry in 1807, the sonnet was made an integral part of the series "Dedicated to Liberty," which Wordsworth insisted be read as a single poem "on the subject of civil Liberty and national independence."[17] If the change in title could be interpreted as evidence of Wordsworth's diminished compassion for the Negro, a headnote added twenty-five years later would surely counteract the impression. Eighteen twenty seven was hardly a radical time for the 57-year old poet, but it was when he chose to introduce the sonnet with a remarkable declaration: "Among the capricious acts of tyranny that disgraced those times [1802], was the chasing of all Negroes from France by decree of the government: we had a fellow-passenger who was one of the expelled." It was an extraordinary statement to come from Byron's apostate "Windermere Treasure." But why did the note not appear in the 1838 edition of the poetry? A cynic might conclude that in 1827, when the antislavery movement was at low ebb, speaking out cost Wordsworth nothing, while in 1838 it was a different story. Years of rioting in Jamaica, Chartist agitation for economic "social equality," the ending of the mandated period of apprenticeship for the emancipated slaves, perhaps even the prospect of laureateship—all these might have caused the future oracle of the Cambridge Apostles, the revered 68-year old Distributor of Stamps, the grand old man of Rydal Mount, not to want to appear to be favoring the implementation of emancipation.[18] A more generous view would simply ignore the 1838 omission and let the sonnet and its headnote stand.

The expression was sincere; it was also superficial. Though a cursory reading of the revisions of "The Banished Negroes" might suggest a growing compassion for Negroes on Wordsworth's part, in fact they show, ironically, why the emancipation effort would falter. In 1802, the person Wordsworth meets on the Channel boat is a "fellow-Passenger" (l. 1) who comes from Calais. Only in line 3 is it clear that the passenger is a "Negro Woman." In the versions of 1827–36 and again in 1840–1848, the "Female" passenger, "Driven from the soil of France," is presented in line 1, apparently strengthening the sense of exile and vulnerability, but Wordsworth typically liked to locate resolution and endurance in the image of a lone and vulnerable female.

Moreover, he would have known from reading Stedman and Newton that it was the men who had the more difficult time of it in the holding pens, and on the Middle Passage and the slave plantations. As both poetry and sentiment, the earlier versions of "The Banished Negroes" are more effective because the sympathy emerges from the situation, and it is people, not politics, that engage the poet's visionary gleam. The poet does intend an indictment of France in the lines about the Negro being "Rejected like all others of that race, / Not one of whom may now find footing there" (ll. 10–12), but the message in 1802 is for England, whose "time is come." Clearly, however, as the years went on, up to and including 1845, to be exact, "The Banished Negroes" continued to engage Wordsworth's attention.

In forever making changes in the sonnet, even if only tinkering with capitalization, Wordsworth seems to have been trying to widen his sympathies as he increasingly felt his country "emasculating" itself with a "freight" of "trespasses" at home. In the process, "The Banished Negroes" would become less particular, more abstract. The female passenger acquires a statuesque dignity not unlike the stoical female personifications of liberty and justice found in contemporary painting and sculpture. She becomes a "white-robed Negro" reminiscent of *The Prelude*'s stately ladies—"spotless," magisterial, too pure to bear the burden of exile or slavery. Meek, "more than tame" in the *Morning Post*, the Negro passenger becomes "pitiably tame" in 1807, and in later versions even loses the "gaudy" array that suggests her African or West Indian heritage. Only in the earliest version is the poet truly angry, demanding in concluding lines to know "What is the meaning of this ordinance? / Dishonor'd Despots, tell us if ye dare." By 1807 the challenge is replaced by reference to an "unfeeling Ordinance," and by 1845 the sense of justice seems at best forced, at worst patronizing: Heaven is called on to be kind to such a woman, Earth asked to feel for her "afflicted race." Wordsworth's strong suit, like Coleridge's, was guilt, his own, the country's, humanity's, but "The Banished Negroes" makes no connection between the plight of the female passenger and the "We" at the start of the poem, to whom the Negro indicates her "poor Out-cast" state. Yet it is clear from the four-part sonnet series "Personal Talk" begun in 1802, that Wordsworth felt some bond with the female passenger, for as he sits without "hope, or aim" in "Personal Talk," preferring *im*personal talk, he is not unlike the female passenger who sits in her exiled state meek, silent, destitute, without "hope or aim." The poet's "languid mind" in "Personal Talk" like the female passenger's "languid speech" is close to the silence the poet cherishes as restorative to the soul, but it is a silence that is also suggestive of escapism—and concomitant guilt, the kind of silence Coleridge toyed with in "Fears in Solitude."[19] On September 1, 1802, Wordsworth had similar fears.

Although the West Indian uprisings of 1802 against the constant enemy France might have been thought motive enough to secure English support for abolition, disorders anywhere were felt to threaten British interests everywhere. Long before the voodoo drums of insurrection had sounded in the northern hills of St. Domingue, igniting the Haitian revolution, the entire West Indies had become a Machiavellian chessboard for nations with investments in sugar and the slave trade. From the government's perspective on September 1, 1802, Wordsworth's sympathies toward the banished Negroes would have put him on the enemy's side. Notwithstanding Napoleon's betrayals, newspaper accounts of blacks murdering French plantation managers would only incite English fears. Indeed, as the rebellions spread from island to island, it was reported that bloodhounds, imported from Jamaica and trained to disembowel black prisoners, were being set loose on St. Domingue. It was all one and the same: Blacks were thieves and murderers, the *Times* reported in a dispatch from Port-au-Prince (November 30, 1803). Neither "mercy nor pardon will any longer be shewn to them." Every Negro in town would now be assumed to be a "brigand" and shot on sight, and "friends," it was hoped, would no longer supply the blacks with ammunition. The "friends" were the arms merchants. There was no need to warn away friends armed with words, for it was not the threat of censorship or stiffer penalties for fomenting dissent that now hushed British pens so much as fear of contagious black violence. Of course, no one bothered pointing out similarities between the ferocity of the black rebels in the West Indies and the blood-lust rioting in French towns a decade earlier, though "mobocracy," Shakespeare's "beast with many heads," would soon give many liberal-minded poets much to think about. It was against this background of political scheming, military violence, and inflammatory news that Wordsworth composed "September 1, 1802" and its predecessor, the sonnet to the "miserable Chieftain" deceived by Napoleon, Toussaint L'Ouverture, who had been arrested in June 1802.

By August, when Wordsworth was working on the sonnet, the "most unhappy Man of Men" lay incarcerated in "some deep dungeon's earless den" somewhere or in a prison in the countryside, where he might hear a milk-maid singing. In later versions, "milk-maid" would be replaced by "whistling rustic" and "Swain attendant on his plough," thus emphasizing Wordsworth's intentions to write not "to" Toussaint but "for" the English. In the late summer of 1802 Wordsworth would have no way of knowing if Toussaint were still alive; it would not have mattered. The "fallen leader" is really superfluous, the "milk-maid" more significant. As Michel Beaupuy had remarked to Wordsworth in the early days of the French Revolution, pointing out a "hunger-bitten

girl" leading a heifer, "'Tis against that / Which we are fighting'"
(9: 511). Failing the good fight, there was always immortality,
which Wordsworth invokes in the sestet. The sonnet to Toussaint is in this sense a conventional elegy: Nature mourns, friends
are summoned, the poet remembers. But the elegiac feeling is
forced. Neither "Toussaint L'Ouverture" nor "The Banished
Negroes" tests out on the pulse because the wrong pulse was
taken, Toussaint's, not the poet's. Toussaint will die in a lonely
prison, a Negro woman and her race will remain in exile. Pity,
as Coleridge had argued in essay "On the Slave Trade," was but
quick-fix emotion in place of introspection, and thus the enemy
of true reform.

In spite of the eloquence of the triumphal last six lines, where
Wordsworth celebrates Toussaint in soul-animating strains reminiscent of Milton—"thou hast great allies; / Thy friends are exultations, agonies, / And love, and man's unconquerable mind"—
the sonnet, predictably compassionate, does not rise much above
typical cliché.[20] In trusting to air, earth, wind and skies and man's
"unconquerable mind" for ultimate redress, Wordsworth was offering Toussaint no better than what Coleridge had offered the
dying slaves in his Greek Ode: the rewards of heaven. Seduced
by Miltonic cadences, Wordsworth overlooked his own principles. The "Preface" to *Lyrical Ballads* held that the mind of man
was far from "unconquerable," the will easily subdued, the heart
misled. It was emphatically to wean men and women from their
appetite for the gross and violent and to enlarge imaginative ca-
pacities, that Wordsworth and Coleridge had composed lyrics
and ballads. Avoiding the "inane and gaudy phraseology" of the
day, they disparaged the rhetorical artifice of contemporary verse
that assimilated feelings to class, and shunned the frantic provocations of gothic fiction that the Lecture on the Slave Trade had

condemned as vulgar and hypocritical. They would also avoid verse written expressly to moral purpose, poetry with palpable design. The sonnets "To Toussaint L'Ouverture" and "The Banished Negroes" are dull because they are dramatically inert. They lack the tension between narrator and tale—and sometimes between author and narrator—that imbues the best of the *Lyrical Ballads* and makes them studies in consciousness and self-consciousness, the essential contribution of the Romantics.

The sonnet to Toussaint L'Ouverture in particular misses psychological opportunity, for the author of *The Borderers* and the former Godwinian may well have intuited something untoward about the black Governor General of St. Domingue. Jefferson was not the only one to observe that the freedom-fighting black leader was not unlike his Corsican antagonist, hungry for power—a conclusion arrived at by some of Toussaint's own followers who were led to betray him. Although "Resolution and Independence" that year prompted Wordsworth to assert, "By our own spirits are we defied," neither "The Banished Negroes" nor the sonnet to Toussaint attempts an imaginative connection between the politics of abolition and the politics of the soul. Yet, if Wordsworth "grieved for Buonaparte, with a vain / And unthinking grief!" at the very time he was composing a statement of grief for Toussaint, what more might he have considered about the "miserable Chieftain" than what was sown in the the key lines of the sonnet on Buonaparte: "'Tis not in battles that from youth we train / The Governor who must be wise and good" (ll. 5–6) but with books and leisure, perfect freedom and the daily talk of man with man. Toussaint was, after all, called "L'Ouverture" not because he opened the way symbolically but because he had opened it militarily, as had Napoleon. Martial achievements, while admirable, were nonetheless not the "stalks of True Power," as

Wordsworth declared in the sonnet on Buonaparte. In fact, such achievements could even lead to new tyranny. The sonnet to Toussaint does not explore this paradox.

It was Southey who, sensing an arrogance in Toussaint, the pride that goeth before a fall, gave voice (albeit briefly) to his suspicions: ". . . is not this vile wickedness about Toussaint and the slave trade," he wrote to his friend Wynn. "If they do not surprize him I trust that by the blessing of God and the help of the yellow fever he will defend St. Domingue successfully *against all power of fame*" (italics added). Clarkson had just been visiting Southey, "the good man who ruined his health and sacrificed two thirds of his fortune in the surprizing exertions he made for the abolition."[21] The contrast between Clarkson and Toussaint could not have been sharper, the one an exemplar of selfless devotion, the other a brilliant tactician yielding to ego. Years later, a perceptive observer of the Haitian revolution, Henry Adams, would make Southey's hint explicit by referring to Toussaint's "morbid lust for power," indifference to means, and extraordinary craft and vehemence of temper, which Adams nailed as Napoleonic.[22] Toussaint, whose canny negotiations with the superpowers were constantly the subject of newspaper reports, would hardly have seemed the type to wear his bonds with "cheerful brow," as Wordsworth imagined, but a patriotic effusion—and the sonnet "To Toussaint L'Ouverture" was just that—was no occasion to inquire into the self-deception of a liberation leader. That more fascinating and challenging theme would have required the breadth and depth of a *Prelude*, or a Shakespearean drama, or— the form that finally would contain such sprawling events as they came to be seen to influence character—the novel. By contrast, neither Toussaint L'Ouverture nor the Negro passenger emerges from the ideas they represent, and those ideas were about freedom in general, not about Negroes. The terrible irony of Wordsworth's sympathy for Toussaint L'Ouverture and the banished Negroes was that it enabled him to see more deeply into the life of English things: What Wordsworth retrieved from the abolition movement were metaphors to advance the cause of the exploited and outcast at home. The working-class movement's gain was the emancipation movement's loss.

Though free in fact, peasants and factory workers, victims of "Oppression," lived like "slaves unrespited," Wordsworth wrote in *The Prelude*.[23] As Southey's *Letters from England* show, Wordsworth was hardly alone in his appropriation of slavery metaphors to describe the plight of the agrarian and industrial working class. Popular social critics like William Cobbett, (1763–1835), the "Peter Porcupine" of radical journalism in his early journalistic years, pressed the issue of the working poor as against paying attention to African slaves, and many literary intellectuals aimed their barbs increasingly at abolitionists for drawing attention away from domestic problems. The implication of investing slavery metaphors with such power that they diminished the reality of West Indian slaves in British eyes seems to have escaped notice. Years after Abolition Wordsworth would proclaim in "Humanity" (1829), a poem with distinct echoes of the abolitionist poet William Cowper in *The Task* (1784), that though "'Slaves cannot breathe in England,'" in effect they do.[24] Wordsworth's insistence that there were indeed slaves in England was his way of showing where he stood on the doctrine of laissez-faire: "Though *fettered* slave be none," he declared in "Humanity," England's floors and soil "Groan underneath a weight of slavish toil." Why? because of the tread of Adam Smith and others of such "heartless schools" of political economy who would elevate free trade above liberating the spirit. In fact, Wordsworth's use of Cowper's image was itself distorting, since Cowper's line had referred to real slaves: Slaves did not breathe in England, Cowper had asserted, because "our air" in "their lungs" made their "shackles fall"—an allusion to the 1772 Mansfield Decision. Cowper was writing about slavery and the slave trade, twenty-three years before Abolition. Wordsworth was writing about "slavish toil" in England twenty-two years *after* Abolition. By then, at the height of the emancipation debates, the claim of an enslaved white working class would only strengthen the hand of those opposing immediate freedom for blacks.

Although a competition of compassion between abolitionists and advocates of the English poor could be discerned in the writings of literary intellectuals before 1807, it was only after passage of the Abolition Bill that the tension between the two freedom movements would become shrill. Adamantly opposed to slavery when the Traffick had been closely identified with atheistic France and barbarous Napoleon, Wordsworth and Coleridge grew increasingly cautious about supporting immediate freedom for oppressed but unchristian black savages. The very month Wordsworth was composing sonnets of sympathy for Toussaint and the banished Negroes, Coleridge was confiding to his *Notebook* thoughts about "Tribes of Negroes who take for the Deity of the Day the first thing they meet of a morning—."[25] Such musings would easily degenerate into "denigration," as fears of the African Other, increasingly a subject in travel diaries and military narratives, presented a more detailed and damning picture of plantation Negroes than the superficial exotica of earlier narratives. At the same time, travel accounts such as Cobbett's *Rural Rides* presented a more detailed and damning picture of "slavery" in the English countryside. Negroes suffering the "Enormities" of the slave trade would seem less abused than the poor and exploited in England who had no legislation to protect them. What could emancipation offer when abolition was seen to have abolished nothing?

On March 25, 1807, the day Parliament passed an Abolition Bill,[26] the first two pages of *Felix Farley's Bristol Journal* carried dire news: excerpts from "private letters" about a "most alarming plot of revolt among the Negroes" on Jamaica the previous December. In two parishes, it was reported, there had been an attempt by a group of blacks to advance their "depredatory and murderous career." The pump was primed, the backfires lit. Abolition would occasion nothing but violations all around. The bill was scheduled to take effect on January 1, 1808, and the ten-month delay left ample time for maneuvering by the opposition, which in fact had already begun with the judicious editing of the bill itself, as it was introduced into the House of Commons. Opponents urged that the phrase "injustice and inhumanity of the African Trade" be changed to "expedient that the slave trade be abolished."[27] They got their way, and why not, since the new phrase better reflected reality? It was "expedient" to stop the Traffick because British capital was being used to aid the enemy every time slaves carried on English ships were sold to the French, a surreptitious bit of business engaged in by sufficient numbers of double-dealing slave traders and virtually impossible to stop. Besides, given the decline of the slave trade itself and the bill's lack of compensation provisions, businessmen and merchants would do well to take what they could—and take they did. Pinney, for one, did not suffer. In February 1807, having valued his slaves at £65 a head, he saw prices rise to £70 by September, with the expectation of diminished imports. It was also expedient to seem to respond to charges of man's inhumanity to man so that business could continue. After Abolition, when blacks on Nevis celebrated what they thought was victory, plantation managers conveniently took their expression of joy as a sign of rebellion and conducted mass whippings in the marketplace. Pinney Sr. knew about the punishments, and knew, too, the reputation of the new overseer, Edward Huggins, as a man of terror. But Pinney defended Huggins when he was brought up on charges of brutality, and plantation life went on as usual.[28]

Despite the overwhelming evidence that political strategems and economic forces conspired to ensure passage of Abolition, some abolitionists did rise above the pro forma prescriptions of Christian morality and act on the belief that ending the slave trade would truly enlarge the heart of man. Sensing that Thomas Clarkson was one of them, Wordsworth honored the husband of his sister's old friend, not only by naming his fourth child Catharine (b. 1808) after Clarkson's wife but, more significantly, by expressing his admiration for the unsung hero in a commemorative sonnet, "To Thomas Clarkson, on the Final Passing of the Bill for the Abolition of the Slave Trade, March 1807," which was published in the collected edition of his poetry that year.[29] Thirty years later, when one of Wilberforce's sons insinuated that Clarkson, now 78, had been paid for his work in the abolition movement and suggested that Wordsworth had been incorrect in asserting that it was Clarkson who "Didst first lead forth that pilgrimage sublime" (l. 5), Wordsworth politely but sternly refused to back down, claiming he had "evidence" to show that the "palm" belonged to Clarkson. What proof he had or thought he had he never said, but he maintained a steadfast attachment to the great abolition leader and did not change one line of the sonnet. Years later De Quincey would angrily denounce "false insidious praise" as an attempt to deny Clarkson his place as "inaugurator" of the "ever-memorable crusade against the African Slave Trade." Others had diffused or popularized the movement, De Quincey contended, but it was Clarkson, not Wilberforce, who "broke the ground"; to him, alone, belongs the "coronet of deathless flowers."[30] Wordsworth was less exercised over the competition between admirers of Clarkson and Wilberforce.

What did it matter who was "first," he wrote, since "both labourers" put forth such rare and high qualities in the fight to end the Traffick? For Wordsworth, Clarkson would always remain what Coleridge had dubbed him, the "moral Steam-Engine" of the antislavery movement, the one who had climbed the "obstinate hill," despite "toilsome" and "dire" consequences. The remarks suggest that in 1807 Wordsworth was familiar with Clarkson's night journeys in Bristol and Liverpool, recounted in the two-volume *History*, which Coleridge would soon review.[31] But something in Wordsworth's sonnet to Clarkson was wrong. The spark between moral force and imagination was lacking.

For all the praise of the "firm friend of human kind," Wordsworth's sonnet is bloodless, hardly reflective of the feisty, ailing antislavery advocate who had only recently demanded of planters and their allies in the House of Lords, "Are you serious in asking for compensation?" Why, you "should compensate Africa!!!" The anger of the exclamation points, the underlinings in his letters, the plodding lunacy of the nighttime wanderings of the docks, the implacable pursuit of the petition drives he led all over the country—Wordsworth captures none of this, and in small but telling revisions over the years, even makes his sonnet more dull. "Duty's intrepid liegeman," originally on a "pilgrimage" becomes a man of "enterprise" (1836), and the "bloody Writing" of slave-traffick testimony turned into "blood-stained Writing"—the double entendre of the description "bloody" as curse and description reduced now to mere description. Rest, perturbed spirit, seems to be Wordsworth's message, as though, with the passage of the Abolition Bill, Clarkson's work was done. Clarkson knew better. So did Coleridge, who nonetheless declared, as though the fight were over, that "every religious and conscientious Briton" was a "debtor in gratitude to Thomas Clarkson, and his fellow labourers, with every African," for on the soul of every individual among us, "did a portion of guilt rest, as long as the slave trade remained legal." Surely the author of "The Rime of the Ancient Mariner" knew that guilt was not that easily expunged—or even acknowledged or identified.[32]

By 1807 Lamb's "damaged archangel," having a difficult time sorting out his own portion of guilt from that of the world, read into slave/master imagery his own predicament. In his short lyric "Psyche" (1808), the soul is said to escape "the slavish trade / Of mortal life!"—a condition Coleridge likens to a life of "much toil, much blame."[33] As for Wordsworth, the new occupant of Allan Bank (June 1808) and the Rectory (May 1811), who now called Sir George Beaumont patron, though still a friend of freedom, a traveler abroad, and a roamer of the North Country engaging in impersonal talk with passing strangers, he no longer had faith that poetry would be able to effect the "reconciliation of opposite or discordant qualities" that Coleridge had defined as the principle of imagination. Compromise was the emerging watchword. Though Wordsworth might show up at Daniel Stuart's "fine new house" in Harley Street in London, wearing "strange attire" and be refused admission, one thing was certain: The views he held were no longer strange.[34] How different from the days of *Lyrical Ballads* when in the "Preface" of 1800 he had eloquently staked out claims for poetry in incantatory words almost interchangeable with those of the abolitionists: "In spite of differences of soil and climate, of language and manners, of laws and customs: in spite of things silently gone out of mind, and things violently destroyed; the Poet binds together by passion and knowledge the vast empire of human society, as it is spread over the whole earth, and over all time."

In fact, differences of soil, climate, language, manners, laws, and customs directed the emerging emancipation debate, which as it deepened became more volatile. Sympathizers now spoke of "bettering conditions" rather than of immediately changing them, and of emancipating slaves gradually in order to preserve freedom. When a slave loses his master, Coleridge would reflect, he loses his soul; therefore the slave must be helped, but not by precipitous action.[35] Emancipation would and should take time. Robert Bowyer's delayed volume of poetry commemorating the ending of the slave trade, to which Coleridge had contributed, was dedicated to the "Society for Bettering the Condition of the Natives of Africa" (1809), which did not, of course, mean that it was not also dedicated to improving the lot of the Negro in the West Indies. Amelioration attracted odd bedfellows: philanthropists, obstructionists, bluestockings, many of whom envisioned a grand experiment of self-sufficiency for the African Negro aided and abetted by British traders who just might coincidentally find new company agents in entrepreneurial blacks. Gradualists tended to focus on conditions closer to home. But no one, friend or foe of the Negro, was surprised at the violations of the Abolition agreement.

Barely six months after the law went into effect, the *Edinburgh Review*'s Francis Jeffrey wrote Coleridge, "I have not quite so much faith in the virtue of our present ministry as some abolitionists have—and shall not be extremely surprised if they were to connive at least some attempt to renew the trade in a clandestine manner." He was right in all respects but one—the "manner" was hardly clandestine. For one thing, the Traffick was still legal among the islands in the West Indies chain. For another, the "daring violations" on the high seas, blatant enough for Parliament to enact stiffer penalties and order heavier patroling of the Guinea coast, continued. On November 24, 1810, the *Liverpool Saturday Advertiser* would announce the readiness of a new ship built at Whitehaven, the *Earl of Lonsdale*, large, fast, with "copper" sheathing, and "well adapted for the East or West India trade."

It had been the slave trade first, and then privateering, that spurred such technological innovation, just as it was an increasing desire for exotic goods from China and India that was encouraging a shift from West Indian to East Indian trade. While Wordsworth's captain brother John Wordsworth might have testified in 1804 that the East India Company had never been engaged in the slave trade, clever questioning might have elicited from him the degree to which the company's complex subcontracting operations with "company ships" close to shore made slave trading possible, particularly near EIC stations in Madagascar, Bombay, and Ceylon. For Wordsworth and Coleridge, even in the treacherous days of Napoleon, such ambiguous policies would have been unthinkable.

Despite William Wordworth's anguish over the death of his brother in February 1805, when John's ship ran aground in the English Channel, John's letters reveal a less innocent soul than Wordsworth's elegies would suggest. John had strong opinions, biases aired without the meliorating intervention of humor. He did not like Jews or Negroes. He did not like America. He warned Mary Hutchinson about her brother Henry's plan to go there, a most "detestable place," and about Americans, a "bad race."[36] Thomas Love Peacock, who like Lamb worked for the East India Company, would sarcastically remark to a friend, "We have only to advert to the conduct of the Spanish Christians in the East Indies and of the Christians of all nations on the coast of Africa, to discover the deeper die of [the] *blood-sucking* atrocities" (of commercial navigation).[37]

Freedom had become a matter of guns: equality, of politics. As for fraternity, it would come to be spoken of more and more as the culture of class, of countrymen unified by church and education. Blacks, a rare few such as Dr. Johnson's Francis Barber, might qualify, for the exclusionary English tradition had not yet become racial. But what had liberty to do with West Indian savages, or savage-acting people in the Midlands and North Country?

CHAPTER 4

Barbary

1816

THAT FIERCE WINTER, when the "icy Earth / Swung blind and blackening in the moonless air,"[1] the upper classes remained for the most part untouched by the high cost of living. They had their bread, their costume balls, their novels and romances. Scott and Byron were favorites, especially Byron's Eastern Tales, rather than the more political "Prisoner of Chillon," "Ode to Napoleon Buonaparte," or early satires, but many in the middle classes also liked Byron's poetry.[2] They glutted themselves on the brooding romanticism of *Childe Harold* and the derring-do of villainous heroes like the Corsair as they sought relief from the growing disorders of the day—unskilled workers out of work and out of control, demonstrating in the streets of Manchester, Bradford, and Birmingham. The irony was that Byron's scornful and sin-surfeited wanderers, for all their arrogance, took a strong stand against despotism, where "the many labour for the one," though Byron, unlike Shelley, would allow that violence was sometimes necessary to be free. It was the wresting of freedom, however, rather than its safekeeping, that absorbed him, the "ravage of the reeking plain," in actuality and in the soul, when freedom was undone that engaged his poetic imagination.

The Corsair, once a slave himself, causes death breaking his "splendid chains," but fighting tyranny requires bold action— "the weak alone repent"—or do nothing.[3] In such a world the Negro is irrelevant, unable to act on his own, and unlikely to compete with the North African, a more apt antagonist in European eyes.

Byron certainly understood the political and social implications of race and color which were reflected in his letters and poetry. His Oriental Tales embrace the period's literary preference for light-skinned exotics, reinforcing the discriminations that beset Toussaint when whites forged alliances with mulattoes, creating blood leagues that intensified after the Haitian revolution.[4] In more than one sense, West Indian rebellion brought race consciousness to the fore in a "dramatic" way. Under no circumstances, Coleridge felt certain, could Shakespeare have intended his "high and chivalrous Moorish chief," Othello, to be played as a Negro. Lamb agreed. Admitting to a "bundle of prejudices," which humor did not disguise, Lamb confessed to not liking "all people *alike*," though he clearly disliked some people more than others: Jews, Scots, Quakers, Negroes. As for Negroes, he would not want to share meat with them or bid them good night, he felt himself forced to confess, for the very reason that "they are black."[5] Still, he acknowledged his prejudices—more than what some philanthropists were prepared to do, as Byron pointedly observed in *Don Juan*. By the time Negro presences start drifting briefly in and out of the middle cantos, pressed into satiric service, Byron had come to feel that blacks were well suited to the exercise of his ironic imagination, for they were victims not only of white slavers but of white emancipators as well; besides, they made wonderful touchstones for white hypocrisy.

The dispassionate truths revealed in *Don Juan* would in effect authenticate the racial divide: a world of white power and black subservience. Racism, it might be said, owed its growing presence not only to the blatant policies and practices of the downright hostile but also, to some extent, to the well-intentioned efforts of humanitarians and liberals, whose celebrations of freedom could appear aimlessly abstract or unavoidably patronizing. If liberty was a classical tradition to be emulated by the elite and patriotic, then only the assimilated African, baptized and educated, could claim to be free. In unintended ways poetry encouraged this expectation. The Byronic outlaw-hero is always "splendid," an attribute of class and character hardly available to the typical West Indian or African black. Though the Byronic hero shines with well-promoted tarnished glory, private sin informing the public posture, his chains are mental, self-imposed, and his fight for freedom a gesture of noblesse oblige dictated by philosophy or social position. As Shelley wrote in 1816 in "The Hymn to Intellectual Beauty," the world was one of "dark slavery," a "dim vast vale of tears, vacant and desolate." Like Shelley, Byron all his life hated man's inhumanity to man, but it was not the world of black slavery that he consistently envisioned, nor did he see himself, any more than Shelley did, in any missionary sense redeeming it. He loved liberty, not libertarians, disliked not abolition but abolitionists. Emancipators, benefactors, bluestockings—the virtuous Lady Byron among them, of course, proponents of missionary zeal—their earnestness and sentimentality roused his suspicions. In any case, that spring, trundling around the Swiss countryside with his library, plates, chests, and servants, Byron had his own exile to attend to.

The myth of the noble black leader should have died with Toussaint's successor, the murdered Haitian dictator Dessalines, but its persistence in popular poetry and drama suggests a general reluctance to acknowledge the growing force of race and culture in the politics of war. It was to be expected that headlines about

"White Slavery on the Barbary Coast" and "enslaved" workers in the North and Midlands would excite British ire more than news of enslaved Negroes in Africa or the West Indies. In 1816, Admiral Sir William Sidney Smith (1794–1840) founded an association of Knights of the Different Orders to work for the abolition of black and white slave trafficking in the north of Africa, "a trade still carried on contrary to religion, humanity, and the honour of Christianity," as the *Times* duly noted. In fact, however, the funds and letters received by Smith were addressed to the President of the Knights Liberation of the "White" Slaves of Africa only.[6] Such inadvertent slips or deliberate shifts in philanthropic reference had already made their way into the poetry and periodical literature of the day, especially the *Times*, which took to reprinting extracts from letters to Smith. "Compassion for the Blacks is worthy of praise," wrote the first minister of His Majesty, the Emperor of Austria, but surely Africans were "more barbarous" than the Europeans who carried on the traffic. The implication was clear: For the sake of civilization (not to mention commercial enterprise), European investment must be in freeing Christian, not African, slaves. In subtler ways, however, the inclusion of the Negro in the brotherhood of man was discouraged.

Coincidental placement of newspaper announcements might incidentally promote de-nigration. On January 1, 1816, Byron's *Poetical Works* were advertised in the *Times* alongside a notice for *Oriental Memoirs* "on Parts of Africa and South America and India," by an anonymous author, a four-volume reminder that the world was as Gibbon had described it, divided into civilized states and barbarous territories. Civilized states, of course, did not practice slavery. "White slavery" was an unfortunate but inevitable feature of war and international competition; black slavery, however, was the natural condition of a barbarous and pagan people. Under the heading "Piratical States of Barbary," the *Times* printed excerpts from eyewitness accounts calling for immediate action to end white slavery (January 2), but it is the "piracy" that offends rather than the slavery, the threat to the British presence off the North African coast and, by extension, to British supremacy on the high seas anywhere that must be stopped. "White slavery" was impressment by another name, a regular casualty of maritime life. In canto four, when old Lambro ships off a wounded Don Juan in chains, "cabined, cribbed, confined," Byron notes that the incident was based on a real event. Just a few years earlier, as he reminded his friend Francis Hodgson, he himself was "almost taken" by Mainnote (Lacedaemonian) pirates off Cape Colonna.[7] There is a kind of excitement in his mention of the possibility, a sense of adventure, a fantasy of foiling the enemy by heroic escape. In short, slavery practiced by Christians or Moorish infidels was merely political and race-free.

"White slaves" had European countries of origin; they had been citizens somewhere. "Blacks," by contrast, were "slaves" forever, in the public mind. Free or indentured, they were "Negroes," and Negroes, or "brigands," as the *Times* liked to call them at times, were merely savages who had exacted freedom by stealth or murder. That other release—the consolations of heavenly reward that abolition songsters and balladeers typically offered dying Negroes—need never have been offered to white slaves, for though white slaves suffered horrible deaths, their fate, unlike that of the Negroes, was not a matter of sustained government policy. White slaves died as unfortunate individuals, not as the individuals of an unfortunate race. The distinction was apparent to world leaders. If the statesmen Clarkson was button-holing in Paris in 1816 on behalf of the Friends of the Negro saw advantage, they could always act to enforce the laws of Abolition, but the statesmen let the violations ride, and no newspaper headlines blazoned forth any complaints. The time was approaching—perhaps it had already arrived—when only the hopelessly naive or the blindly zealous thought that a new Jerusalem or a universal fraternity of souls might reign on earth. The movement for immediate emancipation was forcing into the open discomforting concerns that lay behind the shibboleths of antislavery. In small ways—an image, a tone, a reference, an irony—the poets, Byron preeminent among them, sensed or reflected these darker truths and prefigured, if unknowingly, the racial antagonisms of a future century. Meanwhile, popular poetry and the press would continue to feed, and feed on, the comforting stereotypes that Byron would mischievously exploit without, of course, also invoking his sympathies.

In Thomas Morton's popular three-act musical melodrama, *The Slave* (1816), the governor of Surinam asks Clifton, a good-souled English army captain, what use "revolted negroes" have made of their acquired liberty, beyond exercising a desire to "burn, insult, even massacre their own countrymen." Gambia, a noble black doing sentimental service on the English stage, says that he did not join the rebellious Negroes around him because he recognized that "liberty engendered by treachery, nursed by rapine, and invigorated by cruelty" was not true liberty.[8] Syntax aside, suitable for tawny interpreters of the role, the "super-generous" Gambia, who loves Zelinda, a quadroon, must defer to Clifton, who also loves her, even though, as Gambia well knows, "the white cheek of Europe would be crimsoned" at the "monstrous indignity" of having to acknowledge Clifton's child as legitimate. Years later, recalling a visit he made with Wordsworth to Covent Garden in May 1818 to see *The Slave* (expanded now with additional songs), Henry Crabb Robinson, the lawyer, diarist and tolerant friend of the poets and essayists, remarked that the heroine playing opposite William Charles Macready's virtuous and self-denying Gambia had a fair complexion and was quite unlike an African.[9] Exotica, of course, as Byron well appreciated, had its limits. The Corsair is beloved by the Muslim slave Gulnare, whose "white" arms and "auburn hair" (2: xii) assure she is not beyond the European pale—in contrast to Stedman's "sable" beauty Joanna, who serves and waits, is impregnated by him, and is then selectively edited out of some parts of his published *Narrative*.

Like Leila in *The Giaour* (1813), Byron's Eastern beauties are to the "Mussulman manor" born, and like Don Juan's Haidée, cast in the Circassian or "Numidian vein." Moorish heritage, not Nubian or Sudanese, heats up their blood: north not west or central Africa maps the landscape of their soul. Haidée's mother was a "Moorish maid" from Fez, readers of *Don Juan* are told; thus the Numidean vein triumphs over the European in the love affair between Haidée and Juan, but in the slave market, the African vein triumphs over all: though "twelve negresses from Nubia brought a price / Which the West Indian market scarce could bring," even here distinctions are drawn between East Africa and the slave-raided West. In any case, "Vice spares nothing for a rarity," Byron coolly observes of the shortages in African slaves created by the outlawing of the Traffick. Sarcastically, he gives thanks to Wilberforce, who made the price "twice / What 'twas ere Abolition." Sympathizing no more with Negro slaves than with Jewish bankers, Byron certainly knew—and despised—equivocating money men such as the slave merchants, but he also had little patience for naïve or egocentric do-gooders, "psuedo-philanthropists" whom Peacock rakes over in his novel, *Melincout*—declaimers against slavery who "are very liberal of words which cost them nothing," as the Shelleyan character Sylvan Forester puts it.[10] Byron's tone in *Don Juan* is harsher. Wilberforce's abolitionist haranguing in the House of Commons, it is suggested, winds up serving the enemy. Words, words, words. The satirist's irony deepens with the darkening of skin tone. Exotica not only has its price, it has its limits.

The Nubian women who stand aside in the slave market in *Don Juan* have special value in a merchant's choice of "mistress, fourth wife, or victim," while the African men in this "crowd of shivering slaves of every nation" can anticipate nothing but unrelieved suffering and agony.[11] Then again, as Juan wryly observes, they can stand it. Where other slaves, presumably the whites, are "jaded with vexation," missing friends, family, freedom, the Negroes "more philosophy displayed,— / Used to it, no doubt, as eels are to be flayed."[12] The rhyme reinforces the mocking: Not all slaves, it would seem, are equally unequal. Some may be more naturally suited to their condition than others, more fated to endure their misery. Years later, looking back at the "slave-market at Constantinople . . . as it existed at the opening of this 19th century," De Quincey would note that the "natural aristocracy among slaves," not as evident as in Roman times, was still apparent, and valued "on other principles" than the obvious ones: "Those who were stolen from the terraces and valleys lying along that vast esplanade between the Euxine [Black Sea] and the Caspian had many chances in favour of their proving partially beautiful"—especially those who had a "Mameluke" value.[13] The word reverberates: From Arabic *mamluk*, meaning "slave," it was also used to designate the slaves of the privileged military class. In the old days, there were slaves and there were slaves, but all slaves, regardless of rank, reflected the custom, not the culture, of the country. Ignoring resurgent theological arguments and so-called scientific studies on the Negro's brain being put forward by many of his contemporaries, De Quincey did get the conclusion correct: Slavery in the nineteenth century was not as it had been of yore. It was worldwide, organized, inextricably bound up with racial attitudes as much as with the economy, perhaps even more.

"*Who* would be free *themselves* must strike the blow" was fine advice for Byron to give to the sons of Greece in *Childe Harold*, but such exhortation was certainly not intended for Negroes in the seasoning pens on the Guinea coast or West Indian plantations. Whites rebelled; blacks rioted. Indeed, from the European nations' point of view, black uprisings could only be construed as attacks on legitimacy, since colonial slavery was legal, and legitimacy was God's order on earth. But as Byron recognized, tradition itself, in effect, might be said to separate blacks and whites. In *Childe Harold* Byron links the revolution he would urge upon the Greeks against their Turkish oppressors to "heritage," a word with connotations of property and inheritance. He dares the sons of "Liberty" to remember their "glorious" past and not dishonor their history. They must erase their names from "Slavery's mournful page," he insists ("living page" in *The Giaour*).[14] Yet he would prod them even further to break their Turkish chains. The opening lines of *The Giaour* mock "craven crouching slave[s]" who disgrace their forebears by being "slaves," nay "bondsmen" of slaves, vassals of the panderers and eunuchs of the seraglio! The unsavory associations were intentional. Implicit in Byron's specific goad to the men of Greece in *Childe Harold* is the challenge to pride and virility. "Not thirty tyrants now enforce the chain, / But every carle can lord it o'er thy land" (2:lxxiv). Ye are many, they are few. Shall the sons of freedom fighters continue so . . . "unmanned"? The question would never have been put to blacks, typically portrayed in regional histories, travel narratives, and tales of military exploits as either wild and promiscuous or passive and lazy, but who, as the African slave traders well knew, had been selected out so repeatedly that their tribes were often left with only enfeebled progeny. On West Indian plantations strong blacks fared no better. If they ran away, they were hunted down as instigators and tortured in public. Without heritage (not even the "mournful page" is theirs), deprived of Western light and Christian values; catalogued like flora and fauna by returning adventurers, their presence in Western eyes was essentially as the cargo and property, filling records and reports. It was there that they lived, in misery, correcting the myth of the noble savage.

Abolition for England in 1807 had not meant abolition for the rest of the European slave-trading world, it had not even meant complete compliance by England. Slave trading was frequently conducted on the high seas, under changed flags, in ships near any port where slave traders were not made to feel unwelcome. Writing in the *Gentleman's Magazine* in 1816, Wilberforce estimated that Spain had stolen 25,000 slaves from Africa in the last two years alone. The figure meant little, however, in comparison with smaller numbers given for white slaves, and practically nothing alongside colorful reports of the "deliverance" of captured whites, owing to British skill and bravery. An officer on patrol off the coast of Sierra Leone, writing to the *Times* that summer, reported the end of a four-month siege of slave-raiding piracy by the Spanish and Portuguese, thanks to the capture of four slave ships by the British, who effectively rescued over 1,000 slaves—though what was done with the slaves was never said.[15] Britannia, not humanity, ruled the waves.

Ironically, that spring the *Times* reported that the Viscount Chateaubriand had been urging France to follow the English in the matter of "white slavery" by legislating against the shameful tribute paid to the corsairs of Morocco, Tripoli, Tunis, and Algiers (April 9, 1816), but eager readers of Byron's *Corsair*, panting after heroes sinned against and sinning, might have overlooked the fact that Conrad's real-life prototypes were these very kid-

nappers and slave traders. Moral pronouncements against the
Traffick in England were often undercut by expressions of patriotism, understood as the need to support the British enterprise
against the enemy, whoever it was at the time. Coincidentally,
the *Times* that year noted with distaste the arrival in Cuba of two
vessels with a total cargo of 534 slaves. A month earlier, however,
in a long article on the Spanish slave trade, the paper, highly
critical of King Ferdinand for violating the "interests of humanity," was also conciliatory: "Well, let her [Spain] then trade in
men, if trade she must, to the Southward of the Equator. There
she may find abundant means of crime, abundant supplies of miserable beings, to become still farther brutalised and degraded."[16]
But let her not extend the "hateful traffick" to the "10th degree
of North Latitude." The distinction was significant, for south of
the line lay the Gold Coast, the Ivory Coast, Black Africa,
whereas to the north "we have instituted a grand experiment of
civilisation." In fact, Sierra Leone lay south of the line but was
part of the territory of British influence. Regardless, the "grand
experiment" did not generate much support beyond that advanced by Evangelicals who saw the founding of a black society
in Africa as a way to proselytize, but even missionaries must
surely have paused at reports of the increasing deaths of whites
in the "pestilential colony."[17] Besides, why should Caribbean
blacks want to "go back" to Africa when they had not been born
there? Though the term, *West Indian* applied to an "inhabitant or
native of the West Indies of European origin or descent," blacks
on Jamaica and Barbados could easily see that the planter class
was already an endangered species, often absentee and clearly
outnumbered. Poised between abolition and its violations, the nations of Europe chose to do nothing. That alone was telling, but
Parliament and the press would sustain the myth that England

was different, better, more virtuous. Byron, for one, wasn't buying.

Since Austria, Russia, Prussia, Portugal, Spain, Sweden, and England had all agreed in 1815 at the Congress of Vienna that the slave trade was "immoral in the abstract," they should now persuade Spain to honor that agreement, the *Times* reasoned, lest France realize her "ingenious schemes for African colonisation," and French Benevolence die along with England's "grand experiment." The *Times'* straight-faced appeal to universal brotherhood must have been greeted in many political capitals with derision, however, considering England's own "ingenious schemes." Indeed, in May, the very moment that British planters were complaining about newly enacted slave-import restrictions, blacks on seventy-five estates on Barbados rioted, precipitating one of the most violent and protracted slave rebellions to date in the Caribbean. The British response was fast and furious: 120 Negroes killed, 144 executed, 132 deported to Africa, hundreds more forced into hiding. Reportedly, only one white and one black soldier were slain. Martial law, declared for the surrounding islands, was still in effect in July, when the papers reported subsequent arrests and hangings and—certain to inflame any God-fearing, liberty-loving citizen—the "confessions" of captured Negroes who, it was said, had taken a "dreadful oath, cemented by the taste of human blood," to destroy the white man—though preserve the women and children.

Naturally, the planters knew who to blame for these horrors: the antislavery agitators, but opponents of immediate emancipation found a strange ally in 1816 in William Wilberforce. Seeking peace and harmony, the great emancipator had withdrawn a proposal for a new Registry Bill for slaves, hoping that the planters would submit their own.[18] They did not oblige. Order was the watchword of the day, not humanity. As for freedom, apostrophized by Bryon in the opening line of the "Sonnet to Chillon"—"Eternal Spirit of the chainless Mind!"—well, one first had to have a *"chainless* mind" to ensure that victory would not provoke an *unchained* appetite for power.[19] Did not the Corsican heir to the revolution, having dared the forces of reaction, wind up his own abhorrence? Had not Napoleon deliberately scuttled his own edict to end the slave trade to the West Indies and replaced it with one that would secure the Traffick for France? For Dorothy Wordsworth the revelation that Napoleon had acted in "direct contradiction to [his] former practice and profession" was damning proof of his "weakness." How could one not "smile with scorn" at Napoleon's issuing a "decree of Abolition of the slave trade" and liberty of the press?[20] Coleridge did more than smile. When asked in 1814 by his friend Josiah Wade of Bristol to design a subject for a "transparency," Coleridge suggested a vulture with the head of Napoleon, Britannia standing by, clipping a wing, while off to a side there would be "a slender gilded column, with 'TRADE' on its base, and the cap of liberty on its top." But more than satirical impulse gripped the former lecturer against the slave trade, the watchman of his country's soul. Though Britons might rejoice that the vulture's leg seemed "fetter'd fast" to a rock (Elba), Coleridge warned that "the chain may break, the clipt wing sprout anew." Only a few years earlier, in an inflamatory speech in the House of Commons, Pitt had called Napoleon the "child and Champion of Jacobinism."[21] Napoleon's betrayal of the Revolution haunted the poets. There were lessons here for those who had believed fervently in political change as the prelude to moral reform and social evolution.

Certainly a victim of the slave insurrections in the spring of 1816 was the amelioration theory advanced by many abolitionists that abolition would cause plantation owners to take better care

of their slaves, whose more contented progeny would then buy
their freedom. It had been a fierce winter of insurrection, but the
spring that followed did not give hope that the planters were
doing what they promised. Many, in fact, like Pinney, did not
see that they were doing anything particularly severe in the first
place. Coleridge, however, had disposed of the myth of amelioration soon after Abolition, noting how for many years the public
was "satiated with accounts of the happy condition of the slaves
in our colonies, and the great encouragements and facilities af-
forded to such of them, as by industry and foresight laboured to
better their situation."[22] Amelioration may be the "general tone
of feeling among our planters, and their agents," he allowed, but
as proof to the contrary, he entered into the record, with no small
degree of sarcasm, the "leading paragraph" from a Kingston
newspaper, extolling the great opportunities for slaves to acquire
property: "'Strange as it may appear . . . a number of slaves in
this town have purchased lots of land, and are absolutely in pos-
session of the fee simple of lands and tenements,'" with the happy
result that the men "'manumize their wives, wives, their hus-
bands.'" Strange, indeed, Coleridge must have concluded, and
certainly without influence on the other islands in promoting the
idea that native-born slaves would peaceably evolve into native-
born free men and women. By the time of the Spring 1816 uprisings on Barbados, ninety percent of the slave population had
been born on the island, and had obviously not been convinced
that Abolition improved their lot. Even on Jamaica, the wealthiest of the British islands, with the greatest number of large plantations, the poorest whites enjoyed a power and privilege denied
even to the ostensibly better-off mulattoes and free Negroes. Of
course, years earlier, Bryan Edwards, in his history of Jamaica,
had explained why: "The preeminence and distinction" which
attached to the "White Man" in a country where "the complexion,

generally speaking, distinguished freedom from slavery." Indeed, by 1816 it was apparent that instead of easing up on harsh working conditions and instituting lesser punishments, the planters had toughened up, the *Times* reported, with rules "exceptionally severe" intended to preserve the white advantage.[23]

No advocate of immediate emancipation, the *Times* acknowledged continuing plantation cruelty and thereby in effect confirmed the fallacy of amelioration. On January 1, a story in the "West India Intelligence" column under the heading "Inhuman Treatment of Slaves" was so shocking and gruesome that the editors were moved to exclaim, "Good God!" Could it be that a leading member of the bar, given managerial authority over 150 slaves on a coffee estate in Grenada, had sued for compensation because the torture devices he made his Negroes wear caused their deaths? The paper was pleased to report at least that the judgment had gone against the powerful and well known barrister—"the Achilles of our bar"—whose eloquent pleading of his suit seemed as offensive as his having instituted the action in the first place, but the report did not go on to point out the frequency and pervasiveness of such "inhuman treatment." Perhaps by 1816 there was no need to emphasize the obvious: The case for Negro emancipation had already shifted ground from the moral, religious, and economic arguments of abolition days to psychological and cultural considerations and fears of black vengeance. What could be anticipated from emancipated savages except violence? As the revolutions in France and Haiti had shown, ex-slaves could become enslavers; victims, victimizers. White blood would flow, terror reign. The storms and floods on Jamaica the previous November had hardened attitudes. Dispatches from the Kingston papers reported in the *Times* in January 1816 detailed extensive property damage sustained by the planters—crops, ships, and Negroes "swept away to their death" by the waters. Even the "beautiful" *Earl of Lonsdale* "nearly loaded," had been "bilged and broken almost to pieces," with not a cask of sugar saved and hardly any rum. In such straits, the plantation owners surely would have heeded Monk Lewis' warning to beware the emancipated Negro who would loose a "massacre" on a scale of "the horrors of St Domingo."[24] Would Lewis mention such fears to Byron at Diodati when he came visiting in the summer of 1816?

In 1817, though not with Negroes particularly in mind, Shelley, anxious to see that freedom won be freedom preserved, would articulate the case for going slow on emancipation. A sense of liberty and justice must be kindled in newly emancipated people, he would write, but the fires must be stoked slowly. "Can he who the day before was a trampled slave, suddenly become *liberal-minded, forbearing,* and *independent*"?[25] The question was controversial enough in regard to the recently mobilized peasants and laborers of England. In regard to the Negro, most Englishmen would have answered, unequivocally, no. Slave rebellions in the West Indies would increasingly be seen as dark analogs of the unrest in English cities. Apprehensive over violence in the Caribbean, wary of mobs on the march in the North, property-holding middle and upper classes saw similarities in the impatience of the disenfranchised at home and the restless anticipation of blacks in the West Indies. Though impressions of the Negro as less than civilized certainly did not help the cause of antislavery, it was the sense of white society as less than civilized that mainly attracted Byron. At its most critical and visionary, his poetic imagination would link the two in mutually reflective ways, unintentionally reinforcing stereotypes while also exploding them.

In satirizing the duplicity and vulgarity of the god-fearing Englishman, Byron presents the Negro as a grotesque, to be mocked but also attended to, for what he shows up of his so-called betters. When a "black old neutral personage" of the "third sex," a eunuch eyeing Juan for purchase, is said to be "haggling" with a merchant as if he were at a "mere Christian fair," the reference takes on the unsavory ethnic and commercial connotations Byron intended.[26] "Haggle," with the same root origin as "haggis," Scotland's notorious national dish, could not have been an idle choice for Aberdeen's aristocratic native son. Slave trader, merchant, bargainer, *slave*—they all make Byron sick to his stomach. A similar despising is intended in *Childe Harold*, where a note indicates that the lower-class "idolaters" Byron saw praying at Patras were "negroes," not "Moors." "Pagan" and "not very agreeable" to look at, these "negroes" yet affect a sincerity quite distinct from the practititioners of Western establishment religions.[27] How better to insult hypocrites at home than by comparisons that flatter base and servile inferiors! The Other, thus, becomes a lowest common cultural denominator to serve as mirror image. Though in exile, Byron intuited the mood of his country and shrewdly exploited it to show up hypocrisy. The Negro was already on his way in the Regency period to being cast in the image of Carlyle's "nigger," a word that had been in occasional colloquial use since the late eighteenth century but that Carlyle, with venomous wit, would conspicuously display in his 1849 essay for *Frasers Magazine*, "The Nigger Question." In Byronic hauteur, as in Nietzschean arrogance, racism, though uninvited, would find a not unwelcome home.

But it was not Negroes per se whom Byron would ridicule in *Don Juan* so much as abolitionists—those "serious" and "noble" enthusiasts who busy themselves officiously upon the stage of moral cause, working more harm than good. A favorite target is Wilberforce, who has "set free / The Negroes" and is said to be "worth a million fighters." Of course the fact that Wilberforce was the founding father of the Society for the Suppression of Vice would alone have provoked a Byronic sneer. But the Wilberforce who irritates Byron in *Don Juan* is predominantly the egocentric meddler whose missionary antics make the world forget its more serious problems: that Wellington "has but enslaved the Whites," paving the way for more carnage in his lust to satisfy his ego.[28] Naturally the "Freedom" of mankind should concern the "noblest nation in the world," but Albion, now "first of slaves," must first unchain its own *"mind"*—if that is possible—before it goes about freeing others.[29] Indeed, instead of seeking to emancipate black Africans, England might look to lock up the enslavers of Europe—Alexander I, czar of Russia; Frederick William III, king of Prussia; Francis I, emperor of Austria. The Byzantine machinations of the European powers increasingly excite the caustic narrator of the later cantos, abolition and emancipation not at all. Deepest Africa is a dark continent for Byron, with no claim on his mind or soul. Though well traveled, his narrator says, he has never had the "luck" to "Trace up those shuffling negroes, Nile or Niger, / To that impracticable place Timbuctoo." The tone is sardonic. Though Byron does not say so, readers would have known that the famous explorer Mungo Park (d. 1806) had been killed by natives somewhere near Timbuctoo.[30] The allusion to black savagery, however, is really intended as a blast against colonial adventuring.

Byron consistently uses "Negers" to disparage whites. Writing to Hodgson in 1811 about the hypocrisies of Christianity, he asked and answered his own questions: "Why aren't all men Christians? Why are any!" Of what avail is Christianity if pagan souls in "Timbuctoo, Otaheite [Tahiti], Terra Incognita, etc." can also be saved? "It is a little hard to send a man preaching to Judea, and leave the rest of the world—Negers and what not—*dark* as their complexions, without a ray of light for so many years to lead them on high. . . ." Good will toward men? "[T]en Musselmans" could shame one Anglican.[31] A constant reader of journals and newspapers, Byron was well aware that Europe was ploughing through "Afric" like a *bos piger* (plodding ox), a drive implacable enough to cause the mapmakers dismay. Was there an added fillip in his phrase, *bos piger*—a swipe at the unholy Holy Alliance by way of *Deuteronomy* (25:4)—"Thou shalt not muzzle the ox when he treadeth out the corn"? The biblical expression certainly attracted William Cobbett, who would make it a headnote to one of his "rural rides" around the countryside, observing the effects of the Corn Laws on the poor.[32] For Byron, whose imagination was more readily sparked by outrage over the audacity of tyrants than by the conditions of the tyrannized, the willful cutting up of Africa, inconsequential territory, was hardly distressing. The presumptuousness of the cutters was. Besides, Byron consoles himself—perhaps with a nod in the direction of Iago—had he been to Timbuctoo, he would probably have been told that "black is fair," and while he cannot swear that "black is white," he can easily believe that "white is black."[33] The word play, intended to hit at the hypocrites, would also prove deadly for the Negro, however. The more Byron needled Wilberforce, the more "Negro Emancipation," as it was sometimes called, would be seen as energy wasted on the wrong slavery. If Byron suspected this unintended issue, it did not persuade him in any case to leave off his taunting.

"O Wilberforce!" he baits and puns, "thou man of black renown / Whose merit none enough can sing or say"; you who have struck down "one immense Colossus" (the slave trade), thou "moral Washington of Africa!"—How about perpetrating another "little thing" some summer's day? How about setting "the other half" of the Earth to rights? "You have freed the *blacks*—now pray shut up the whites." The reference is to leaders of the unholy Holy Alliance, imprisoning and enslaving people in

Greece and Italy, but there are other suggestions as well for the misguided Wilberforce: Why not also shut up George IV's pavilion?—It's bleeding the nation dry.[34] Of course, Byron would really like to shut up George, in more senses than one, but he adroitly maneuvers around such a treasonable suggestion with a passing reference to the bloated monarch's extravagance at Brighton. Byron's main target in these cantos is not George but Wilberforce and the abolitionist pack in Parliament leading the public astray. Given all the problems of the day, Negro emancipation hardly merits such attention. The theme is snidely reinforced in a final bit of additional advice to Wilberforce: Why not "Ship off the Holy Three [the Alliance] to Senegal?" Teach the powers that "'sauce for goose is sauce for gander,'" show them what it means to be "in thrall!" "Senegal" was a nice touch: Given over to the French by the time canto 14 was composed, Senegal was not only strategic for the slave trade, it was central in the European grab for gold—and also, not incidentally, the perfect snake pit for one's enemies. So much for abolition and emancipation and for do-gooders who would save the world with "new inventions" such as Negro colonization or population control: Thomas Malthus, meet William Wilberforce. Byron would put such saviors into the same handbasket and send them all to hell: "Timbuctoo travels, voyages to the Poles / Are ways to benefit mankind, as true, / Perhaps, as shooting them at Waterloo."[35] It was a trenchant critique, if a bit too late for full effect. Abroad for three years when *Don Juan* started to appear, Byron may not have fully appreciated the competition. In 1816, the "slavery" that was beginning to capture the headlines in England had nothing ostensibly to do with Negroes on West Indian plantations or piracy along the Barbary Coast.

The sale in just two months' time of 200,000 copies of William Cobbett's "Address to the Journeymen and Labourers," which appeared in the November 2, 1816 issue of the *Political Register*, unofficially signaled the start of a working-class movement that would increasingly claim the attention of the British reading public and the government, with unfortunate effects for the antislavery movement. In *Rural Rides*, that amazing collection of miscellania on political, economic, and social life in the southern counties of England—and the most widely read of all the pieces dashed off for the *Political Register*—Cobbett would put forth the case of the "enslaved" English worker, while blaming "dead-weights" like Wilberforce for diverting the public gaze from the miseries of the working class in order to cover up connections between slave traders and bankers and merchants. Negro slaves, Cobbett held, were better off than English laborers. There were slaves, poor weavers; slavemasters, "Lords of the Loom"; and slavery, the condition of the miserable and the impoverished. Cobbett was, as he entitled a projected series, "The Poor Man's Friend."[36] That meant in effect not being a friend of the Negro. It also suggested that friends of the Negro were dangerously undermining domestic reform. Writing to Catharine Clarkson about the recent Corn Law riots in Suffolk, Dorothy Wordsworth expressed the hope that her friends were out of harm's way. Though she knew that the disturbances were worse in the North, she had obviously heard enough about the growing division between abolitionists and workers to be concerned: "surely the Poor could not by any possible means take the fancy that *Mr. Clarkson* was their enemy!"[37] Indeed, they could. By 1816 Southey was certain that between them, Cobbett and Henry Hunt, who had been in prison with Cobbett in 1810— those "low, designing, dirty levellers," Byron would call them— had so incited the masses that there would be a "convulsion in three years!" Crabb Robinson saw Southey's fears as "alarmist," but he was mistaken. Southey feared the mob, Byron despised it, Shelley, ambivalent, was still hopeful. It was a politically explosive age, a *"memorable age"* Shelley would proclaim in 1819 in "A Philosophical View of Reform." He would still carry the hope expressed in the preface to *Laon and Cythna* that he might "kindle a virtuous enthusiasm" for the doctrines of liberty and justice, and awaken the nation from its "slavery and degradation to a true sense of moral dignity and freedom."[38] But the candle would flicker, the hope would not easily be sustained.

On the Continent, increasingly removed from the English political scene, Byron and Shelley may not have fully seen why the winter of domestic discontent back home would only grow colder, and the image of peasants and factory workers working like "slaves" displace the reality of West Indian Negroes and enslaved political prisoners in North Africa in popular literature, though they clearly saw the common truth that freed people everywhere were not necessarily free. Even in the New World, long the symbol of freedom, the Old World had begun to exercise its deadly charms. America, Cobbett would goad in 1819, after having returned from brief exile on Long Island, "only saddled the white people with a charge"—free Negroes who constituted a "disorderly, improvident set of beings" swelling the ranks of the impoverished. The antislavery movement was taking on new enemies, friends of the working poor, and a new battleground, the western territories of the disunited United States.

CHAPTER 5

Hampstead
1819

L IKE OTHER TOWNS along the Ohio at the close of the second
decade of the nineteenth century, Louisville, Kentucky was
drawn into the darkening debate over slavery. The fifteenth state
would stay in the Union, but it was clear that wealth and power
belonged to those who owned or engaged in the interstate transportation of slaves.[1] The "western countries," as the Illinois-
Indiana-Kentucky territories were called, had become anti-slavery
battleground, though there was no doubt which side was win-
ning. Clarkson's *Essay on the Slavery and Commerce of the Human
Species, Particularly the African* (1786) had been recently reissued
by a preacher in Kentucky, who insisted it be "given away" so
the greatest number of people could read it, but even the clergy
saw how difficult it was for businessmen to refuse the benefits of
the "peculiar institution."[2] George Keats, for one, did not refuse.
A rainy spring in Devonshire in 1818, the lack of prospects for
work, the strain of nursing his younger brother Tom, all turned
George's thoughts to the American Midwest, which he had been
reading about in Morris Birkbeck's popular *Notes on a Journey in
America.*[3] That June, George and his young bride Georgiana left
for America. Three years later, in 1821, the year John Keats died,

24-year-old George Keats was on his way to becoming Louisville's first millionaire. That meant also being a slave owner.

Birkbeck, an abolitionist Quaker from Yorkshire, had stressed
the advantages of emigrating to America, but Cobbett blasted
"Friend Morris" for misleading readers and luring them to hard-
ship settlements in the Midwest. Friend Morris, meanwhile, was
busy accusing neighboring farmers of buying up tracts of land to
sell at inflated prices for slave plantations.[4] Birkbeck had harsh
words for slavery, "that broadest, foulest blot which still prevails
over so large a portion of the United States," a "leprosy" which,
if not soon eliminated, or at least stopped in ambiguous regions
such as Kentucky, would propel the nation into violence.[5] On the
short journey taken in 1817, "From the Coast of Virginia to the
Territory of Illinois" (the subtitle of his *Notes*), he recorded distressing scenes: female slaves and children brutalized and sold at
auction, chain gangs herded south, and numerous examples of
black depravity, the inevitable consequence, he felt, of the white
depravity of owning slaves. Cobbett's attack on Birkbeck in the
October 1818 issue of the *Quarterly Review*, the very same issue
in which *Endymion* was trounced, had no effect on George in dis-
suading him from staying in America. "I see Cobbet [sic] has been
attacking the Settlement," Keats wrote in December 1818, concerned that he had not heard from his brother in a while.[6] "I must
steer myself by the rudder of information"; he was anxious for
news. George, however, though he did not say so, had already
drifted into southern currents.

The summer they arrived, but telling no one, the young couple had headed down the Ohio into Henderson, Kentucky, an
area sparsely settled and only recently made safe from Indian forays.[7] Unaware that George and Georgiana had never gone to
Birkbeck's, and hearing rumblings from returning settlers, Keats
grew worried. In the long intervals between letters, he took to

writing journal accounts to them, entries stretching over weeks and months that were filled with local facts and fancies, musings, chitchat, and verse. Serious passages were often undercut with fun. In one, charming as it was inaccurate, he wonders if George and Georgiana are shooting buffalo, chasing pheasants, and pursuing rabbits and wild boar. Underneath there was unease, sometimes anger, at what he didn't know. No sentimentalist, Keats knew well enough from reading Robertson and Voltaire that "man, inheriting a place uncontaminated with civilization" would not be free of the "usual ill and injury." He had no illusions about wilderness landscapes as benign or especially suited to generate natural piety. Indeed, an often-reprinted "Moral and Political Chart of the Inhabited World" at the time, made in Philadelphia (1821), showed America to be a land of ten million Europeans, a vague number of "Unsubdued Indians," and one-and-a-half-million African slaves. American "Europeans" were concerned about tomahawks, not chains.

Nature could be full of "hardships and disquietude," even worse than "Baliffs, Debts and Poverties of civilised life," and could exact "mortal pains," Keats joked to George and Georgiana in the spring of 1819.[8] Even Wordsworth, still and always an influence, had shown that "ills" and "evils" could befall those who lived in the eye of nature, especially in America. The young man in "Ruth," (1799) who comes from "Georgia's shore" had known wondrous freedom but also war—and, worse, "wild men's vices." There was the gorgeous earth, there was the "world of woe." In "Ruth" the wild land stirs the young man's "impetuous blood." He comes back from America with a hat of Cherokee feathers "brought" from the Indians, but he's been a soldier boy and is no innocent. Like Othello, he wins his Desdemona with tales of adventure of how he roamed through "savage lands" with "vagrant bands / Of Indians in the West."[9] However, he himself becomes a savage, "as if let loose from chains," a free spirit who turns into a "slave of low desires." He deserts his young bride and returns to the wild. "God help thee, Ruth!" a narrator interjects, recalling the cry of the wedding guest listening to the Ancient Mariner, but no "fiends" plague Ruth, other than the ones that plague her errant husband. Abandoned, vagrant, mad, Ruth is finally released from imprisonment to wander lonely on the Quantock hills. She endures because she is not "a slave in soul," manacled to hate or vengeance. Wordsworth's faith, however, was not Keats's.

Keats had doubts about America even before he learned that George did not go to Birkbeck's. "The humanity of the United States can never reach the sublime—Birkbeck's mind is too much in the American stryle [sic]," he reflected. Franklin, for example, typical of the American spirit, though a "great Man doubtless," and a practical genius, was no Milton or Sidney. Mulling over distinctions between the "understanding" and the "sublime," Keats concluded that Franklin, a "philosophical Quaker full of mean and thrifty maxims," was not so fine a man of achievement as Shakespeare, and so, he teased, since the mantle of poetry was yet to be worn across the Atlantic, perhaps George's child might become "the first American Poet."[10] George, however, had other realms of gold in mind. Though land was relatively cheap in southwest Kentucky, George borrowed on his inheritance from Keats and quietly changed his plans at the urging of a new friend with whom he had stayed for a short while. He bought into a steamboat enterprise, an experience that would soon prove deeply unsettling for him and for Keats. The friend was the not-yet-famous but already infamous John James Audubon (1785–1851), whose floating schemes for success George would only belatedly come to regard as suspicious. Audubon certainly appreciated the conflict raging over extending slavery into the Kentucky Territory. The son of a onetime planter and slave dealer in St. Domingue, Audubon surely knew that Kentucky slaves destined for New Orleans were usually sent downriver by steamboat. And his sharp and practiced eye would have spotted in young George Keats an innocent, new to America and financial dealing.[11] Although the 1807 United States Act to Prohibit the Importation of Slaves clearly forbade fitting out vessels for the purpose of slave trading "from any foreign kingdom, place, or country," Audubon would have spotted the loophole permitting lucrative business in interstate slave traffic.[12] When did Audubon learn that the boat he had induced George to invest in lay irretrievably at the bottom of the Mississippi River? He never said, but Keats, when he finally heard from George what had happened to their money, wasted no words on the slick American entrepreneur: a "dishonest" man, that Audubon, who "fleeced" his brother, with the result that their precarious financial condition was now made worse. As for George, whose details about the transaction had been guarded and minimal, he did not seem "fit to deal with the world; or at least the american worrld [sic]." The incident intensified Keats's hostility toward America, now associated with money woes, disappointment in George, and dislike of Audubon, not to mention the on-again, off-again animadversions of Cobbett. There were indeed savages in America, none noble.

George, an emigré with no political passions or pantisocratic dreams, had little to say to Keats about life in the new land.[13] In 1822, somewhat on the defensive, he would tell others that he had gone to America only to earn enough money to return to England, an impression given to Keats and no doubt reinforced by some "very pretty [critical] pickings" about America Keats reported receiving now and then. Cool, aloof from public affairs, a wee bit arrogant perhaps, George and Georgiana expressed an impatience with America, "this vortex of petty meannesses and low vices." They were, after all, a proper middle-class English couple, part of the English immigrant wave to the Midwest, generally skilled and middle class. "A complete Bond-street beau and belle" was how they struck one observer in Philadelphia when they passed through in 1818, a remark that suggests that Mr. and Mrs. George Keats were not exactly prepared for farming at Birkbeck's. In any case, four years later, George Keats felt comfortable enough to display a critical dismissiveness about America. The politics of the American people vary "every day," he wrote, and would be of interest only to "lovers and haters of democracy." It would appear that George did not count himself in either group, but in fact the "lovers and haters" of democracy had already begun to polarize the western territories over the issue of slavery, and in Kentucky it was impossible not to take sides. The Jeffersonian fantasy of an agrarian democracy led by a benevolent, property-holding elite had already collapsed into the volatile issue of states' rights. Lovers of this reconceived democracy were, perforce, haters of abolition.

Keats was amused by George's occasional comments on America, but what he made of them in connection with George's pursuit of happiness he did not say. The truth was, he and his "dear friend and brother" had drifted apart. "From the time you left me," Keats wrote, "our friends say I have altered completely—am not the same person— . . . I dare say you have altered also—every man does—." The letters betray an unease over lack of information, an undercurrent which inevitably seeped into his poetry. Barely one month after completing the sensually beautiful "To Autumn," he composed the haunting lyric "To Fanny," which begins, "What can I do to drive away / Remembrance from my eyes." It was a cry that linked his tragic sense of being in thrall to Fanny Brawne with thoughts about "that most hateful land," America, the "Dungeoner" on whose "wicked strand" the lives of his "friends" were being "wreck'd" by "sordid" afflictions. Such a place of "rank-grown forests, frosted, black, and blind," proved that "great unerring Nature" could indeed be wrong. Keats showed the poem only to Fanny Brawne, and it was not published until some years after George's death, but it did show that Keats was questioning not nature, but human nature.[14] Anything might sadden him now, and little would prove surprising.

Though he had always taken the "Liberal side of the Question," he no longer felt moved to press political sentiments into poetry. Three years earlier, in the verse epistle "To My Brother George," he had boldly announced, "the patriot shall feel / My stern alarum, and unsheath his steel; / Or, in the senate thunder out my numbers / To startle princes from their easy slumbers" (ll.73–76). That feisty, if politically adolescent, optimism belonged to the days of Leigh Hunt's influence.[15] In the May 1818 issue of the *Examiner* and by way of Shelley, Hunt had praised political enthusiasm as the answer to the despairing cynicism of the conservative Lake School (which included Wordsworth). What could one man ever do? Hunt asked himself. "Let a glorious and living person answer"—Clarkson—who, thinking upon "the horrors of the Slave Trade," had dedicated his life to its overthrow. Laughed at, violently opposed, Clarkson "has *lived* to see the Slave-Trade, aye, even the slavery of the descendants of the 'cursed' Ham, made a Felony." Keats concurred in such views, but he would not lecture readers or force metaphors to accommodate policies or programs. His refusal to be a political poet came not just from hostility to poetry of palpable design but from a natural "negative capability." Though young, he had already glimpsed a world of dark passages, where the balance or resolution of good and evil was not readily apparent, a world of "Misery and Heartbreak, Pain, Sickness and oppression," in which the needs of the world and the self were often indistinguishable.[16] In 1819, the poetic challenge for a politically sensitive man of imagination was to resist being transformed into an unacknowledged legislator of the world.

Like George, John Keats might boast an "aristocratic temper," but "Notwithstand[ing]," he felt "very much pleas'd" with the anti-aristocratic "proceedings" of workers and radicals in the northern towns and the triumphal entry into London by Henry Hunt before an estimated crowd of 200,000.[17] "Proceedings" was hardly the word; rioting was more like it. Keats's sympathies were clearly with the workers, and he wrote to George about the newspaper accounts he was reading that September of the growing number of workers' assemblies. George seems to have been uninterested in the nascent English working-class movement, though much of what was happening that late summer and early fall in England had to do with the victory of the Cobbett over the Birkbeck camp. In fact, Cobbett was wildly successful in stealing abolitionist rhetoric. Controlled by lords of the loom, also known as "congregating manufacturers," "rich-ruffians," and "*white slave* holders*,*" English "*slaves*" suffer far more than Negroes in Africa or the West Indies, Cobbett asserted. He was relentlessly insistent on this point, scoring his essays with italics, hyphens, exclamation marks, alliteration. He could hardly contain himself: "Talk of *vassals!* Talk of *villains!* Talk of *Serfs!*" Not even in feudal times were men "so debased, so absolutely slaves" as the poor creatures in the "*enlightened*" North working fourteen hours a day in 84-degree heat! Here was Hell. Where was outrage? Cobbett knew exactly where it was: misplaced at "*humanity-meeting*[s]," at gatherings called by abolitionists, "*showers-offs*," and "humanity people"—like Wilberforce! If political leaders really wanted "to *free slaves*," Cobbett fumed, let them "*look at home*." His fury was unabating, particularly when he contrasted provisions for slaves with those of the working man. "There is not a negro in the West-Indies, who has not more to eat *in a day*" than the average English laborer has to eat "in *a week*, and of better food too."[18] Cobbett has nothing but "contempt" for those who "busy themselves with compassion for the negroes," while the wretched of the English earth continue to be more wretched "than any negro slaves are, or ever were, or ever can be." If conditions were not improved for English workers, Cobbett predicted, they would be not just "slaves" but slaves "of the lowest and most degraded *cast*"—an interesting word, connoting as it did hue and shadow, and applicable to either Indian or Negro. In short, if nothing were done to correct abuses, workers would become Negroes without the so-called protections of the plantation. Image was eclipsing fact. To be *like* a Negro was even worse than being one. The ironies would continue.

If servants and workers could become "slaves," why could "slaves" not become workers and servants? "*Mutato nomine, de te historia narratur* [names have been changed to protect the innocent]," the *Morning Chronicle* slyly commented on a recent government proposal to encourage emigration to South Africa. Prospective emigrés could then take with them hired or indentured laborers, who "must not be *called* slaves" but servants.[19] The advice became the *de*vice, recalling the days before the Mansfield Decision when slave ship captains suddenly freed their slaves on paper before entering freedom-loving English ports. If similar semantic sleights were not being practiced in America, then George Keats was simply being more circumspect with English acquaintances than with American: A few years after Keats's death, he would write about his "servants," who were in fact his "slaves," as his will and tax records showed. Slaves or servants, prospective English emigrés to South Africa would not have to worry about such distinctions, nor about the "Caffree hordes" recently rebellious, now suppressed. "Caffrees"—from Arabic *Kaffir*, meaning "infidels"—were a "very feeble" enemy, an "uncivilized" people, easy to repress and conciliate, the *Times* pointed out. Killing, after all, was not enslaving, and servants were not slaves. By contrast, Europeans on the Continent were still making victims of the sable natives of Africa, proof that twelve years after Abolition, the "cruel and mercenary habit" was hardly dead. Colonization was not to be confused with colonialism. The inflammatory words in the paper were "on the Continent." The growing agitation by the workers' assemblies no doubt prompted the government's call for emigration to the Cape, where, it was said, there was better opportunity for work than in America, but no doubt there was thought as well of extending imperial influence. The missionaries had not been too successful in that regard.

Although France had declared the slave trade anathema in 1814, an extract from an anonymous letter to the *Times* from St. Malo, dated August 8, 1819, indicated that "Notwithstanding all that has been said and done upon the subject of the slave-trade, there is now fitting here [the northwest coast of France] one of the finest schooners I ever saw, and which I have no doubt is for this traffic." The item would appear to have gone unheeded; there was no follow up. England in 1819 was concerned less with slave trading to the West Indies or America than with disorders in its own towns and cities. The St. Malo dispatch, printed on August 14, was placed directly under an editorial critical of the swelling demonstrations. The number of workers' assemblies was alarming, the *Times* kept reporting, fearful of what would soon become incendiary fact. And indeed, on August 15, 1819, at St. Peter's Field in Manchester, violence erupted as hundreds of protesters were suddenly sabred by nervous cavalry and militia. The event would become a rallying cry and be forever remembered in history and song as the Peterloo Massacre, an incident even more explosive symbolically than it was in fact. No slave trading by Continental enemies, no West Indian rebellions, no Negro atrocity, no tribal revenge had ever evoked such outrage and regret. Foreign wars had ended: wars at home had begun.

In the Midlands, the machine had invaded the garden, but no one except the farmer-landlords and the manufacturers seemed to be benefiting. A decline in trade, a fall in grain prices, a rise in population, an increased tax burden on the poor (Cobbett's particular abhorrence), and new corn laws—all came together to make the hard lot of the peasant and laboring classes even more difficult. The "dangerous" once roused, the common people would prove "the most formidable of enemies," Crabb Robinson had predicted in 1816.[20] Here was slavery, as Cobbett had claimed. What had "Negro" servitude in the West Indies to compare with such exploitation on native ground? As far back as February 1807, one month before passage of the Abolition Bill, *Felix Farley's Bristol Journal*, welcoming Samuel (the Ale-maker) Whitbread's sober proposal for poor relief, had urged that charity begin at home. Abolition of the slave-trade would indeed be "a most noble example to the rest of mankind," the newspaper observed, since, like all efforts at "amelioration of our Poor," abolition was founded on doctrines "consonant to the spirit of Christianity," but the poor (white) working class must come first. Who was paying attention to such remarks? Certainly not the abolitionists, Cobbett disdainfully pointed out.

That reform had come to such a competitive pass in Manchester was ironic, for it was here, in 1788—in the "metropolis of manufactures," as Crabb Robinson called it—that 10,000 people, moving more effectively with their hands and feet than philosophers and political economists had ever done with their ambivalent proposals and equivocations, had "launched" the petition campaign to end the slave trade—one of the most remarkable mass movements in English history.[21] But the decline in antislavery fervor was owing to other reasons beside the growing discontent of the English class and the provocations of the periodicals. The contest between the followers of Birkbeck and the partisans of Cobbett could not alone have depressed the movement. Something else, something insidious, was taking new hold in the British consciousness which no amount of conscience could unlodge, though it would be some years before it would become pervasive. In 1794, the Manchester Literary and Philosophical Society had held "disquisitions on the inferiority of the Negro," a series of talks led by the physician Charles White, a Fellow of the Royal Society, whose late-eighteenth-century *Account of the Regular Gradation in Man* would become a standard reference for British racism.[22] Between "scientific" disparagement of the Negro and the provocations of Peterloo, the movement for immediate emancipation would be set back significantly. Even white slaves in Barbary were forgotten. "White Slavery at home," claimed the headlines.

Workers' advocates saw in factory owners not just "Kin to the Guinea traffickers" but men more dangerous, since "Slave-merchants on the English soil" constitute themselves "'honorable men'; / Legal in all they do, and scrupulous. . . ." The words were Joseph Cottle's, the Bristol printer of *Lyrical Ballads*; the context, an excerpt from his volume of poems, "Malvern Hills" (1798), a forgettable but heartfelt attempt to rouse his countrymen to the plight of "Domestic slaves, who raise no uproar rude, / But calmly suffer, far from public gaze . . . leagued with death." It was particularly the children who had moved Cottle, wagonloads of the "friendless destitute," whom he remembered seeing in Bristol in 1793, "close-pack[ed] as on a slave-deck," and totally dependent "on the tender mercies of their Egyptian task masters!"[23] *"Merchandise," "commodities,"* part of the "enormities" of the factory system, such terms were certain to call to mind abolitionist descriptions of Guinea cargo, but with the ironic effect of heightening the sense of horror for the "slaves" of England, not Jamaica. The sight of a factory child blackened with grime would expunge the image of a West Indian child torn from its mother. Metaphor was devouring reality.

"Slavery in Yorkshire," the radical *Leeds Mercury* would proclaim, referring to children in the worsted mills of North Bradford. "We have slaves at home" and merchants who wield the "oppressor's scourge," the "tyrants' rod," the "chains" of economic exploitation.[24] Indeed, shortly after Peterloo it was proposed that a Peterloo medal be made from the melted-down bugle of the commanding officer. The trophy would show a kneeling demonstrator being hacked to death, with the famous words "Am I Not a Man and a Brother?" scrawled along the base, and the answer "No! You are a poor weaver."[25] That the famous Wedgwood medallion, official seal of the London Abolition Society, might be appropriated, even satirically, for the cause of the English working class showed the ease with which the antislavery movement had been eclipsed, or absorbed, by the wider and more popular workers' movement for political and economic reform. The shift, however, from concern about the plight of oppressed Negroes to agitation against the horrendous conditions of the oppressed masses was an inevitable consequence of the displacement of liberty by equality, an effect in part of the emancipation movement itself, as questions of race sharpened considerations of class. The hard truth was that both movements were compelling, though the urgency to right wrongs that were visible, immediate, and threatening to the well-being and conscience of the nation understandably led to a concentration of attention, political and literary, on the inhumane working conditions on poor farms and

in the factories. In Bowyer's 1809 anthology of abolitionist poetry, Abolition had been hailed as "one of the most important
events in the history of British legislation," "a test by which to
measure the debasement or exaltation of moral feeling," and
"triumphal proof that private patriotism has been the source of
public philanthropy." Such hyperbole had served the cause of
abolition well as effective rhetoric, part of a ballad-and-broadside
drive rallying the public for twenty-five years. A decade later,
the "test" to measure "moral" feeling was no longer felt to be sen-
sitivity to the plight of the Negro, whose *im*moral life, it would
increasingly be said, was the ruination of the country's prospects.
Peterloo was hardly an unexpected or unwarranted eruption.

In September, obviously in response to a suggestion, Keats
wrote George that it would not be a good idea to return to
England now, given the "immense difficulties of the times."[26] Of
course, talk of a brief trip to London meant that George needed
money, but the timing for Keats could not have been worse. Virtually without resources of his own, in debt to friends, secretly
engaged to Fanny Brawne, when he could ill afford to marry,
and writing poetry that did not sell, Keats now declared the writing of "a few fine Plays" to be his "greatest ambition." That was
where the fast money was, as he knew from his stint as a drama
critic for the *Champion*. "A Tragedy would lift me out of this
mess," he wrote George, and "mess it is as far as it regards our
Pockets—."[27] It was not just Reformer Hunt in the northern industrial districts whose course Keats had been following in the
press, that summer, but Edmund Kean, whom he hoped to get
for *Otho the Great*, a "tragedy" he had just completed with his
friend Charles Brown, though he heard that Kean might be going
to America. The famous actor, for Keats the most wonderful "in
London and Europe," had recently finished a run at Drury
Lane—to "absolute rapture of applause," the papers reported.

The vehicle was *Carib Chief*, a five-act "tragedy" about a former slave on the island of Dominica whose ruling passion is revenge. A melodrama of little value, *Carib Chief*, which made its debut in May, owed its "success" to the genius of its star, whose "burning vehemence" seemed to redeem the play's talkiness and bombast. But the theme and main character of the historical drama, set in the reign of Elizabeth, might well have reminded Londoners of contemporary concerns. The "Carib Chief" was noticeably out of stereotype: He was as savage as he was noble.

Nothing could have resonated more against immediate emancipation or seemed better designed to stall it than a popular production about a West Indian tribal leader who, for all his past sufferings, is still a "wild beast."[28] Given recent reports of outrages committed by blacks in the West Indian islands, *Carib Chief* might well have prompted thoughts about culture and freedom. What good could be expected of freed slaves on British territory when Sierra Leone alone, a "grand experiment" to establish an African colony that would attract free and emancipated Negroes, was proving the impossibility of changing "10,000 ferocious savages into peaceable, orderly, and industrious citizens"? Long articles casting doubt on the African Institution's investments in colonization efforts filled the pages of the *Times* that summer and fall, coinciding with daily accounts of mobs massing in Manchester. In any case, the success of *Carib Chief* probably encouraged Kean to walk away from Drury Lane in an argument with manager Elliston, who had financial troubles of his own, and Elliston would have been looking to Kean's Richard to shore him up, not Keats's Ludolph. Thus Elliston's provisional acceptance of *Otho* for the 1820 season would have seemed to Keats like rejection. He needed money now, and in a pique, he withdrew the play, submitted it to Covent Garden and found himself summarily turned aside.[29] It would not have been the first time, however, that he had written for money or created a fanatic character whose only love is for the "treasured deep."[30] George, meanwhile, continued blissfully unaware of what his innocent scheming with Audubon was costing.

Persuaded by a remark in a lecture by Hazlitt that translations from the *Decameron*, particularly "Isabella," could not "fail to succeed [financially] in the present day," Keats, a year earlier, had taken a seventeenth-century English translation of the Boccaccio story of true love destroyed and set it to verse. Though he would soon dismiss the tale as "mawkish" and "smokeable" (a favorite word, meaning vulnerable to ridicule), he invested in it in an unusual way. Departing from his source in Boccaccio, where Isabella's brothers kill her lover when they discover her secret relationship with him, Keats turns the brothers into sadistic merchant adventurers, "ledger-men" of "hungry pride and gainful cowardice" who make capital of flesh, and for whom "many a weary hand did swelt / In torched mines and noisy factories, / And many once proud-quiver'd loins did melt / In blood from stinging whip."[31] With an empire extending from flooding African rivers to Ceylon shores to regions cold with ice, the brothers are said to be enriched with "ancestral merchandise," a phrase evocative of African forebears and the origin of the slave trade: And "for them alone did seethe / A thousand men in troubles wide and dark: / Half-ignorant, they turn'd an easy wheel, / That set sharp racks at work, to pinch and peel." The characterization, the imagery, and the explicit social criticism were entirely Keats's devising, and suggestive of the scheming, fortune-obsessed, Volpone-like Conrad in *Otho* who calls the good (but weak) Albert a "slave."

The Ceylon reference alone reflected Keats's determined interest in updating the Boccaccio tale. Boldly taken by British forces in 1795 and annexed by treaties in 1802 and 1815, Ceylon was very much a public issue in 1818, a prime example of the East India Company's widespread corruption and repressive rule.[32] But the new lines on Isabella's brothers move on psychological ground as well. "Why were they proud?" an unidentified narrator asks about them. The question is posed five times in one stanza, but never answered, a rhetorical device of the ballad recalling "The Rime of The Ancient Mariner" in its signaling of swift brutality to come. And come it does in "Isabella," fast and violently: "There was Lorenzo slain." Isabella's brothers become "well nigh mad" when they discover not their sister's love affair but the fact that her lover is their own servant. Killing Lorenzo is not a crime but a business transaction—to get rid of bad property and save their sister, property herself, for marriage to a nobleman with olive groves. After all, slavery and slave trading had a long and acceptable tradition in the Mediterranean, aided and abetted by piracy from the North African coast to the Italian colonies. Where Coleridge's odd ballad redeems its murderer by making him a penitent, however, Keats leaves Isabella's vicious brothers as they are but gives them a disquieting feature: fine taste. "[M]oney bags," slave traders, the brothers are also said to be "Great wits in Spanish, Tuscan, and Malay." Overtly evil, they live "self-retired" with a store of art, wealthy Florentines, connoisseurs of beauty. Here was complication beyond typical abolitionist verse, a view not of the noble savage but of the savage noble (or bourgeois aspirant), and of iniquity incarnate which no amount of political reform could meliorate. The brothers anticipate Count Cenci, whose perverse energies turn on "Strength, wealth, and pride, and lust, and length of days / Wherein to act the deeds which are the stewards of their revenue" (I, i:313). In "Isabella," love is underdone by economic forces, murder motivated by commodity mentality and greed. Despite its embarrassing sentimentality and sometimes awkward phrasing, "Isabella," though a warmed-over romantic narrative, displays the ambivalent power of money to sustain both the best and the worst in man, as George Keats would discover. Shortly before leaving for America, George read "Isabella'"s "capitalist stanzas," as critics would later call them, and he probably reread the poem, when it was published two years later in July in *Lamia, Isabella, The Eve of St. Agnes, and Other Poems* (1820). By then, however, a more self-critical Keats worried that "Isabella," written for money, about the corruption of money, might jeopardize the volume's chances of success because it was immature (though Lamb loved the poem). Keats's style, his tone, and his dedication to poetry had changed from the commitment made in "Sleep and Poetry" (1816) to write verse that would address "the agonies, the strife / Of human hearts" (ll. 124–25). After "Isabella," Keats avoided compositions "of a political tendency," verse explicitly "wielded in the cause of Reform," poetry that would vex the world by reductively concentrating on strife and agonies. The triumph of the ode "To Autumn" was its acceptance of the life of sensation and death-driven gorgeousness.[33]

Certainly, by the end of 1818, impatient with poetry that betrayed "any irritable reaching after fact & reason," Keats had also begun to turn away from the kind of Miltonic cosmopolitics that marked *Hyperion*. There, imitating Milton, Keats had explored the relationship between power and beauty: fallen gods, "Dungeon'd in opaque element" like slaves, miserably unaware that life is not evolutionary but cyclical. As Shelley was unbinding Prometheus, Keats felt himself increasingly restrained. To George in the spring, he admitted he was not "in great cue for writing lately," which was true. A related truth was that he did not know how to proceed: "I know not why Poetry and I have been so distant lately I must make some advances soon." Coleridge, who went walking with Keats in April, remembered a "loose, slack, not well-dressed youth," a change, it would seem, from the jaunty, robust appearance Keats had given his first publisher two years earlier.[34] By the spring of 1819, George weighed heavily on his mind. The papers were reporting hard times in America, especially for "farmers," and Keats still did not know for sure that George had gone to Birkbeck's. But there were other reasons for distance from his muse—anxiety over Fanny Brawne, depression over negative reviews, and the enervating effects of frequent bouts of coughs and fever, not to mention his unease at abandoning *Hyperion*, his most ambitious work so far. Too "Miltonic," he said of it repeatedly to friends and family. He meant the poem's structure and style, but an additional problem may have been that *Hyperion* was not darkly Shakespearian enough, or Blakean. Gods "Dungeon'd" in despair, teeth clenched, limbs "Lock'd up like veins of metal, crampt and screw'd" were fine for epics, but something at once more dramatic and personal was needed to reflect the new kind of "negative capability" that had begun "yeast[ing]" away in him that year.

Hazlitt, whose literary and political lectures Keats had been attending or carrying off in manuscript form since the beginning of 1818, excited in Keats a more dispassionate view of the agonies and strife of human hearts. Like Hunt, Hazlitt had sung the praises of Clarkson, whose portrait he painted, calling him "the true apostle of human Redemption." But it was Hazlitt the dazzling lecturer of gusto and bite, the radical voice against tyranny, the author of "Prince Maurice's Parrot Or, French Instructions to a British Plenipotentiary," a satiric bill of rights on slavery and the slave trade who caught and fixed Keats's admiration. No less kind to hypocritical England than to France, Hazlitt's essay included among its declarations the right "to rob and murder on the coast of Africa" as part of the "internal rights of legislation and domestic privileges of every European and Christian state."

Unlike some of his contemporaries who moderated their anti-slavery passions after passage of the Abolition Bill in 1807, Hazlitt never wavered from the position he had taken when merely a boy visiting Liverpool: "The man who is a well-wisher to slavery, is always a slave himself."[35] But more than abolitionist sentiment, which would have already been endorsed for Keats by Hunt and his circle, it was Hazlitt's psychological perspective on tyranny and slavery that attracted Keats, Hazlitt's sense of the futility of legislating morality, with its implication of a more intense and fleeting humanity than Keats had otherwise considered.

Where many antislavery sympathizers turned their gaze outward, toward suffering victims, Hazlitt focused on what Wordsworth in *The Prelude* called "the hiding places of man's power." There, in the deep recesses of mind, lay ambiguous associations of beauty, terror, power, and truth, which Hazlitt found brilliantly dramatized in Shakespeare. Particularly in his observations on *Coriolanus*, which he unleashed again, almost verbatim, in the corrosive "Letter to William Gifford, Esq." Hazlitt paraded philosophical and aesthetic notions that confirmed Keats's own: that truth is beauty, beauty truth, and that that was all one could ever know on earth and all one need to know.[36] The gods, of course, know more. Heroic figures on earth strive not to dominate but excel,[37] but they overreach and despair. Lesser tyrants, such as Coriolanus or Napoleon, blinded by the "egotistical sublime," mistake their energies and think that truth is power, power truth. They are thus better and worse than others. Like Coleridge, for whom *Coriolanus* was full of "wonderful philosophic impartiality," Hazlitt saw the play as also inexorably prescient, expressive of the spirit of the age. So delighted was Keats with Hazlitt's comments on the play, not to mention the acerbic counterattack on the journal that had laid waste to *Endymion*, that over a two-day period he copied out extensive "high season'd parts" and included them in the February 1819 journal letter to George and Georgiana. He trusted that his brother and sister-in-law would "like" the excerpts, an understatement, considering the amount of quotation. At the very least, however, George would have seen the growing influence on Keats of a critic of great "force and innate power," whose "demon" had been lately fired up against slavery but who saw that though the battle might be fought by way of legislation, the war for changing attitudes and feelings would not be won that way.

"I have a hatred of tyranny," Hazlitt declared in 1819 in the introduction to a collected edition of his political essays. "I have no mind to have my person made a property of . . . I deny that liberty and slavery are convertible terms."[38] But he also saw how easily one contained the seed of the other. Lashing out in the "Letter to Gifford" (Keats relishing every word) and defending his remarks on *Coriolanus*, Hazlitt shot back at his critics, calling them government toadies. There were indeed "tyrants" and "slaves" abroad in the world, each feeding the appetite for oppression, but Gifford (1756–1826), the editor of the *Anti-Jacobin*, a "cat's paw," would "hush the matter up," and pretend there is no such thing. What Gifford could or would not see because of political bias or stupidity was that *Coriolanus* was a "storehouse of political commonplaces," existing by simple contrasts, and it was not Shakespeare's job, so to speak, to take sides, though he did lean a bit to the "arbitrary." Keeping a careful eye on the probable impact of his remarks, Hazlitt had led off his original essay on *Coriolanus* with the remark that any one who studied the play could save himself the trouble of reading Burke or Paine or the debates in Parliament. "The Arguments for and against aristocracy and democracy, on the Privileges of the few and the claims of the many, on Liberty and slavery, power and the abuse of it, peace and war" were in *Coriolanus* "very ably handed, with the spirit of a poet and the acuteness of a Philosopher." His argument was, in effect, for an imaginative view above and beyond the usual polarizing dialectic of tyrants and slaves. By such reasoning, the democratic tribunes in *Coriolanus* might be said to be more tyrannous than the tyrant.[39] These were not observations liberals or abolitionists with ready programs of legislative reform and abstract dedications to benevolence would find attractive. What Keats saw in Hazlitt was not politics but psychology, a kind of dark humanity that tested out on the pulse.

"The love of power in ourselves and the admiration of it in others," Hazlitt observed, anticipating Nietzsche, "are both natural to man: the one makes him a tyrant, the other a slave," though it was the tyrant who was the more dramatically interesting. "We had rather be the oppressor than the oppressed," he commented. "Wrong, dressed out in pride, pomp, and circumstance, has more attraction than abstract right." Coleridge had tried to say as much (with no success) to Mrs. Barbauld: Beauty is truth, truth beauty, and neither one need bear the freight of morality. As Keats had written to George, a fight is destructive, but the energies displayed in it are "fine." By exciting the passions, a poet lays bare force, energy, and imagination, not morality.[40] This was both a cathartic and an empathic idea. The poetic imagination is thus beyond good and evil. In *Coriolanus*, it routs its subject with an aristocratic, monopolizing, exaggerating power, whipping all circumstances into a "right royal" ("anti-levelling") effect. Imagination "rises above the ordinary standard of sufferings and crimes" and aligns itself with "excess." Blake would have been pleased with the expression. A year earlier, Keats had written that great literature proceeds from "negative capability," the state of being in "uncertainties, Mysteries, doubts, without any irritable reaching after fact & reason." Here in Hazlitt's essay on *Coriolanus* was "negative capability" with a vengeance, imagination as a burning bright that would almost consume a poet by taking him into regions he could not easily order or negotiate. Negative capability meant seeing beyond political passions, no matter how morally imperative, and rejecting finally the certain programs of good hearts whose partisan cause would save the world.

Hazlitt, keen observer of Napoleon and Robespierre, sensed that if Shakespeare despised the populace, he also saw danger in men of too passionate will and arrogant virtue. Like Byron, Hazlitt detected in Wilberforce "a fine specimen of *moral equivocation*" and "ostentatious humanity," a self-indulgent righteousness that *Don Juan* mocked as typical of evangelical missionaries. Taking Cobbett's views over Birkbeck's, Hazlitt denounced Wilberforce in *The Spirit of the Age* as one who "preaches vital Christianity to untutored savages and tolerates its worst abuses in civilized states," one who "conquers other countries, and makes this a plea for enslaving his own."[41] Wilberforce would unbind the chains of Africa while helping "to rivet those of his own country, and of Europe." He was an egocentric opportunist, one for whom "the great question of the Abolition of the Slave Trade" could be colored by a "fluctuating, time-serving principle"; a patriot and philanthropist who votes on the side of conscience when he can do so with impunity. What difference finally was there between such a man and the Tyrant? Puffed with pride, Wilberforce was even "at one time, half inclined to surrender [the Abolition Bill] into Mr Pitt's dilatory hands" when he thought "the gloss of novelty was gone from it, and the gaudy colouring of popularity sunk into the *sable* ground from which it rose," Hazlitt spewed. "Sable" indeed—the connotation may not have been intended, but it fit Hazlitt's theme.[42]

By way of Hazlitt, Keats came to see acutely how the "Chief Poet" he had so admired in "On Sitting Down to Read 'King Lear'

Once Again" had been causing "a change" in him, a "very gradual ripening of the intellectual powers" that he associated with a desire to write "great productions."[43] The language of imagination "naturally falls in with the language of power," Hazlitt wrote, because it is attracted to "strong excitement," while "pure reason and the moral sense approve only of the true and the good." Man was more complicated than the abolitionists and moralists had shown (or would admit), the drive for power pervasive and ambiguous. In Hazlitt's highly charged "Letter to Gifford," Keats may have felt confirmation of his own growing sense that "great productions" turn not on the subtle dramatization of the current political scene, though drawing on it perhaps, but on a more interesting and complex politics within, richer ore to mine. Keats was delighted with the "Letter," which he called a "feu de joie," and with Hazlitt's wonderful damning, in "a style of genius." But it was the cooler descents into what Hazlitt had called "the subtle sophistry of the human mind, that tolerates and pampers evil in order to guard against its approaches," that may have helped refine for Keats where he now wanted to go with poetry. He mused out loud in his letters about beauty and truth, fancy and imagination, knowledge and power. The speculations were decidedly loose, conversations with himself, not statements intended for prefaces of biographiae literariae. And the speculations were not entirely new, for "the subtle sophistry of the human mind" was what he had been already exploring in some of the 1819 odes, showing how distance or abstraction cool the affections, making them remote, and divesting them of sensation in order to reconstitute them as thought. Possibly, in Hazlitt's suspicions of "philosophic fanatics," Keats saw his own presentiment that ideas could destroy the very humanity they would represent. "Cold Philosophy," as "Lamia" had shown, for all its stated good intention to reason men away from enslaving passion, could free the self but kill the spirit. The philosophers were wrong: There were no universal truths to which mankind might aspire, no ideals won that would be constant. The road was rougher, harder, darker, winding back upon itself. The implications for the antislavery movement were obvious: Gradualism at best, for true emancipation would have to be won over and over again, as the ending of *Prometheus Unbound* makes clear.[44]

Whatever the philosophical or literary persuasions that year, whatever the influences of anxiety over Fanny and George, Keats's reforming impulse in 1819 began to undergo a change, cautious doubt and careful reappraisal of what it meant for a poet to know what a nightingale would never know—"hungry generations," weariness, fever, and fret. In Hazlitt's analysis of *Coriolanus* Keats may have felt a prompting to move beyond expression of aching hope to the embrace of a sorrow or woe too huge "for mortal tongue, or pen of scribe," as the priestess Moneta commands in *The Fall of Hyperion*.[45] Personal, medical, and financial occasions were beginning to weigh on him. If he was beginning to see his way more clearly to a different kind of poetry, something more epic or more dramatic, it would be through a glass darkly, or too late. Reflecting on his lack of steady purpose that spring, Keats had written to George, "I am young, writing at random—straining at particles of light in the midst of a great darkness." But "give me this credit"—he used the money expression twice—"Do you not think I strive—to know myself?"[46] It was more a rhetorical question than not, a search by way of self-accusation and doubt. A few months later, in *The Fall of Hyperion*, Keats would make self-indictment central in his inquiry into the nature of a poet, and himself one of the "human sacrifices" on the "altars" of Poetry, prostrate before the priestess with the "gilt and blood-stained" head. The image was from Hazlitt's essay on *Coriolanus*; so was a certain testing of the limits of political passion. Tyranny could come in subtle guise when belief was at its most fervent. Coriolanus was right, though hardly humane, about the mass of humanity.

"Fanatics have their dreams, wherewith they weave / A paradise for a sect," as the opening verses of *The Fall of Hyperion* shrewdly observe, but the warning is followed by lines that seem to encourage poets to become fanatics and "love their fellows even to the death." The metaphor of the manacles of the mind now receives its most ironic treatment, as poets who "feel the giant agony of the world" are likened to "slaves to poor humanity" who "Labour for mortal good." The poet is trapped in a dilemma. The old conflict of vexing the world or soothing it has returned, renewed at the extremes. A bleeding heart who would "venom all his days" with visions of woe and guilt could wind up like the young and solitary spirit in Shelley's *Alastor*, who falls upon the thorns of life and bleeds. On the other hand, recoiling from a world where "but to think is to be full of sorrow / And leaden-eyed despair," a despairing poet might yield to "dumb enchantment" (l. 11), where an admirable poet would seek to enchant with "the fine spell of words. . . ." A provocative Moneta has it both ways. A true poet, she imperiously declares, knows that the miseries of the world "Are misery, and will not let them rest." But she also holds out as desirable a poet who "pours out a balm upon the world" and clearly excludes the suppliant poet from her pantheon of sage-humanist-physician. And what of the dreamer of this "dream," the subtitle of *The Fall of Hyperion*, the poet who would so define himself? His state of mind can be imagined as he restrains himself from blasting George and knows that he must restrain himself from loving Fanny. Meanwhile, the literary mode that might have wonderfully contained his paradoxes (as well as pay his bills) was there before him in Hazlitt's essays, but not by way of Kean. It was no idle shift that the goddess of

Hyperion in 1818, Mnemosyne (Memory), became "Moneta" in *The Fall of Hyperion*, an admonitory *belle dame sans merci* "Dea Moneta," the muse of money and the Roman mint.[47] The tyrant money was, of course, much on Keats's mind that year. The world, the world of poetry, the world of the self, were inextricable.

In May, Keats had heard the nightingale, the "deceiving elf" who sang of never knowing weariness, fret, or fever. In September, weary and full of a kind of "pleasant pain," he wrote George that he now wanted to compose without "fever." Did the shift signal a diminution of power? "Some think I have lost that poetic ardour and fire 'tis said I once had—the fact is perhaps I have."[48] In May he ended a four-month journal letter to George and Georgiana with a plea to know everything happening to them and with a faintly elegiac farewell: "God bless you my dear Brother & Sister." Over the last few months he had been moving from Hampstead to the Isle of Wight and back again, in spurts of creativity, but he was restless, depressed, and increasingly anxious over George's money problems as well as his own. In June he wrote Haydon, asking to "borrow or beg." Though always "much in want of Money," he now felt "driven" to "necessity" on learning that a distant relation was about to "file a Bill in Chancery." "Nothing could have in all its circumstances fallen out worse for me than the last year has done, or could be more damping to my poetical talent—," he wrote George, just one day after breaking off composition on *The Fall of Hyperion*.[49] "As badly off as a Man can be," not even able to "mortgage" his intellect "in the Press," Keats left for London to discuss debts and loans with his guardian, Abbey. But George kept pressing, concerned that a delay in more financing for him might mean "immediate opportunity being lost." Keats advised him not to "fret," for "in a new country whoever has money must have opportunity of employing it in many ways"—he surely had Audubon in mind.

The nagging question now finally surfaced: How could Audubon have so deceived people into thinking he was "A Man of Property"? Four days later, in the same journal letter, his suspicion and disappointment no longer repressed, almost sputtering, Keats asked bluntly for an account about how one could succeed in America, meaning in effect how George could have been tricked by Audubon. "It appears to me you have as yet been somehow deceived. I cannot help thinking Mr Audubon has deceived you. I shall not like the sight of him—I shall endeavor to avoid seeing him—." George "puzzled" him, he confessed. There was "no meridian" to fix him to. "[T]hose Americans" continued to fill him with unease, and he was reluctant to see George "become one of them" but in fact, he feared that the change had already occurred. Perhaps out of guilt, George suggested that Keats visit Louisville, not really expecting the invitation to be acted on. Keats replied, "You will perceive that it is quite out of my interest to come to America—What could I do there? How could I employ myself?" Indeed, the question really was, How was George employing himself? "You do not mention the name of the gentleman who assists you," Keats persisted—this was "an extraordinary thing." "How could you do without that assistance? I will not trust myself with brooding over this."⁵⁰ Had Keats known who was assisting George that fall, he might well have brooded, for the "gentleman" was Audubon's brother-in-law (and another Audubon victim), Thomas Bakewell, a successful businessman who had ties with the wealthy French community in America, and with shipbuilding and merchandising interests in Liverpool. Years later, Bakewell's name would turn up on subscription lists with others—Taracon, Berthoud, along with that of George Keats—the founding fathers of Louis-ville. Not surprising, the Jefferson County tax list for 1821 would show that Thomas Bakewell owned slaves.

In 1819 Louisville was growing fast, with new businesses forming along the riverbanks. Kentucky and Virginia, with a sur-plus of slaves, had already become slave-trading centers for plan-tations in Alabama, Louisiana, and Mississippi. There were whipping posts in town, but also meeting rooms for abolition and colonization societies. Especially in Virginia taverns, where the intellectual and cultural elite would meet for talk and ale, "Negro slavery was the prevailing Topic—the beginning, the middle and the end—an evil uppermost in everyman's thought; which all deplored, many were anxious to fly, but for which no man can devise a remedy." Although Kentucky's slave population was growing rapidly, however, there was still time to right the wrong. Birkbeck's tone was more fervent than hectoring. "This curse has taken fast hold of Kentucky, Tennessee, and all the new states to the South," though it had not yet endangered freedom in the swing states.[51] If wise heads prevailed (not to mention warm hearts), slavery could be defeated because it was economically unsound—a debatable proposition, however, for many of the Midwest "Europeans," as it was for the West Indian planters and their allies in Parliament. For Birkbeck, emancipation was a mat-ter of moral principle and corrective legislation. What he did not see, or would not acknowledge, was that slavery had gone beyond being agrarian practice or economic policy in the South and bor-der states like Kentucky. It had become a way of life, a myth and culture, working a subtle sophistry on many well-intentioned minds—including that of George Keats. Based on economic pol-icy, slavery had come to make economic sense. George was hardly in a class with Thomas Cooper (1759–1840), doctor, chemist, and onetime ardent radical, pantisocrat and abolitionist who had been an inspiration for Coleridge and who, once in Columbia, South Carolina, wound up owning two families of slaves and in 1826, writing a constitutional defense of the peculiar institution.[52] But such conversions were not uncommon.

If literary intellectuals in England were slow to comment on slavery in the West Indies and America in 1819, it was because the "crisis" superseding "every other topic of political interest and discussion," as the papers were reporting, was not emancipation but unemployment and poverty. Peterloo cast a long shadow. The fall of 1819 was hardly a "Keatsian" season of "mists and mellow fruitfulness."[53] The word *slavery* was now used almost exclusively for the exploited poor, whose plight was traced to the treachery or indifference of government. "Slavery," Shelley caustically intoned in "The Mask of Anarchy" after news of Peterloo reached him in Italy, "'Tis to work, and have such pay / As just keeps life from day to day." The abolition movement had ironically proved its success in the way slave imagery was now being appropriated for petition drives on behalf of children and factory workers. Descriptions of black Africans in chains, miles away in Guinea and the Caribbean, yielded to images of beggars sleeping on the streets of London and wandering the dingy back roads in the Midlands and the North. England was a poorhouse, a madhouse, a parliamentary house divided about what to do. Against this confusion and degradation, Cobbett continued to needle: "Who *ever* saw a beggar in America?"[54] In 1819 the implication was clear: Freedom should not be the right to starve to death in Birkbeck's wilderness. "Take out the *foreigners* [largely the poorer British immigrants drawn to the western countries] and the [free] *negroes*," Cobbett advised, "and you will find, that the paupers of New York do not amount to a *hundredth part* of those of Liverpool, Bristol, Birmingham, or London, population for population." For Cobbett, America was the promised land precisely because it had no "tax gatherers," no money draining politicians, no bankers, and, most important, "No Wilberforces. Think of that! No Wilberforces!" Abolitionists only deflected attention away from the farmers and factory workers, the honest poor who were working for slave wages. Keats was impressed. Oh! that he had "two double plumpers [votes]" for Cobbett, he exclaimed, once Cobbett was back in England and running for Parliament.[55] Birkbeck, despite his abolitionist stance, would always be associated in his mind with George's troubles in America.

In the letter dated November 8, 1820—it would be the last that would be sent from America—George began, "Again, and Again I must send bad news," meaning business. Keats, dying now and far away in Naples with the painter Joseph Severn, waiting out a quarantine on their way to Rome, never read it. But a cousin of Severn, who had seen George and Georgiana in America around that time, wrote that they were "very happy," living very comfortably, and only desirous of getting back to England.[56] Regardless, in a few short years, "Geo. Keats and Co." would be well on its way to making George Keats First Citizen of Louisville.[57] Convenience and the expectations of Southern culture helped fix his way of life. A few years after Keats's death, George expressed pride at being the brother of "the distinguished British poet" who would inevitably be inscribed in English literary history. Perhaps he needed to justify himself, to answer critics and old acquaintances of his brother who were accusing him of heartlessness, and of bleeding his brother dry, and to prove that John Keats's anguish over him had not been in vain. If so, the defense was unintentionally ironic, for it showed how much of an insider George Keats had become in Louisillle society, by becoming an outsider in ways that would have concerned his brother as a "friend to man."

Though only twenty-one, back in the summer of 1818 when

he first made his tentative way along the Ohio River, George felt that his character, manners, and habits then were already those of the "completely formed" Englishman. He had been and still fancied himself "more free from national prejudices than most men," by avoiding "that American tone which seems to have become engrafted on that of all my countrymen." But where Keats took the philosophy of Americans to be utilitarian, and therefore inimical to imagination, George seems to have looked no further than manners and mores for his cultural definitions. In April 1825 he wrote to Keats's old friend C.W. Dilke that he had "attended enough to Politics to be able to see the bearings of our lax governments upon the morals of a People already sufficient corrupt." A "Resident not unfriendly to America," George was in no hurry to establish a closer relationship.[58] By 1828, he regarded himself still as "an *Englishman*" and "obstinately *such*," preferring an English education for his children as "more favorable to the[ir] morals as well as the[ir] health."[59] The touch of the snob may have reflected Georgiana's attitudes more than his own, but undoubtedly George saw himself as a cut above. He looked to move to a better area, he wrote, where, among "a more congenial people," he might better cherish "sociable virtues." His business associates, after all, had all along been Bourbons and political conservatives, the heart of the slave-holding South. And so, effortlessly, innocently enough, he would write that year that for some time now he has been surrounded by "numerous negroos servants" in his household who, though they "impose upon us," do not "fret us."[60]

Land alone was no longer an index of status and wealth. Acquisition of blacks in a household was. There was money enough, however—a "profusion" in fact—so that George and Georgiana could scatter their dollars in a "congenial" mood, without sighing at their disappearance. Though his slaves did "impose" in both senses of the word, taxing him financially and psychologically, larger considerations had obviously worked the "subtle sophistry" that allowed George Keats to become a generous and forgiving slave master. As Cobbett had pointed out, the natural state for slaves, unbaptized and uneducated, was criminal. Now they could be saved. As it was, the comforts of life in Louisville relieved George from feeling burdened by his generosity, while paternalism assured that he would take responsibility for his slaves' welfare. Thus was Louisville linked to the West Indies, for Kentucky gentlemen, like West Indian planters, saw emancipation as a threat not only to their purse but to their way of life. Full and immediate freedom for blacks would only create upheaval. Such were the lessons of the French and Haitian revolutions. Carib chiefs might be noble, but they could also be avenging. And no black in Lousiville had even been a Carib chief. It made better sense to appease the mobs of Manchester.

In 1833, the Kentucky General Assembly would enact a resolution forbidding the importation of slaves for resale to New Orleans. By that time, George and Georgiana were prospering with lumber and flour mills and living in the most desirable part of town. Fanny Keats had married the young Spanish liberal Valentine Llanos, who glimpsed Keats in Rome three days before he died, and Fanny Brawne was wed to Louis Lindo, from one of the oldest and most esteemed Sephardic families in Britain, some branches of which had strong mercantile connections with the West Indies. Though readers then and for years afterward would prefer the romantic tales of Scott and Byron to Keats's sonnets and odes, his reputation grew, owing in some part to George's promotion.[61] Ironically, however, America's Keats, and England's for a time, would be the aesthete, the celebrant of leafy bowers and easeful death, Shelley's suffering *Adonais* made immortal by aimless struggle in a vaguely hostile world. Moneta's acolyte, poised between the impulse to vex the world and soothe it, would have to wait for recognition until such time as more subtle explorations of his poetry would begin. In *The Fall of Hyperion* Moneta says a poet must "die" into life. This was an empathic idea, deeper and more enduring in its effects than particular social or political programs. Still there were gestures worth making, the protests of the man, not the poet. Dying in Naples, Keats asked to be hurried on to Rome, it was said, so as not be buried in a place where sentries hovered on political watch, even at the theater.[62]

CHAPTER 6

Exile

1822

J ULY 8 WAS A MUGGY DAY, the first in the dry summer to promise rain. Shelley and Edward Williams had set sail in the
twenty-four-foot boat Byron christened *Don Juan* but which Shelley preferred to call *Ariel*.[1] No magic, however, would ever undo
the disaster wrought by the storm that came up that afternoon,
ten miles off shore. Shelley had been on his way back from Leg-
horn to San Terenzo on the Gulf of Spezia, where a financially
anxious Leigh Hunt, editor of the newly conceived periodical *The
Liberal*, was waiting for him. It was his volume of Keats's 1820
Poems that Shelley had with him when he drowned. Compared
with Byron's yacht, the *Bolivar*, the *Don Juan* was small and tricky
to handle in bad weather, it was said, though it was never clear
from conflicting eyewitness accounts if Shelley had reefed or not
when the winds came up and the waves started shooting high over
the deck.[2] The storm was one of the worst in years and sank better
ships than Shelley's. Still, there had been talk about Shelley's
casual interest in points of sail, as opposed to his apparent greater
interest in points of philosophy in the books he brought along to
read. Ironically (fatalistically, some would say), just that June he
had written to John Gisborne that he felt "too little certainty of

the future, and too little satisfaction with regard to the past, to undertake any subject seriously and deeply."[3] He had finally abandoned the play he had been working on intermittently for two years, *Charles the First*, and had not answered the enigmatic question posed in *The Triumph of Life*—"Then, what is Life?"—when he drowned.[4] Play and poem, fragments both, suggest that doubts and ironies were shadowing the celebratory prophecies of *Prometheus Unbound* and *Hellas*. What had lain uneasily about Keats's heart as "the burden of the mystery" had been deepening for Shelley into the burden of the *misery*.

There was, of course, private cause for the depression that had begun to infect the Pisan circle and drive it slowly into eccentric orbit in its last years. The ephemeral nature of passionate love, the deaths of children, the loss of friends, quarrels with publishers, debts, legal entanglements, exile, intimations of mortality—all aggravated a philosophical restlessness in Byron and Shelley that was showing itself as nostalgia, resignation, moodiness, at times despair.[5] Scenes of despotism and evil unfold in their dramas and poetry, threatening the primacy of imagination. In fanciful retrospect, it might even seem that Byron's boat had been the better named: It was possible to effect change as a Bolivar, none as an Ariel. Though a *libertador* might turn into an "autocrat of bondage" and a battlefield hero become a mass murderer behind palace walls, the slave of a benevolent master was still a slave, untutored in freedom. In *The Tempest*, the last line is Prospero's dubious command to the faithful but impatient Ariel: "Be free, and fare thou well!" What the poets clearly saw in 1822 was how frequently the newly free failed to live up to the expectations of liberation. "We had rather be the oppressor than the oppressed," Hazlitt had shrewdly observed. Though Shelley insisted all his life that we should be neither, he understood how slavery warped the disposition to fellowship. "Allowances must be made for emancipated slaves," Byron declared, but he had the followers of the exiled Prince Alexander Mavrocordato in mind, not lowly black Africans. Shelley extended the argument: If the Greeks were "degraded, by moral and political slavery" such habits "which subsist only in relation to a peculiar state of social institution may be expected to cease so soon as that relation is dissolved."[6] In other words, freed slaves who had been familiar with freedom were capable of reverting to freedom. Unfortunately for the rebellious blacks and runaway slaves in St. Domingue, descriptions in travel narratives and newspapers more than suggested that Negroes were incapable of managing what they never had. That view would gain strength in the decades to come, reinvigorating opposition to immediate emancipation. Meanwhile, the truth of Hazlitt's deadly observation impressed itself on the Continent. By 1822 it was apparent to the poets that progress was illusory, and blood would triumph over imagination.

Three years earlier, in Venice, lazing about on gondola rides with Shelley in a "fast-falling rain," Byron might allow how he was sometimes like his world-weary pilgrim Harold, but Shelley still clung to "those philosophical notions which assert the power of man over his own mind" (preface to "Julian and Maddalo"). Greek myth might avail in explaining warring forces within, but in two important particulars Shelley held that the modern world surpassed the ancient: the abolition of slavery and the elevation of women. The analogy was not unlike that drawn by Mary Wollstonecraft in *Vindication of the Rights of Women* (1792): "'Is one half of the human species, like the poor African slaves, to be subject to prejudices that brutalize them . . . ?'"[7] The intent was honorable, the effect unfortunate: Where women became metaphors for victims, blacks became metaphors for women and victims of rhetoric. Only an imaginative reader would see in the oppression of women "poor African slaves."[8] In *Laon and Cythna* (1817), the Tyrant Otho rapes the freedom-fighting heroine; in *The Cenci* (1819), the sadistic, power-crazed count violates his daughter. But though nothing yet was won, all was not yet lost: Where Wordsworth's poor females are real and representative of political and economic oppression, Shelley's violated women are emblems of a violated body politic that might still be cleansed. They serve a philosophical ideal by challenging its opposite: "Revenge," says Cythna, is "but a change and choice / Of bonds."[9] The revolutionary spirit in *Laon and Cythna* is audaciously enacted by brother and sister, also lovers, for revolution is the breaking of the "mortal chain / Of custom," and custom is the "queen of many slaves." To Shelley in the early buoyant years of exile, everything was possible. Out of Europe's dark night of the soul America was born, "England's chainless child."[10] Blake alone intuited a darker destiny: In "America, A Prophecy" (1793), the shadowy daughter Urthona stands before an enchained Orc, the image of God dwelling in the darkness of Africa, and intones, "On my American plains I feel the struggling afflictions / Endured by roots that writhe their arms into the nether deep." The stunning presentiment would go unread, though some years later, comparing political economies, De Quincey would remark that the New World was indeed like the Old World, maybe worse, where "slavery has assumed a far coarser and more animal aspect" than in Roman times.[11]

In 1819, the coarse animal behavior that mainly roused concern was associated with Peterloo, though the slave trade was not forgotten. That February, Coleridge, exercised over the "dreadful slavery" of the Middle Ages and the vassal slaves of our ancestors, conceded that such slaves were hardly in a league with the "miserable victims of the West Indies." But though "far from wishing to exculpate or palliate the evils of slavery"—the "deepest stain upon civilized man," Shelley called it in "A Philosophical View of Reform"[12]—it is primarily the evil of commerce as the oppression of the "little white slaves in the cotton factory," that rouses him in his prose and poetry. He deeply felt the horror of flesh-and-blood slaves in the Caribbean, but it was the horror of Manchester that moved him to the battle cry, "Ye are many— they are few."

Rebellion could veer two ways, however: toward freedom or toward anarchy. The tragedy of Peterloo was not only the precipitous panic of the militia but the frenzied massing of the mob, whose only social bond had been anger over exploitation. Abroad, reading about Peterloo and incensed over the killings, Shelley declared himself ready to abandon the "odorous gardens of visionary verse to journey across the great Sandy desert of Politics."[13] Deserts real and symbolic were much on his mind since "Ozymandias." In 1820 he expressed an interest in acquiring "Arabian grammars, dictionaries, manuscripts"; a year later, he was thinking about getting a "respectable appointment" in India "or any where where I might be compelled to active exertion" and be employed "politically."[14] But already by 1819, the condition of the "enslaved" peasants and workers of England seemed to be pressing the visionary poet to becoming an *acknowledged* legislator of mankind. The fierce, explosive exhortations of "The Mask of Anarchy" almost deny the "calm, lawful, and inflexible preparation for resistance in the shape of a protesting multitude" that Leigh Hunt claimed was the poem's theme.[15] "Slaves" of England work under conditions that not even savage men or wild beasts within a den would endure, Shelley charges in "The Mask," though he was hardly unaware of the connection between British imperialism and exploitation at home. In a related poem to "two political characters of 1819," the poet unleashes hatred on "Sidmouth and Castlereagh," whose politics encourage a cal-

lous toleration of the slave trade: "As a shark and dog-fish wait /
Under an Atlantic isle, / For the Negro-ship, whose freight / Is
the theme of their debate, / Wrinkling their red gills," Sidmouth
and Castlereagh, "vultures," "scorpions," "bloodless wolves,"
"crows," "vipers" permit it all.[16] When Hunt would note in 1832
that Shelley's countrymen still had not come to appreciate his
advocacy of reform through passive resistence, there was good
reason.

In "The Mask of Anarchy," when the weak see tyrants ride
over their wives, leaving blood on the grass like dew, they are
overcome with revenge, "Fiercely thirsting to exchange / Blood
for blood—and wrong for wrong" (xlviii). Could stanzas of murderous excess be counteracted by one line of prosaic advice—"Do
not thus when you are strong"? Perhaps, but the history of Haiti
since Toussaint had already provided an answer. The tyrant, the
despot, the enslaver were evil; the mass, the mob, the demagogue
were dangerous. Racial fears would only accelerate anxieties
caused by working-class rioting in England and tribal violence
abroad. Class and culture would increasingly become considerations of Freedom. In *The Prelude*, Wordsworth had coolly dis-
tanced himself from "slaves unrespited of low pursuits" who lived
"amid the same perpetual flow / Of trivial objects, melted and
reduced / To one identity," with "no law, no meaning, and no
end."[17] To Shelley the age was one of war, "the oppressed against
the oppressors," oppressors now including "pelting wretches"
who feed on the hard work of others. To Byron, it was an age
when "ignoble fowls" passed themselves off as falcons and were
hawked at by mobs of "mousing owls."[18] It was inevitable that
with the rising tide of revolution and anarchy, violent advocates
of emancipation and reform would find truth and beauty in a mirror. Shelley saw, as Wordsworth and Coleridge had seen the year
Shelley was born, how easily the fall of tyrants could usher in a

reign of terror and test the hard truth of *Prometheus Unbound*: "All spirits are enslaved which serve things evil."[19]

Though work had been proceeding in Liverpool and London in 1822 to establish a British and Foreign Anti-Slavery Society, supporters did not see any contradiction in urging at one and the same time immediate emancipation and more humane treatment of slaves.[20] But confusion in the politics of how to proceed already told the story. Humanitarianism was not necessarily a prime motive for antislavery outrage. On July 8, the *Times* argued that there was "no more fitting season than the Present, at which to rouse the public vigilance to abuses in the management of our distant colonies." But it was not slavery as such, the abuse of humankind, that provoked the *Times* so much as misuse of the profits of slavery—the corruption, bureaucracy, and waste that attended the slave trade and its backup banking companies and businesses in London. "It is a perverse truth that this country, which has prosecuted the colonial system with more zeal than any other, and which has appeared to make the acquisition of colonies a more vital principle of her whole political career, should likewise be that country of all others which has sacrificed with lavish folly the *benefits* desirable from the system," the *Times* asserted. Notwithstanding all nature of criticism, the antislavery enthusiasts plowed on, setting up regional societies, printing pamphlets, and arguing for high import duties on sugar not only from the West Indies but from the East as well. If they were aware that demonstrations at home and rebellions in the West Indies were intensifying suspicion of the Other, they made no mention of it. In fact, the myth of the Other, fostering the impression of the Negro as culturally alien and racially inferior, had just about replaced the myth of the noble savage. The "obeah" man of Caribbean voodoo who had helped move the message of revolution through the Haitian jungles would have been as foreign to the black who had been in Britain for generations as he was to the evangelical missionary in Barbados and Jamaica. But to the typical white Englishman, blacks in Britain were either invisible or beneath contempt, an attitude that would be innocently reflected in an account by De Quincey of an odd incident that occurred one day in London when he and Hazlitt were out walking.

The duke of Cumberland on his way to Pall Mall, was about to pass a line of common folk waiting to see him. The custom was that those directly in his path would remove their hats in a gesture of respect, while the royal personage, in turn, would bow back in acknowledgment. De Quincey and Hazlitt happened upon the crowd as the lines were forming. A "negro sweep," however, was also in the street, apparently oblivious to what was going on or what was required of him. What would the duke do in the face of such indifference by a mere Negro, De Quincey wondered. The Negro was part of the "great fact" of humanity living in London, a "rather muddy" fact, but a fact all in all, and one known to the person himself who repeated a thousand times a day that he was a "nigger" and a sweep. De Quincey posed the question dispassionately to Hazlitt, as though the "fact" before them were a counter in a game of chance or a problem in elementary logic." If human at all," which some people doubted, what might be expected? Blacks were "pretty nearly as abject a representative of our human family divine as can ever have existed," he remarked to Hazlitt. Nonetheless, he concluded, the Negro was a man, "however a poor one," and was protected by the law of the land.[21] Still, there he was, this "fact": How could the duke condescend to acknowledge such a "grub," and such a "very doubtful grub, as this"? The word at the time was not without its literal meaning of larva of insects, especially of the beetle, but it is not unreasonable to imagine De Quincey intentionally swiping at "Grub-street," where there were congregations of antislavery propagandists and literary hacks Dr. Johnson once defined as mean and needy writers of "temporary poems."[22] In any case, the encounter between duke and Negro would reveal the sympathetic differences between Hazlitt and De Quincey, each representative of positions held by leading literary intellectuals of the day."[23]

What the duke did in fact was stop in front of the sweep and give him half a crown, no paltry sum. De Quincey felt vindicated. Had the duke done otherwise, he explained to Hazlitt, had the duke bowed, or given money and bowed, he would have "vulgarised" the salutation and insulted the people. Could any honor be taken if the same bow given to the populace had been associated with a "paralytic negro sweep"? The crowd, as De Quincey remembered the scene, was pleased with the duke's decision, and everyone applauded the action—all, that is, save one: William Hazlitt. The black might be a fool, a mere scavenger, Hazlitt replied, but "I insist upon it that he was entitled to the bow, since all Pall Mall had it before him, and that it was unprincely to refuse it." De Quincey argued back that the bow would have been useless to the Negro, compared with the half crown, and that avoiding a sense of contamination and a dishonoring of the entire proceeding counted for much more.[24] To Hazlitt the Negro was a "bona fide specimen" of *Homo sapiens*, though "damaged," to be sure: Was the black not the equal of the white, he quizzed his companion, as capable of working, of paying taxes on his tobacco and broom and . . . of committing treason? Hazlitt, angry, was at his most brilliantly provocative and humane.

It would be the "greatest enormity in history, the stupidest and the most barefaced insult that ever was practised on the understandings or the rights of men," Hazlitt would explode in *The Liberal* in 1823, if "we should interfere in this quarrel between liberty and slavery, take the wrong side, and endeavor to suppress the natural consequences of that very example of freedom we [English] had set."[25] Hazlitt meant, of course, England's not interfering on the part of European "despots" and their "flagitous system" of provoking uprisings they could then say they were forced to suppress. The word *enormity* would surely invoke the slave trade, as would phrases about "hold[ing] mankind as a property in perpetuity" and committing outrages against "common sense and human nature." But Hazlitt keenly saw in the politics of slavery different kinds of wrong—political expediency, racial arrogance, narrow-minded assertions of property rights. He warned his country not to take the "wrong side," but was it clear which side that was? Leaders of reform sometimes seemed no more freedom-loving than tyrants and the mob.

There were distinctions to be made among those who put themselves forth as friends of the Negro. Coleridge clearly saw that Wilberforce was no Clarkson and thought enough of the difference to note it.[26] Asked whether he had ever thought of "his probable fate in the next world, Clarkson had replied, 'How can I? I think only of the slaves in Barbadoes!'" The answer prompted Coleridge to a comparison that would have warmed Hazlitt's heart and Byron's. Clarkson was sincere, but "Does Mr Wilberforce care a farthing for the slaves in the West Indies, or if they were all at the devil, so that *his soul were saved*?" For Byron, Wilberforce, the vigilant custodian of his country's virtue, remained an object of scorn and ridicule, a "canting Ludro," and "that son of a bitch." In *Detached Thoughts*, notebook entries covering the period from October 15, 1821, through May 18, 1822, under the heading "Orators," Byron wrote, "I do not admire Mr Wilberforce's speaking—it is nothing but a flow of words— 'words—words alone!'"[27] It was not just Wilberforce's rhetorical style that provoked Byron, but Wilberforce's substitution of words for deeds. Though Byron did not comment further on what appropriate action might be, the entry in *Detached Thoughts* stands as a strong statement against African slavery, particularly significant because it was a private reflection. It makes his "blood boil," he wrote, "to know that there are slaves. I sometimes wish that I was the Owner of Africa—to do at once—what Wilberforce will do in time—viz—sweep Slavery from her desarts—and look on upon the first dance of Freedom."[28] Like Hazlitt, Byron could attack with double-edged irony. Only an "Owner" can at once disown his property, while moral carpetbaggers can take their time. While Byron's antislavery sentiment is genuine, so is his skepticism: He had little faith that Wilberforce would move "in time," and therefore that the world would ever see free slaves dancing. Meanwhile, such stereotypes of the Negro, and worse, were taking deeper hold on the British consciousness, separating the issues of emancipation and freedom.

For Byron, as for most Englishmen of the day, the African Negro was a native of the "desarts" of the Sahara and the Sudan, from Niger to Nile, and images of liberated Negroes in happy dance were certainly consistent with depictions of tribal culture in contemporary journal narratives and travelogues. To note this fact is not to discredit Byron but to acknowledge him in his time.[29] Byron may have read the travel books of John Barrow, a friend of Murray, who had undertaken several expeditions for the Crown. One, a best-selling account of Barrow's five-hundred-mile journey east from Cape Town, taken in 1797 for the Admiralty, describes tribes of Negroes, in defiance of the white gods of the missionaries, worshiping black gods by dancing. Genuinely sympathetic to the plight of the Africans he saw, and holding slave traders responsible for degrading and demeaning them, Barrow might nonetheless have given opponents of abolition ammunition by remarking that domestic slaves at the Cape were much better treated than peasants in Europe.[30] The Empire was

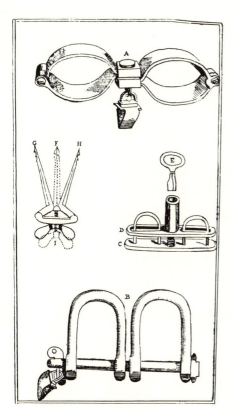

8a. (left) "These were specimens of articles in Liverpool . . . different iron instruments used in this cruel traffic. I bought a pair of the iron hand-cuffs with which the men-slaves are confined. The right-hand wrist of one, and the left of another, are almost brought into contact by these, and fastened together . . . by a little bolt with a small padlock at the end of it. I also bought a pair of shackles for the legs. . . . The right ancle [sic] of one man is fastened to the left of another, as the reader will observe, by similar means." Clarkson's History, Vol. I, p. 375. Courtesy of The New York Public Library.

8b. (below) Devices for restraint, torture, or punishment of slaves are not readily distinguishable. The exact purpose of this slave collar cannot be determined, though it probably had multiple uses, depending on the overseer's mood. From James Walvin, Slavery and the Slave Trade: A Short Illustrated History, 1983. Courtesy of The Macmillan Press, London.

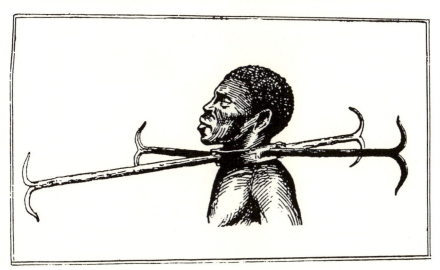

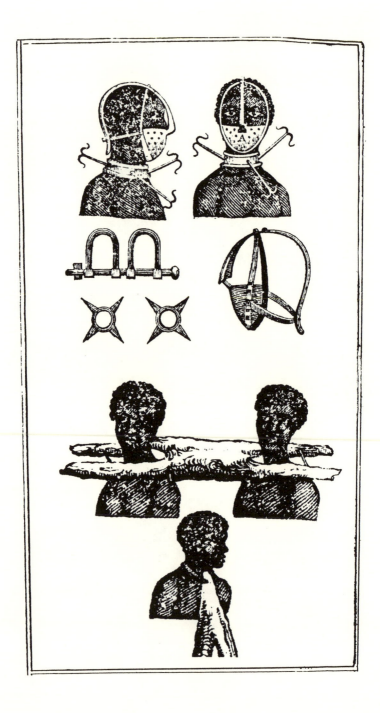

9. *An undated anti-slavery tract published in London shows and explains the use of "Log-Yokes," the "Head-frame and Mouth-piece . . . with Boots and Spurs," and assorted iron devices used to restrain or torture slaves. From Liverpool Packet No. 5, "Slavers and Privateers," Scouse Press, Liverpool.*

10. Establishments such as the Black Boy Inn were evidence of the pervasiveness of Guinea cargo in Bristol. The port was also, however, home to inquiring minds and crusading spirits: Clarkson began his abolition work taking testimony on mutilated black corpses and cannibalism on the slave ships, while Coleridge's 1795 lectures at the Black Boy Inn set a course of dead reckoning against the trade. This photograph was taken c. 1874, when the inn was demolished. Courtesy of The M. J. Tozer Collection, Bristol, England.

HERE
Lieth the Body of
SCIPIO AFRICANUS
Negro Servant to y Right
Honourable Charles William
Earl of Suffolk and Brador
who died y 21 December
1720 Aged 18 Years

I who was Born a PAGAN and a SLAVE
Now Sweetly Sleep a CHRISTIAN in my Grave
What tho' my hue was dark my SAVIOR'S sight
Shall Change this darkness into radiant light
Such grace to me my Lord on earth has given
To recommend me to my Lord in heaven
Whose glorious second coming here I wait
With saints and Angels Him to celebrate

*11. These eighteenth-century tombstones in a suburb of Bristol, England, suggest
Africans may be as good as whites in the sight of God—after they are dead, if they
have adopted the ways of civilization, and assuming they receive God's grace. Until
that time, slavery is presumably a divinely-ordained state. The grave markers
corroborate the religious geopolitics of the 1821 "Moral and Political Chart of the
Inhabited World" among these illustrations. Courtesy of the Bristol Reference Library,
England.*

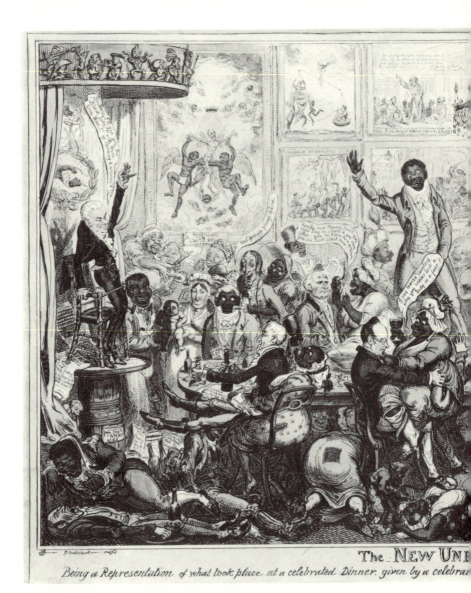

The NEW UNI

Being a Representation of what took place at a celebrated Dinner, given by a celebra

12. *Cruikshank's "New Union Club" (July 19, 1819) parodies Gilray's "The Union Club"
(1801), with Negroes substituting for the Irish, and a different set of Englishmen. The general
theme, that abolitionist philanthropy is merely a disguise for greed and gain, is portrayed in the
riotous club scene, and also in the pictures-within-the-picture. To the left, William Wilberforce
(the meeting's chairman) leads the toast: "Brothers, I'll give you the 'Black Joke,'" referring to a
lewd song. The journalist John Stottard, bottle in one hand and broken decanter in the other, is
below and to the right, bouncing in the lap of a Negress. Seated at the table, with his back to the
Negro prince, a severe and dignified expression on his black-smudged face, is Wilberforce's brother-
in-law, James Stephens; a Negress grins (or leers) at him, saying, "Really now Massa Teven, you
right say be* sham'd you own Color! you no know how amsum you bis look* black now."
Zachary Macaulay, the noted philanthropist, is at the near side of the table, peering through his*

,UB.

society. ———— *Vide Mr M.c...t's Pamphlet entitled "More Thoughts" &c &c"*

Pubd July 19 1819 by G Humphrey 27 St James's Street London

spectacles at a fat Negress whose haunches he is attempting to grasp; she has raised a large bumper of wine, asking, "I say Massa 'Caulay why you nebber look a body in the face?" The gentleman whose pocket is being picked of a letter addressed to Smith Esq. M.P. is William Smith, M.P. for Norwich, and a leading abolitionist.

As a group, the abolitionists are seen as great promoters of fighting, lechery, drunkenness and miscegenation. In the foreground, lower left, a Negro footman vomits into the open mouth of an unconscious Quaker; in the background, the pictures-within-the-picture further mock the four identified protagonists. Courtesy of the British Museum.

ORIGINAL POETRY.

SONNET.
No.-III.
TO TOUSSAINT L'OUVERTURE.

TOUSSAINT ! the most unhappy man of men,
Whether the rural milk-maid by her cow
Sing in thy hearing, or thou liest now
Alone in some deep dungeon's earless den,
O miserable Chieftain ! where and when
Wilt thou find patience ? yet die not ; be thou
Life to thyself in death ; with chearful brow
Live, loving death, nor let one thought in ten
Be painful to thee. Thou hast left behind
Powers that will work for thee, air, earth, and skies !
There's not a breathing of the common wind
That will forget thee : thou hast great allies :
Thy friends are exultations, agonies,
And love, and man's unconquerable mind.

W. L. D.

13. Wordsworth's sonnet "To Toussaint L'Ouverture," as printed in the Morning Post, February 3, 1803. Deceived by Napoleon's forceable attempt to re-enslave the blacks of St. Dominigue, Toussaint led an heroic and bloody revolt in which the French army and plantation managers alike were slaughtered. After setting himself up as a quasi-emperor, Toussaint, the "most unhappy man of men," was captured and incarcerated in a French prison, where he spent the brief remainder of his life. Although Wordsworth offers the "miserable Chieftain" the joys of heaven, the genius of Romantic poetry is to avoid palpable or overt moral purpose, and explore the imaginative consciousness of both the poet and of humanity. Courtesy of The Newberry Library, Chicago.

moving east. Ceylon, Mauritius, Malta, and the Cape were growing more important than the West Indies. Besides, if so many Negroes were slaves, there might be good reason. God's will, it would be said, was that the sons of Ham should be in servitude, an attitude inadvertently suggested in a drama Byron was working on that June, one of his darkest compositions.

In Part One of *The Deformed Transformed*, a derivative Faustean folk drama, the devil appears as a "tall black man."[31] "Dusky [black], but not uncomely," the description is hardly flattering, alluding as it does to the opening verse of the Song of Solomon, where the words are traditionally attributed to a harem girl (ll. 5–6). Gratuitously—and therefore tellingly—the devil, who calls himself the "Stranger," volunteers the information that if he wanted to, he could be "whiter," but he has, you see, a *"penchant"* for black—it's "so honest, and besides, / Can neither blush with shame nor pale with fear," he tells the physically deformed protagonist, Arnold. The broad hint is taken by Arnold, a hunchback, for when he agrees with the Stranger that they should change appearances, the devil willingly assumes Arnold's shape, asking to be addressed as "Caesar," a great name for "bloodhounds," while Arnold rejects the form of the "tall black man" and elects to be Achilles. In fact, however, a second transformation seems to have been intended in the unfinished play, as Arnold, no longer physically deformed, yields increasingly to morally deformities. *The Deformed Transformed* breaks off at the opening scene of a third section, but before it does, there are suggestions that Arnold, not unlike Othello, a subject of conversation between Byron and Shelley that year, will succumb to self-loathing, jealousy, and "tyrannous hate."[32] For a drama begun at the height of revolutionary movements, the implications were not promising: Arnold and his Virgilian "bloodhound" become witnesses to history as tableaux of blood and gore, and the Stranger sounds not unlike the despondent poet in Shelley's pageant of the "triumph" of life. [33] A culture of despair seemed to be taking root in the lovely garden of Italian exile, political as well as personal disappointments tempering the philosophical ideal. Shelley's own dramatic fragment at the time was no more auspicious.

In January 1821 the *London Magazine* had promised readers a play on the subject of Charles the First by "the illustrious poet, Percy Bysshe Shelley." [34] Though no converts to the poet's "creed," the editors expressed confidence that Shelley's new play would be even better than *The Cenci*. But, as Shelley explained, *Charles* was a "hard nut to crack," and he left off composition in the middle of a short fifth scene. Had he gone on with it, however, it may have borne bitter fruit, for brief and disjointed as it is, it more than hints at the impossibility of realizing the God-wininan philosophy of *Political Justice*, with its hopes for the perfectability of man. In *Charles the First* there seems to be only the certainty of recurring violence and the failure of moral reform. Hazlitt's Charles, high priest of the ignorance and superstition of divine right, is for Shelley more Hume's monarch in the *History of England*—a "well-meaning but imperfect man" who is hardly a match for evil counselors and bloodthirsty citizens. Shelley's Charles seems more like Hazlitt's Coriolanus, while a grim song, sung by Archy the fool, recalls Keats's "La Belle Dame Sans Merci" in its lament that no birds sing but the "widowed bird." Additional lines even seem to mock the elegiac joy of "The Intimations Ode," where birds do sing and the meanest flower that grows can give thoughts too deep for tears: "There was no leaf upon the forest bare, / No flower upon the ground, / And little motion in the air, / Except the mill-wheel's sound." [35]

Though barely five tentative scenes, *Charles the First* suggests that Shelley had moved away from allegorical prophecies and toward dramatic representations of "negative capability," but with-

out Keats's hard-won tentative peace. Hazlitt, no admirer of
Shelley, particularly the "philosophic fanatic" of *Prometheus Unbound*, would probably have been pleased with *Charles the First*,
where despotism is all-encompassing, the privilege of royalty and
ecclesiastics, and rebellion but the violent desire of ordinary citizens for vengeance.[36] There seem to be no heroes on the horizon:
Everyone suffers the corruption of the world's slow stain. Both
the vicious Archbishop Laud and the victimized "Second Citizen" would dine on carrion. The entire cast of *Charles the First*
seems destined for the deathcart in *The Triumph of Life*. Of the
three groups that contend for power—King, Parliament, mob—
all are tainted. In the opening scene, a group of manipulators and
intriguers from the Inns of Court parades past a group of un-
scrupulous and intolerant libertarians. An older citizen, once a
"slave in Egyptian bondage," now looks to blood and war to solve
problems. A younger citizen, idealistic youth, will probably fall
upon the thorns of life and destroy himself or be destroyed.[37]
Then there is Archy, whose cryptic utterances are ignored. He
is the poet as skeptic, the seer as impotent, the prophet in vain.
His remarks sometimes strike "what eludes philosophy," yet he
dare not aim his "archer's wit" beyond his "gilded prison" for fear
of being understood (sc. ii). By 1822, in the wake of conspiracy
attempts and repressive acts reported to Shelley by his friends,
it was clear to publishers at least what could happen to those
whose barbs struck too sharply at government targets. Manuscripts could be censored, dramatic compositions not be per-
formed, and, of course, men and women could be arrested.

Abandoning *Charles the First*, Shelley wrote that a "slight circumstance" had shattered the "fragile edifice" of the "concep-
tion." He did not explain, but added, "What motives have I to
write.—I *had* motives—and I thank the god of my own heart they
were totally different from those of the other apes of humanity

who make mouths in the glass of time."[38] The tone is resigned, the Promethean spark sputtering. Hunt recalled no physical change in Shelley that year, except the brown hair becoming slightly touched with gray, but clearly there had been inner change in Ariel, seen in the tone and the diction of *Charles the First* and *The Triumph of Life*. An impulse to enslave and tyrannize may lie deep in the human condition, and save for small moments in the history of time, spasms of hope in the early days of revolution, there was little evidence that imagination had redeemed anything or any one but a "sacred few." What Hazlitt complained he missed in the poet of 1819—a sense of life as "worn-out, thread-bare experience" that might "serve as ballast" to the mind—had now become a heavy load. In addition to noting the "vivifying soul" of *The Triumph of Life* when he reviewed it, Hazlitt commented also on its "morbid genius."

At the start of the following year, Byron yielded to "the worm, the canker, and the grief" in more sentimental ways.[39] In *The Island; or Christian and His Comrades* (January 1823), his nod to the mutiny on the *Bounty*, South Sea idyllic life is achingly invoked in a love story that replicates the Haidée episode of *Don Juan* but is set against rebellion prompted by pleasure-seeking, not the rights of man. An unheroic Fletcher Christian appears briefly as the ringleader of a group of sailors whose only motive is to avoid the "toil and tumult" of contemporary life. His role is minimal, his cause piracy not politics. Against such indolence and lawlessness, Captain Bligh's appeal to order and command is understandable, even admirable. No Corsair, no Harold, no late-canto Don Juan, this rebel *malgré lui* is merely a narrative device to get to the island, where, in the fantasy love tale of a "blue-eyed Northern child" and a young "gentle savage of the wild"—the "New World" stretching her "dusk hand" to the Old"—a poet's heart and soul might be temporarily renewed. Byron seems to have grown tired of the satiric chase or, as the late cantos of *Don Juan* demonstrate, at least of the chase. The Regency outlaw, the poet whose work the *Literary Gazette* called licentious" and full of "moral vomit," in *The Island* seems to look on authority as a civilizing force, sentimentality as a necessary antidote to history, and rebellion as a waste of energy and time.[40] Nostalgia rules *The Island*, an opiate longing to ease into a world of no pain. Though young Torquil is finally captured and drowns in an attempted escape, the lovers are reunited in death in Neuha's wondrous cave beneath the sea.

So cleanly severed from politics and real life at sea is *The Island*, that the vision of "Peace and Pleasure" in its last canto—a Shelleyan-like paradise as "only the yet infant world displays"— suggests the ultimate impossibility of escaping from the mundane world with all its pain and sorrow. Perhaps writing *The Island* was cathartic. After writing it, Byron set sail in the summer of 1823 for a very different kind of island and in January 1824 arrived in fever-ridden Missolonghi. Dying, devising military plans for hapless independence armies, cadging money for the Greek cause, and working untiringly for the self-interested philanthropic Greek Committee in London, Byron well knew what happened to the "dusk hand" of the New World when it was extended to Europe, and to all revolutionary movements once they succeeded. On January 22, completing his thirty-sixth year, he wrote of seeking a "soldier's grave" in Greece, "land of honourable death." Three months later, on April 19, he was dead. Coleridge, who had slipped away from Dr. Gillman to buy opium, silently watched Byron's funeral cortege winding by Highgate Hill on its way to Hucknall in the north. This Byron, the politically engaged disbeliever, returned to England at last, was still in exile.

If Wordsworth and Coleridge did not flirt with fantasy or

descend into doubt or despair, it was because they willed themselves a faith in God and country which Byron and Shelley would or could not. Steadfast conviction, however, did not translate into action; unswerving devotion to liberty did not issue in support of West Indian Negroes or the working-class oppressed. To a request from the abolitionist James Montgomery to contribute to an anthology in aid of chimney sweeps, Wordsworth writes that he feels for their "unhappy situation," and hopes to see the practice of employing such helpless creatures abolished, but that at no period of life has he "been able to write verses that do not spring from an inward impulse of some sort of other."[41] It was so; what was also so was an obstinate integrity, which could lead him to hold on forever to moral principles whose means of realization he had rejected. Slavery was wrong: so was immediate emancipation. In 1829, at the height of the renewed emancipation debates, Wordsworth composed a verse epistle, "Liberty," taking for an epigraph Abraham Cowley's distinction between the liberty of a people and the liberty of a private man. The first was when people were governed by laws they made for themselves, Cowley had written, the second when a man was the master of his own time and actions, "as far as may consist with the laws of God, and of his country." It was the second liberty that defined Wordsworth's stance on emancipation, for without the right exercise of freedom, freedom would be lost. For all his sometimes cranky complaints about cities and change, the conservative bard of Rydal Mount seems to have spent more time thinking about emancipation than radical Wordsworth spent on abolition.

More versified piety than poetry, "Liberty" nonetheless reinforces Wordsworth's lifelong belief in freedom, understood as unrestricted movement in the natural world and as free choice consistent with religious and national culture (Cowley's second example). "Liberty'"s theme—that all living creatures must be free, no matter how comfortable the confining conditions—had been the topic of an overwhelming number of poems Wordsworth and Coleridge composed in their West Country period. That same theme now constituted, in effect, an answer to those who offered to ameliorate slave conditions rather than eliminate them. One cannot make a prison cell pleasant, as Toussaint L'Ouverture or the Prisoner of Chillon might have testified. Though the ostensible subject matter of "Liberty" is trivial—fish swimming freely in a pond—it is for that very reason that it is significant, recalling the Ancient Mariner's blessing of water snakes. Observing fish recently released from enclosure in a "crystal cell," the poet imagines how they have been saved from the certain death that would have awaited them in their "bauble prison."⁴² To be at liberty is the natural and instinctive desire of all living things: The "emancipated captive" bird will not return to captivity, regardless of the luxury, and "No sea / Swells like the bosom of a man set free; / A wilderness is rich with liberty." Although the poem is obvious, even monotonous, in its insistence on physical freedom as the primary condition of liberty, several lines also suggest a more subtle point: that power is arrogance, no matter how generous the intention. Power corrupts, and a benevolent dictator is a dictator still.

"Humanity," a companion piece to "Liberty" composed at the same time and originally intended as a part of it, suggests that the impulse to enslave reflects a failure of the empathic imagination. Between a caged lark and a slain albatross lies a difference not in kind, only in degree. Tempering wrongs by offering so-called palliatives can therefore make matters "worse" and create "deadlier" effects ("Humanity"). If the "high-minded Slave" must spurn a kindness that would make him less forlorn, if he must affect a "look of pitiable gratitude" because his bondage may be made somewhat lighter—the very argument the "humane" planters were still making to Parliament—then wrong is done not only to the slaves, by turning them into feigning and vengeful beings, but to the enslavers, depriving them of an opportunity to exchange pity for empathy, sentimentality for sentiment. Not unknowingly had *Lyrical Ballads* focused attention on the tellers of the tales, on the narrators who come upon the destitute and the miserable and whose responses become the imaginative centers of their poems.

"If Power could live at ease with self-restraint!" Wordsworth exclaims in "Humanity," then "*harsh* tyranny" would cease and "unoffending creatures find release / From qualified oppression, whose defence / Rests on a hollow plea of recompense. . . ." A bit convoluted syntactically, to be sure, but Wordsworth was composing (though not yet publishing) "Humanity" at a time of impassioned pleas against immediate emancipation, and he may have wanted to separate his own preference for gradualism from the kind of go-slow policies being put forth by obstructionists. "Humanity" stresses two words and two words only—*harsh* and *fettered*. If willful instincts could only be chained, then slaves might be unchained and the "fettered" and the exploited, slaves in fact and enslaved labourers, "find release."[43] But, as Wordsworth saw it, Power could not "live at ease with self-restraint," and "qualified oppression" only allowed the planters' allies in Parliament to define freedom according to formulas for "recompense." Though hardly a memorable outpouring of imagination, "Humanity" is a remarkable verse statement. It connects all manner of slavery, linking the occupation of Greece, "Bright Galaxy of Isles," to the exploitation of workers in England, where "floors and soil / Groan underneath a weight of slavish toil," and these with the audacities of African Slavery: "Shall man assume a property in man? / Lay on the moral will a withering ban? / Shame that our laws at distance still protest / Enormities, which they at home reject!"[44] In "Humanity," the sixty-year-old stamp collector of the Lakes hardly seems the self-centered turn-coat his political and literary enemies were making him out to be. For a poet whose sympathies were continually reaffirmed by the vagrants and beggars he happened to meet, the Negro was a rare encounter—an exile on a boat from Calais ("September 1"), an incidental sighting in the motley of a London crowd (*The Prelude*, book 7). Concentrated in towns and cities or below stairs in country homes, blacks, though they certainly existed in the North Country, were not a natural or habitual part of Wordsworth's experience. Thus he could drop into thoughtless expression, as he once did with a parody of a Ben Jonson lyric, "Queen and Huntress chaste and fair," mocking the widow of the Haitian dictator Henri Christophe. On October 24, 1822, Dorothy wrote to Catharine Clarkson that William and Sarah had had a hearty laugh over a poem they "threw off last Sunday afternoon," which she "*must*" send on for her friend's amusement.[45] They had all been talking about Clarkson's compassion for all human beings, especially his "perseverence in the *African* cause, and of his last act of kindness to the distressed Negro widow and her family," even inviting the Queen to stay at Playford Hall, near Ipswich, in Suffolk. Well, they talked about it and then, "Oh! how they laughed" at the "tender" image of the "sable princess" at Clarkson's fireside, prompting Wordsworth to mocking verse. In "Queen and Huntress," "Hayti's shining queen" is presented full of "pomp" and pretension as an "ebon" figure with "diadam" sitting in a "British chair." Each of the three stanzas ends with an incantatory tribute to the shining black presence sitting opposite her "champion." Beneath the lightly mocking tone, however, there is affectionate regard for Clarkson, who obviously put no barrier between his principles and his actions. The poet of "September 1" still appreciated the man who had climbed abolition's "obstinate hill," and who was now attempting the even rockier ascent of emancipation. The "sable" princess is advised not to let "Willy's [envious] holy shade" get in the way. "Willy" was William Wilberforce, of course, and by using a nickname, Wordsworth, like Byron, was signaling the difference between Clarkson's "faithful heart" and Wilberforce's giant ego, while also, unintentionally, revealing the persistence of Negro stereotyping.[46] A few years later, in the otherwise powerful blank verse "On the Power of Sound," Wordsworth would write of "the tired slave" for whom "Song lifts the languid oar, / And bids it aptly fall, with chime / That beautifies the fairest shore, / And mitigates the harshest clime" (iv)—sentimental drivel that belonged to an earlier antislavery age, but that now lived anew in the patronizing tone of indifference that eased the way for racism.[47]

By 1829, Wordsworth, like Southey, and the rest of England, would have had his stereotypes reinforced by well-intentioned but condescending journal accounts such as *Six Months in the West Indies* (1825), written by Coleridge's "harum scarum nephew," Henry Nelson Coleridge. Though Sara Hutchinson, Coleridge's adored "Asra," would dismiss *Six Months* as that "conceited work about West India," Henry, who became engaged to Coleridge's daughter, revealed enough of British attitudes toward Africans to suggest that such attitudes were taking hold.[48] Shortly after meeting Sara Coleridge in December 1822, ill health forced Henry to travel to a warmer climate, and in 1825 he went to Barbados with another cousin, William Hart Coleridge, who had just been appointed bishop of Barbados and the Leeward Islands the year before. "The Black Bishop," Southey referred to him in the spring of 1824, noting how unusual it was that so rich and well-educated a young man of unlimited opportunity would choose to go to the West Indies out of a "sense of duty."[49] But in fact, William Hart Coleridge was in the grand tradition of service, which the American Quaker John Woolman had popularized in his own *Journal* (1775), recently reissued in London. Crabb Robinson, who had been at Lamb's in January, looking over his library— "such a number of first-rate works in very bad condition is, I think, nowhere to be found"—commented on Woolman's *Journal*, a favorite of Lamb: a "perfect gem," a work of "exquisite purity and grace," whose author, not incidentally, was one of the first to have had "misgivings about the institution of slavery." Henry surely saw West Indian blacks through William Hart Coleridge's sympathetic eyes, but these were also the eyes of the establishment that had appointed him, and of a government still ten years away from legislating emancipation. *Six Months in the West Indies* is hardly a tract against slavery. Some even found its tone in part flippant or vulgar, but *Six Months* did find an admirer in Coleridge's son Hartley, who wrote his younger brother Derwent that he found Henry's journal "very clever" and "tolerably sensible," which meant, in fact, that it took a careful "gradualist" line toward freeing the blacks.[50] Striving to be fair, Henry has strong advice for planters: Do better by your slaves, lest the law do worse unto you. This was not morality talking so much as practical politics. It was clear that some law, sometime soon, would pass Parliament. Clear and forthright on the issue of slavery as an evil, Henry also argues that it is a necessary evil until education prepares Negroes for self-government. Such counsel no doubt pleased his uncle, Samuel Taylor Coleridge, though Hartley Coleridge wondered if Henry felt "sufficiently the moral enormity of the slave system."[51]

For certain, as the preface to the third edition of *Six Months* would reveal, Henry Nelson Coleridge was aware of how publication in 1832 might reflect and possibly influence the Emancipation and Reform bill debates. He refers to the "awful crisis" of the country at a time "when the right hand of the colonial power of England is hacked at with a pertinacious hatred, of which there is no example in the history of domestic treason or foreign hostility." He has a "deep conviction" of the "immense importance of the West Indies to our maritime superiority," and "of the truth of the political views of which, in respect of the conduct of the abolitionists, the events of every day and hour more and more persaude me." The die was cast; sides finally had to be taken. Though criticizing planters on several of the islands for their cruel ways, Henry chooses to be first a politic, not a moral, man. The voice throughout *Six Months in the West Indies* is not that of his hellfire preacher uncle from Bristol days or of "Mr. Slave-Trade" Clarkson, but that of a conspicuous conciliator. It is the voice of reason, not rhetoric, seeking to inform, not move. For its very moderating tone at a crucial time, its arguments would give aid and comfort to the enemy of the Negro.

Freeing 800,000 slaves was a "mighty work" that must be done, Henry writes, but in an orderly manner. He makes it clear that he does not like Methodist and abolition types holding forth in taverns. On the other hand, he recognizes that the planters do not see, and do not want to see, the miserable conditions on their plantations.[52] Still, he falls out on their side. He defends them, stating that his fellow countrymen who have not been to the West Indies cannot appreciate all the little kindnesses extended to the Negroes by the planters and their representatives. Yes, he has heard reports that planters are "monstrous," but the slaves in the West Indies are better off than people think. Cobbett, in this year before Emancipation, must have been smiling. Negroes work less, eat and drink more, have more money, and dress more gaily than "nine tenths of all the people of Great Britain under the condition of tradesmen, farmers and domestic servants," Henry writes. Though Henry's final word is for the planters, encouraging them to move quickly, he is is forever balancing his concerns. No Emancipation Act can turn slaves into citizens, he argues, the very point Wordsworth and Coleridge had been urging in opposition to the stifling, bureaucratic Poor Laws. To be habitually industrious, Henry points out, one needs "moral stimulus," which means education, and here, he feels certain, the planters can take the lead by providing instruction and clothing and opportunity for slaves to purchase freedom.[53] The planters had other ideas: They would ignore such advice and simply dig in.

The year an Emancipation Bill finally passed Parliament, Coleridge would look back on the era of abolition as crucial in the history of slavery. In the margin of William Fitzwilliam Owen's *Narrative of Voyages to Explore the Shores of Africa, Arabia, and Madagascar* (133), he would write that after reading such an account on the "state of the negroes in their own country," surely Englishmen could be "pardoned" for thinking that if only the power and wisdom of law had regulated the Middle Passage and secured kinder treatment for the Negroes, "gradual Christianizing and final emancipation of the Slave after his arrival in the Colonies" would have been provided, and the transportation to the West Indies could have been looked upon as "a blessed Providence for the poor Africans."[54] Otherwise, the poison of the old slave society would leach into the new (slave) society and into the general body politic. Not only did "civilizing" education not occur, however; not even minimal religious instruction was permitted on many of the islands, and where it had been, it was often withdrawn for fear of fomenting dissent and encouraging strategies of violence. International slave trading continued, as Henry well knew it would, and West Indian slaves were worked harder in proportion to diminishing supplies, economic conditions, and planter independence. The poets, unable to reconcile the promises of imagination with the starker evidence of their senses and their reading, retreated to revising earlier commitments. The human heart could not be legislated.

Abolition had exacted his most fervent emotions, Coleridge would recall on the eve of Emancipation. ". . . I then stated in the Watchman—and I lost some friends by it—that no good will be done by applying to Parliament—that it was unjust—and that in twenty years after a Parliamentary Abolition—the horrors of the Trade would be increased twenty-fold. Now all acknowledge that to be true. *More* Africans are now transported to America for Slavery—the Middle Passage is more horrible—and the Slavery itself worse."[55] But nowhere in *The Watchman* did Coleridge make such an ominous prediction, nor do his letters mention the loss of any friends because of the lecture or the essay "On the Slave Trade." His comments do, however, show the degree to which the more complex and threatening issue of emancipation caused gradualists to rationalize their position by pointing to their earlier embrace of abolition and not unsubtly reminding readers of God and country. In one of Wordsworth's more insistently virtuous pieces from this period, "The Armenian Lady's Love" (1830), the lovely daughter of a Muslim ruler who falls in love with a young Christian slave recognizes the better way, which is white and Western. He, of course, is a slave only in body; his soul is freely married to that of a countess in Venice.[56] The young Armenian nonetheless undoes his chains and vows to convert. The message of the poem is internally inconsistent, however, for the young woman's act of charity springs from imagination and impulse, nurtured somehow among the pagan "misbelievers" of her native land. Had the young man been black, she would not have freed him. Ending the slave trade meant seeing morality when there was no longer economic advantage; ending slavery meant confronting questions of culture and class.

A half-century after Abolition, De Quincey—who had gone

out of his way to indicate that his father, a West Indian merchant, had not been a slave trader, the same De Quincey who had so adamantly celebrated the untiring efforts of Clarkson—would now cluck his tongue impatiently at how easily people still confused *"slavery* with the *slave trade,"* as though the two prongs of the antislavery movement were the same![57] He had been conversing with a "very respectable and well-informed surgeon in the north," who simply assumed that Wilberforce and Clarkson had been engaged in*"emancipation."* Nothing could satisfy him to the contrary, in spite of efforts to convince the gentleman that "however *ultimately* contemplating that result [emancipation]," Clarkson and Wilberforce disowned it as their "express and immediate" object.[58] The breach was widening, even among gradualists. Crabb Robinson took another view. Clarkson, he wrote, hardly "anticipated" that slavery itself would be abolished by government in his day, but nevertheless Clarkson's "exertions to accomplish the first step," the abolition of the *slave-trade*, his "great work," were absolutely essential to the ending of slavery.[59] What Crabb Robinson saw was that there never could have been a difference in the aims of abolition and emancipation. The younger poets would have said there never *should* have been. If not cause, certainly the motive that drove men to enslave on the high seas and on West Indian plantations was the same. But of course, there were now more than two sides to The Negro Question. The kind and degree of gradualism was no longer the main issue.

CHAPTER 7

Rydal
1833

IRONICALLY, THE WORD *Negrophobia*, meaning "an intense dislike of negroes," seems to have been born with the vote for emancipation: The OED cites a first recorded use for October 1833 in the *Westminster Review*, just two months after the passage of "An Act for the Abolition of Slavery Throughout the British Colonies."[1] Though there never was a comparable noun *negrophilia*, *negrophile* had already appeared in an 1803 issue of the *Edinburgh Review*, where it was applied to those whose mischief-making "revolution" had brought about the ruination of the "colonists." Though *negrophile*, used only in a disparaging sense, did not take on the vicious racial connotations of *nigger lover* that would emerge later on in America, the term *negrophobia* did bring together matters of race and class.[2] At the center of often fiery Parliamentary debates over work rules for slaves and compensation for planters simmered the potentially explosive issue of the nature of the Negro or, as Carlyle would put it in *Fraser's Magazine* in 1849 with his usual sarcastic indelicacy, "The Nigger Question."[3] Carlyle, solidly in Cobbett's camp against abolitionists, ranted that Emancipation was just a prelude to "black Anarchy" and Social Death." He praised Cobbett for his militant defense of humanity and the poor," but the poisoned quills he himself shot at West Indian blacks made Peter Porcupine's barbs seem like mere pinpricks.[4]

The West India Plan, as the Emancipation Bill tended to be called, would not only mandate the elimination of slavery in the colonies but would also promote "the Industry of the Manumitted Slaves" six years and older, including those at sea, and compensate "Persons Hitherto Entitled to the Services of Such Slaves." In the charged atmosphere of the debates, however, there were odd alliances pro and con. Planters and their allies made it clear that they doubted the ability or willingness of freed Negroes to work as hard as slaves, while Benthamite liberals and many abolitionists argued that ex-slaves would work harder when they worked for their own land and profit. Though Southey referred to the emancipation fight in the extreme, as a squaring-off between obstinate planters and rash abolitionists, somewhere in between there were gradualists, put off by the strident racism of the colonists and pseudoscientists but offended also by the base materialism offered by proponents of immediate freedom who were often also advocates of laissez-faire. Among the gradualists was Coleridge, who determinedly saw himself in June 1833 as an "ardent and almost life-long Denouncer of Slavery." He referred to the bill ambiguously as the "Ministerial Plan," suggesting that it was a government contrivance more than a parliamentary negotiation, but his real objections to it, like Wordsworth's, were on cultural and psychological grounds. In its assumptions the plan was, simply, "insane." "The World has not been [the Negroes'] Friend, nor the World's Law," he caustically observed. Thus the world's *"motives"* would have little force for Negroes in making them work hard or not.[5] Believing that freed slaves would indeed work as hard—and as miserably—as any other farm or factory worker, the gradualists also differed among themselves about how long such training would take beyond the apprentice-ship period, and whether or not it should be accompanied by Christian education. In any case, by 1833 it was brutally apparent in Jamaica that private Negro ownership of land had not acted as a restraint on social license or political upheaval. And Haiti, of course, to those like Wordsworth who had looked for "exulta-tions" to follow "agonies," was proving a political and economic disaster.

Unlike agitation for abolition, when economic and humani-tarian interests had the happy fate to coincide, the prospect of emancipation divided friends of the Negro while drawing to-gether a variety of opponents. Some saw in the loss of slaves the loss of colonial power and thus a weakening of international ad-vantage. Others sensed ominous parallels in black rebellion and working-class alliances and feared the growing power of the mob. Still others saw in the rivalry between advocates of the working class and abolitionists an eventual competition between the work-ers themselves, with ex-slaves taking jobs away from whites. Then there were the dubious theological arguments: God and country might command the immediate release of enslaved peo-ple, but God and country could also argue for protecting church and state, order and tradition. To many in the government, Tory and Whig alike, the growing empire seemed to make manifest England's destiny to export light to the darker continents, but missionary work took time. Fear of social change already wrought by political and industrial revolution overflowed as recollections of hostilities. Only the propertied, it was said, were responsible citizens, though only the propertied owned slaves. Countering eighteenth-century ideas about universal benevolence, the dark side of Enlightenment had been expressed by Gibbon, who ar-gued that the "savage nations of the globe are the common ene-mies of civilized society."[6]

In June 1833, embracing a sentiment he had flung aside years earlier, Coleridge wrote that although he did not object to talking about the "*rights*" of Negroes in the West Indies, as a way of stimulating the people "*here,*" he "utterly" condemned the frantic practice of declaiming about the rights of the blacks themselves. "They ought to be forcibly reminded of the state in which their brethren in Africa still are," he sputtered, and taught to be thankful "for the providence which has placed them within reach of the means of grace." Rights flow from a sense of Christian duty, and "it is under that name that the process of humanization ought to begin and be conducted throughout."⁷ Clearly, almost a half-century after the French Revolution, it was apparent that equality had never been intended as the philosophical equal of liberty, and that brotherhood did not flow from gaining freedom. Not even Toussaint had had the word *fraternity* embossed on his official documents, which did bear the other two watchwords of the revolution.⁸ As Wordsworth told the Reverend Dewey that July, shortly before the vote on emancipation, the world was "running mad" to find answers in politics,"whereas the great evils, sin, bondage, misery, lie deep in the human heart."⁹ And possibly in the descent of man, others would soon suggest.

Far from England and the Caribbean, Charles Darwin, on board the HMS *Beagle* in 1831, had been making notes on geological and zoological evolution that would strengthen the position of outspoken racialists, though such an application of his hypotheses and findings had never been his intention. Indeed, sounding more empathic than either Wordsworth or Coleridge now, Darwin wrote in his Diary that those "who look tenderly at the slave owner and with a cold heart at the slave never seem to put themselves in the position of the latter; what a cheerless prospect, with not even a hope of change!" Darwin invoked God and conscience in his expressions of sympathy, sure to irritate the negrophobes who looked to the Bible for justification. In words reminiscent of *Detached Thoughts*, where Byron wrote that it made his "blood boil to know that there are slaves," Darwin declared, "It makes one's blood boil, yet heart tremble, to think that we Englishmen and our American descendants, with their boastful cry of liberty, have been and are so guilty."[10] That slavery is "palliated by men, who profess to love their neighbors as themselves, who believe in God, and pray that his Will be done on earth!" struck Darwin as grievous abomination. Though his own scientific inquiries would be misappropriated to make a biological case against the Negro, in fact the Negroes Darwin observed on his voyages, grown more European and "civilized" because of missionaries, convinced Darwin that historical progress in the form of social improvement was possible, though "improvement," of course, was understood as taking place in a Christian culture. Byron, no more overtly friendly in *Don Juan* to the Negro—or to the Jew, Arab, or Papist either, for that matter—saw missionaries and philanthropists as earnest egomaniacs intruding on native populations. Still, where Evangelicals abroad might *im*pose their patronizing ways, radicals at home, like Cobbett, would *dis*pose of black rights altogether, and not without the support of the Poet Laureate: "I sent up a petition . . . in favour of our little white slaves and refused to sign one for the immediate emancipation of the black ones," Southey wrote on the eve of the Emancipation vote. "The next insurrection will settle the question of slavery in Jamaica."[11] The remark would definitely have hit home, referring as it did to the Christmas rebellion that had swept western Jamaica in 1831—violent uprisings, suppressed in kind, with a vehemence that had jolted the nation. Reportedly 20,000 to 30,000 slaves were involved from over 200 estates. Sparked essentially, it was believed, not by ignorant, miserable, and mistreated slaves but by a more educated Creole elite, aided and abetted by evangelical missionaries (in some quarters the revolt was called the Baptist War), the aftermath was greater polarization of the races. Free Negroes were now a powerful force in Jamaica, outnumbering whites three to two, and Creoles formed a substantial part of a population rife with racial tension. A "siege mentality" gripped the remaining whites on the islands, the papers reported, including white fears of black "retributive brutality."[12] In the wake of the Jamaica riots Southey's caveat would hardly have gone unheeded: "God grant that the miserable conditions of our own poor may not one day . . . lead to consequences quite as dreadful in this country!"

Race wars had become class wars; class wars were becoming race wars. In September 1831, following the defeat of another Reform Bill, demonstrations had broken out again in the Midlands among the unemployed and poor who saw nothing in the Reform Bill that spoke to their interests. Government leaders blamed the middle class for inciting riots; the middle class blamed the lower class; and advocates of the working class blamed the upper-class abolitionists.[13] Common people, *mobs*, were inheriting the earth. Byron, dead seven years, would not have winced at Coleridge's unfortunate comment in August 1833: "Men of genius are rarely much angered by the company of vulgar people, because they have a power of looking *at* such persons as objects of amusement of another race altogether."[14] To Coleridge, the Reform Bill was the "mad and barbarizing scheme of a delegation of individuals" responding to the masses, and the masses were now associated with the Negro, a class mob with no humility, no fear, no reverence, "like Ham the accursed."[15] Wandering out from time to time in his black breeches, discoursing still on the sins of man, a clergyman without a pulpit, Coleridge never sought to rekindle the antislavery outrage of his earlier days. Holding forth in the various homes he rested in, or from his bed at Dr. James Gillman's, Coleridge would declaim against indolence, particularly the Negro's. Such men will not work harder even if they feel an incentive for greater opportunity and a chance to better their condition, he contended.[16] Wages offered by planters would not stimulate industry. He knew: He had calculated that West Indian Negroes could get all they needed working only twenty days. Why, then, would they want to work more?[17] Although there was none of the arrogant impatience or mocking challenge in his remarks that tended to mark the hostile outpourings of the negrophobes, literary history would not be kind to Coleridge in his later days. He would be accused of "tergiversation," to use one of his own favorite words, and worse. Clearly the opium patient of Highgate was no longer the abolitionist firebrand of Bristol, but he was no doctrinaire bigot, either. Indeed, in his frank, sometimes prejudicial, comments on Negroes and emancipation, Coleridge openly avowed sentiments that some liberals in a later age would bury in slippery hypocrisies.

In June 1833, with passage inevitable, Coleridge's cautious comments took on heat. "Have you ever been able to discover any principle in this Emancipation Bill for the Slaves, except a principle of fear of the Abolition Faction struggling with a dread of causing some monstrous calamity to the empire at large?" he wondered. "Well! I will not prophecy; and God grant that this tremendous and unprecedented act of positive enactment may not do the harm to the cause of humanity and freedom which I cannot but fear!" But yet, what can be hoped, "when all human wisdom and counsel are set at naught, and religious faith—the only miraculous agent amongst men—is not invoked or regarded!"[18] Coleridge well knew that where there was "religious faith" Christian feeling need not follow—the Ancient Mariner instinctively blesses the water snakes, but his piety at the end is merely compulsive, and his presence among good Christian folk elicts only shunning and fear. Like Wordsworth, Coleridge thought that trusting to acts and amendments to rectify moral wrongs was illusionary, and the Emancipation Bill seemed more a matter of political expediency than "religious faith." Without "miraculous" agency, there could only be relentless necessity, enslavement to fate. In this sense, Wordsworth, Coleridge, and Darwin were one: The triumphal march of humanity could evolve only under the banner of God—except that once upon a time Wordsworth and Coleridge believed that imagination was a God-given faculty, awful and sacred, and that poetry was its visionary representation on earth. The sadness—Coleridge once called it "dejection"— was that he had lost the "miraculous" power. He confined his outpourings now on liberty and emancipation to friends and visitors. The public debate that spring and summer of 1833 was carried on without him in articles and reports, anecdotes and dispatches, and the occasional doggerel that had attended Abolition. There were no prophetic raptures from the poets, no imaginative light cast on the dim and perilous way of progress.

Excerpts from the parliamentary debates ran the length and width of pages in the oversize *Times*. The regional presses and the periodicals followed with reprints and articles. The *Post* objected to the "emancipation scheme," saying that it was "calculated" to alarm the colonies. The preference was for a gradual extinction of slavery, during which time a police force could be established, moral and religious education instituted, and colonial legislatures urged to promote industry. The Liverpool *Albion*, however, reprinting arguments in favor of emancipation, insisted simply that its time had come because slavery violated every principle of justice and humanity; even the duke of Wellington had declared that Emancipation would mean the "advancement of the negro character and intellect." On August 24, after the vote for emancipation but a year before implementation, the *Westmorland Gazette and Kendal Advertiser* reprinted a not untypical letter from the *Times* in which one "Justitia" suggested that immediate emancipation would only injure the poor Negroes. As slaves, Justitia pointed out, the Negroes did not have to worry about clothing, housing, weather, or food, and besides, since most people would not distinguish between Negroes free and enslaved anyway, ex-slaves from the West Indian islands could never be united with whites in a free peasantry in England.[19] If the English constitution could not be proclaimed on different soil, for different people, if it could not be the law of Spain or Sicily, how could it possibly apply on Jamaica? Rely on it, Justitia concluded, a freed Negro population would only mean an idle population, slothful, miserable, troublesome. It was a "harsh view of human nature," Justitia allowed, but, alas, a true one. Fifteen years later, in his damning essay "Occasional Discourse on the Nigger Question," Carlyle would make no such apologies: His West Indian Negroes were "pumpkin" eaters who let the sugar cane rot, dooming the island and, by ominous extension, the nation and empire. Theories of racial superiority fed imperialism; imperialism fed theories of racial superiority.

Despite the number of articles on emancipation, the average citizen in 1833 remained relatively uninformed about how slaves really lived in the West Indies, and content with explanations of Negro torpor as justification for slavery. Recognizing the psychological problems inherent in the condition of slavery, "the habit of abject obedience," Coleridge attributed the apathy of slaves to their having been "*brutified*," which was the "dire effect" of slavery, not its justification, and which he held was therefore cause for "bitterest condemnation."[20] In fact, as he well knew, the myth of the planters' Eden and of sullen and lazy slaves, particularly on Jamaica, had been deeply impressed on the public

mind by whitewashed reports from plantation managers, sentimental stage plays, and pallid, topographical accounts by occasional visitors. Only in the years directly preceding Emancipation
did relatively accurate reports on the order of Henry Nelson
Coleridge's emerge, though even here the striving to seem objec-
tive precluded accusation. Not widely seen were accounts such
as Henry Whiteley's *Three Months in Jamaica* (1833), published for
the Anti-Slavery Society, in which one Bagster, a Methodist,
tells how he came to Jamaica on September 3, 1832, knowing only
what he had read in the papers, then dramatically changed his
mind. Before his arrival, he said, he had been under the impression that the slaves on Jamaica were well treated and that abolitionists in Parliament were making much ado about nothing,
especially considering the graver problems of factory life, child
labor, and the evils of manufacturing. Surely, he thought, the
condition of the Negroes on Jamaica must be preferable. Then
he saw: cart whippings, beatings "severe beyond description,"
white men coupling with black women as "the custom of the
country." When he left, he was threatened.

The year closed on a less than sanguine note for the future of
the Negro. On December 31, 1833, the *Times* filled its entire third
page with summaries of the "Slavery Abolition Bill" and of the
legislative measures yet to be taken to enact it in the colonies.
Reports from the different colonies showed how complicated the
issue was, for each colonial jurisdiction required a separate model
to meet its different needs, though foremost among them was
provision for an "effective police establishment" based on the Jamaica Police Act of 1831. As the framers of the Emancipation
Act had anticipated, in order to make emancipation work, there
would have to be an adequate supply of officers on all the islands
and sufficient means of imprisonment in rural areas. Suprisingly,
when the Jamaican House of Assembly ratified the Slave Eman-

cipation Bill, there were protests but no incidents. On St. Vincent, however, objections were vociferous and on Tobago, the lieutenant governor read out a threatening proclamation against breakers of the peace, demanding also that slaves show "unqualified obedience to their masters." The *Times* ended its roundup of the colonial response with an apparently irrelevant comment: "A considerable quantity of rain had fallen at Barbadoes, and the crops were, in consequence, in a most flourishing condition." That was about all that would be flourishing.

No one for or against the bill had really doubted that Emancipation would come to pass, but disagreements over monetary obligations, terms and conditions of apprenticeship, and maritime and commercial interests were serious. Conditions for Negroes were not the concern so much as compensation for the planters. Near the final vote, a "long desultory debate" was begun that continued for a week, a raucous exchange over prices and regulations. What would happen to sugar, to revenue collections, to the 18,000 seamen involved in West Indian trade? At the last minute, petitions deluged both houses of Parliament. On August 1, 1833 The *Liverpool Gore General Advertiser* reported that two days earlier, in Commons, the gallery had to be cleared because of "strangers" shouting "downright robbery." The planters knew the die was cast, but the death-rattling could be deafening. They were infuriated by Lord Mulgrave's reference to His Majesty's slave population as property of the Crown, not theirs, but King William IV was conciliatory—what else!—a far cry from his maiden speech in Lords when as duke of Clarence, he had warmly supported the slave trade. Clearly, when the bill passed, no one felt vindicated, and debate continued. On August 21, 1833 a new theme was introduced, and though not pursued, it would prove incendiary in the decades to come: Was a Negro good enough to sit in either house? someone asked. Meanwhile, as dispatches from Jamaica showed that August, despite the relative quiet that attended the local ratifications of the Emancipation Bill, panic and dismay were mounting. Various orders were read out to slaves on all the islands, reminding them that Emancipation did not mean immediate freedom. Though the Negroes were addressed in various proclamations by governors and officials as "friends," they were told to honor their owners, lest their "friends" impose stiff penalties for disobedience and insubordination. And of course they would understand that despite an Emancipation Act, they would be obliged to work for nothing for several years. Attitudes hardened all around. The Emancipation Act freed no one. It compensated owners, though hardly the black slave owners of Africa, where tribal traditions of blacks enslaving blacks went on unimpeded by European law or politics. Neither the planters nor the poets seemed to notice this anomaly, but governments did.

On August 1, 1834, in relative quiet, the Act to Abolish Slavery in the British Colonies, IV William 2 & 3, went into effect. The vote had been the issue, not the date of implementation, which many papers ignored. On July 29, the *Tyne Mercury; or Northumberland, Durham, & Cumberland Gazette* carried a notice of a public meeting of the Friends of Negro Emancipation and Religious Instruction in Newcastle under the heading "Abolition of Slavery." In honor of the event, it noted, money would be collected for the rebuilding of chapels destroyed on Jamaica during the rioting. The *Berwick Advertiser*, deep in Walter Scott country, on July 31 waxed sentimental—"tomorrow's sun will not strike upon the eyeballs of a slave." It was as though time had stood still, and the happy prophecies of abolition days had returned. "Slavery is no more" will be heard from isle to isle, the *Advertiser* proclaimed, as it offered a verse of thanksgiving full of recycled clichés for the return of the beautiful isles ravished by "adventurous strangers" raiding "Afric's shores." History wondrously succumbed to revision: God, wroth with such inquity, had sent hurricanes, earthquakes, and evils to the island until such time as the British flag restored freedom. What the *Advertiser* not untypically advertised was a longing for the good old days. The celebratory couplets concluded with an insipid "eve o'emancipation" soliloquy in the voice of a noble savage counting the moments to liberty.

The *Liverpool Chronicle and General Advertiser*, similarly overcome by the significance of the day, reprinted Cowper's "beautiful little poem," "The Morning Dream," because it was "so singularly prophetic of the lst of August, 1834, that most glorious day for England." The inanity of Cowper's allegory in which Freedom, a lovely woman, causes Demon Oppression to die would do nothing, of course, to address the specific problems that Emancipation would present to nation and empire. On July 26, 1834, *Felix Farley's Bristol Journal* reprinted on page one without comment on "either the reasoning or the facts," an *Edinburgh Evening Post* article, "West India Compensation." No comment was necessary, but the substance of the article was sure to rouse British ire. According to the *Edinburgh's* calulations, it would be at least two years before any money voted by Parliament would be available for the "oppressed and ill-used planters," and years before there would be any reliable information from the colonies about slave prices from 1823 to 1830, on which compensation would be based. Could the poor colonialists have been "misled" into passing the act, the *Edinburgh* wondered out loud. "From our hearts we pity the planters and their families" who are suffering, not from "actual privation," admittedly, but from "cruel anxiety." The *Kendal Mercury*, on August 9, 1834, quoting *Fraser's Magazine*, asked under the heading "The Poet's Condition," "Where are the poets?" Wordsworth apparently had had nothing

to say, and the "great man, Coleridge," as Crabb Robinson recorded with "sorrow" that July, had just died.[21]
Ironically, but not surprisingly, it would be Wordsworth
with his opposition to immediate emancipation but commitment
still to the moral life, who would prove the most consistently humane.[22] Insistent always that moral life could not be legislated,
Wordsworth stopped short of the anger that could engulf Hazlitt,
the philosophical confusions that could daunt Keats, the frustration that could overtake Shelley, the resignation that could grip
Byron close to death, the guilt that tranquilized Coleridge. Continually invoking the revisionary gleam, Wordsworth rewrote
himself, easing his way, philosophically, politically, and poeti-
cally to the conservatism of the later years. But his humanity remained constant. Admittedly, it was easy to think otherwise
about the tall, wiry, harsh-looking figure in the long brown sur-
tout, the conservative Anglican surrounded by his court of
friends, family, and faithful followers at "Idle Mount."[23] How
could the poet of "Toussaint," "The Banished Negroes," sonnet
series to freedom oppose the immediate emancipation of the Negroes? How could he who once drew breath from revolutionary
days turn away from those who would overthrow tyranny? The
answers were always in the poetry. "Perilous is sweeping change,
all chance unsound," he would declare in the sonnet "Blest Statesman" (1838). The line—from Spenser's "All change is perilous,
and all chance unsound"—emphasized the dangers of "sweeping"
change. For a poet who had dedicated himself to the spontaneous
overflow of powerful feeling recollected in tranquility, time and
reflection were crucial in distinguishing between transitory rapture and eternal joy. "Blest Statesman" counterposes "slave of
fate" and "Servant of Providence," the servant being the "blest"
statesman. By linking "slave" and "fate," Wordsworth was reminding readers of the state of the *un*blest, of the dangers of living

immoderately, enslaved to the senses—the lessons of "Laodamia." The betrayal of the French Revolution still haunted him. Gradualism was not just a political position but a psychological necessity.

In a heady essay, called a "Postscript" (!), meant to accompany a new volume of poetry in 1834, Wordsworth would argue that his sentiments were the same as they had always been, but that too many poor were now being encouraged to seek relief in ways that could not lead to lasting happiness, and that matters would only worsen were current political sentiments like the new Poor Law act to prevail. To Crabb Robinson he wrote in February 1833, "you mistake in supposing me an anti-Reformer, *that* I never was, but an anti-Billman, heart and soul. It is a fixed judgment of my mind that an unbridled democracy is the worst of all tyrannies."[24] Wordsworth associated the oppressed with the mob and the mob with easy manipulation by those who pretended to good intentions. As the populace increasingly embraced the cause of emancipation, and antislavery clubs, committees, societies, and tea parties grew, he remained adamant in his caution but never lost sight of the difference between metaphor and reality. In the sonnet "The Dunolly Eagle," written in 1833, he renewed the theme of "Liberty" and "Humanity" that being free means, first, being free in the eye of nature. An eagle "kennelled and chained" seeks the "sea blue's icy depths," more so if by storm he is driven into a "castle dungeon's darkest mew." "Poor Bird!" Nature can indeed betray the heart that loves her, but it is not nature that the poet blames. The sonnet ends with the observation that it is "man" who makes his brother a creature "[t]hat clings to slavery for its own sad sake."[25] As in *Lyrical Ballads*, the attention in "The Dunolly Eagle" is on the captor not the captive, the victimizer, not the victim.

As usual, Wordsworth saw into the heart of things, though

what he saw did not prove comforting. In a letter to Benjamin Dockray of Lancaster in April 1840, ostensibly thanking him for sending on a copy of his "valuable paper on Colonial Slavery," Wordsworth in effect provided his own little lecture on "this important subject."[26] In the question of slavery, he began, "there are *three* parties—the slave, the slaveowner, and the British people." Tellingly, he left out a fourth party, Negroes who were now no longer slaves but certainly not part of "the British people." But he did pose a critical question: Should a slave owner in the present state of society, "as a matter of private conscience," retain property in the slave "after he is convinced that it would be for the slave's benefit, civil, moral, and religious, that he should be emancipated"? His answer should have confounded his enemies, for whatever the pecuniary loss, Wordsworth says unequivocally that the slaveowner, "taking a right view of the case, ought to be prepared to undergo it." Here was the Wordsworth who would eventually help convert a reluctant Ralph Waldo Emerson from proslavery to abolition. Here, also, was the uncompromising poet of "Resolution and Independence"—a slave should make "a good use of his liberty," the only way of truly recompensing his master for his "sacrifice." Wordsworth wanted no law but that of the human heart, not only because he knew that legal recourses were no solution to moral problems, but because he mistrusted the law. It could be used to imprison freedom fighters like Toussaint, expel Negroes, and impose or excuse cruelty. It could not make peace in a way to prevent future violence and revenge. Anticipating by 150 years conditions in twentieth-century America, Wordsworth wrote that, without a sense of the moral obligation due masters as people who acted in accordance with the laws and habits of their country, whether or not those laws were right, freed slaves could easily feel that their "late oppressors" had been delivered over to them to do with as they pleased. Such a proceeding would be a "wanton outrage upon the feelings of the masters, and poverty, distress, and disorder could not but ensue." Failing thus to show "caritas" toward their former oppressor—Keats's negative capability—the oppressed would become the new oppressors and, as in the West Indies, continue to move the races further apart, while inflicting injury on their own.

In 1840, in response to Haydon's request to include him in a painting honoring the Anti-slavery Society, Wordsworth declined, saying he could not be in the picture because he had played no active part in the antislavery movement, despite his lively interest in it.[27] Nonetheless, he feels compelled to speak out: "[N]o man can deplore more than I do a state of slavery in itself. I do not only deplore but I *abhor* it, if it could be got rid of without the introduction of something worse, which I much fear would not be the case with respect to the West Indies, if the question be dealt with in the way many excellent men are so eagerly set upon." There was some yielding here from the 70-year old eminence, though not much. Negroes were better off as slaves than as free men, he explained to Dockray, because as free men they could be exploited. No law can protect animals from the cruelty of their masters, the weak from the strong. In fact, such a law would only increase the evil: "The best surety for an uneducated man behaving with care and kindness to his beast lies in the sense of the uncontrolled property which he possesses in him."[28] The comparison was unfortunate, to be sure, and thoughtless, even asinine, but Wordsworth was no negrophobe. Though he hardly had illusions about the tyrannies practiced by the educated, he was as impatient with the myopic expectation that laws could legislate feelings in the "uneducated" as he was adamant against the expectation that poetry be propaganda. He would have been dismayed but not surprised at the fact that in 1992, in the old mining village of Frickley in Yorkshire, a place that seems not to have changed from the days of the Boer War, clubs would proudly bear the names of the patriotic past with a kind of "xenophobic defiance"—"The Empire," "The Pretoria," "The Niggers." "You won't see any black faces in Frickley," a local snarls.[29]

The fear of the "introduction of something worse" than slavery, the certain perpetuation of violence that Wordsworth wrote about to Haydon, had in fact by 1840 seriously infected the British Empire and the New Jerusalem across the sea. In 1845 Crabb Robinson would report that at Rydal certain topics were now excluded from conversation, among them "the American question"—slavery, Texas. A Tory atmosphere reigned at Rydal, but not a Tory mentality. Wordsworth had always been uneasy with the "precipitate course." He would prefer that slaves purchase their freedom in stages. Place freedom within reach of all who desire and deserve it; otherwise the sugar islands will know "the horrors of insurrection, devastation, and massacre. . . ." Peterloo would come to the West Indies. There was, in short, a paternalistic obligation to educate and prepare people for freedom. Wordsworth sensed that immediate emancipation would only accelerate and intensify rioting in the Caribbean. He would have been critical of the violence, but like Coleridge, Byron, Shelley, and Keats, he would not have blamed the victims.

With Emancipation, the political goal of the most fervent moralist, radical, and idealist was achieved. But the imaginative complexities which had caused the poets to regard mere politics as a distraction—even as a fraud—would long persist and would long continue to manifest themselves with great intractibility. Shortly after passage of the Abolition Bill in 1807, Coleridge, in a playful, self-deprecating mood, found himself mulling over advertisements for runaways that had appeared in the July and August 1801 issues of the *Kingston Mercantile Advertiser*. The notices, without distinguishing among their objects, called for the recapture of Negroes, horses, and mules.[30] The ads, about twenty such, had been clipped and tucked away among "the wrapping papers in the trunk of an officer just returned from the West India station." One feels a pause in the reflections, a shudder of truths sinking in. "What a History!" Coleridge exclaims. "Horses and Negroes! Negroes and Horses! It makes me tremble at my own Nature!" His own nature, the nature of man, had been, and would always be much on his mind. Announcing to himself yet again a magnum opus he would never get around to write, a history of the progess of morality from the time of William the Conquerer to the present day, he muses, mockingly, "Flattering News for Anno Domini 2000!" as it compares itself with the seventeenth and eighteenth centuries. It was his imaginative sense of his own century that made him "tremble," but the cursed gift of all the Romantic poets that they could out of fears in solitude predict the destiny of nations.

Notes

CHAPTER I

1. *Felix Farley's Bristol Journal* (FFBJ) 20 June 1795, p. 1 gives thanks for the "late rains." *Sarah Farley's Bristol Journal* and *Bonner and Middleton's Bristol Journal* also refer to "late seasonable rain."
2. The image, sails thin and sere, is taken from "The Rime of the Ancient Mariner," fytte 7.
3. The descriptions are from the essay "On the Slave Trade," *The Watchman*, in *The Collected Works of Samuel Taylor Coleridge*, ed. Lewis Patton, Bollingen Series LXXV (Princeton: Princeton University Press, 1970), and Herman Melville's *Redburn, His First Voyage; Being the Sailor Boy Confessions and Reminiscences of the Son of a Gentleman in the Merchant Service* (1849; reprint, New York: Anchor Doubleday, 1957). *Redburn* contains brief but significant passages on free blacks in Liverpool and at sea. On a more insidious note, Carl Bernhard Wadström, chief director of the Royal Assay and Refining Office in Sweden, noted some of the different ways nations had of thinning out slave cargo on the Middle Passage: The English threw them overboard; the French poisoned them them first. See *Observations on the Slave Trade and a Description of Some Part of the Coast of Guinea* during a voyage made in 1787 and 1788, in company with Doctor A. Sparrman and Captain Arrehenius (London: 1789), 30. Healthy Negroes were also jettisoned if cargo needed to be lightened, as was the case in the notorious *Zong* affair

in 1783 when 133 Negroes were thrown overboard in order to make up for poor sailing time.

4. From Coleridge's "Reflections on Having Left a Place of Retirement," first published in the *Monthly Magazine*, October 1796. The poem describes how a passing stranger looks with "pleased sadness" at Coleridge's honeymoon cottage and is thus "calmed" for a moment in his "thirst of idle gold" (ll. 11–14). The poem suggests that the author may have been feeling guilty for lazing around in the countryside while his unnumbered brethren abroad toil and bleed. *The Complete Poetical Works of Samuel Taylor Coleridge*, ed. E. H. Coleridge, 2 vols. (1912; reprint, Oxford: Oxford University Press, 1975), 1:106; hereafter referred to as Coleridge, CPW.

5. Melville, *Redburn*, 138, 149. In 1814, the year he became Poet Laureate, Southey celebrated Roscoe as a known "enemy to the slave trade, the peculiar disgrace of Liverpool." Coleridge also saw Roscoe as a man of "most delightful manners" but shied away from disclosing the fact that Roscoe and his associates ruled Liverpool, which in effect meant that they had to have something to do with the slave trade.

6. Thomas De Quincey, *Autobiographic Sketches* [also known in variant form as *Autobiography*], in *The Collected Writings of Thomas De Quincey*, ed. David Masson, 14 vols. (1852; reprint, Edinburgh: Adam and Charles Black, 1889), 1:18–19; hereafter referred to as De Quincey, CW.

7. François Vigier, *Change and Apathy: Liverpool, and Manchester During the Industrial Revolution* (Cambridge, Mass.: MIT Press, 1970), 53. See also S. G. Checkland, who notes that many of the leading citizens of Liverpool were selected on their "willingness and capacity for the slave trade and its auxiliaries." "Economic Attitudes in Liverpool, 1793–1807," *Economic History Review*, 2d ser. 5 (1952): 74.

8. Rushton was looking back to 1787. Preface to *Poems and Other Writings to which is added "A Sketch of the Life of the Author,"* by the Rev. Wm. Shepherd (1806; 2d ed. London: 1824). In 1797 the indefatigable abolitionist wrote "An Expostulation Letter to George Washington," protesting the American president's ownership of slaves.

9. The name of the black was John Dean. Two years after the notorious incident, which took place on July 1 [1787], Clarkson recorded having heard that the slaver *Brothers*, bound for Africa, was having trouble getting and keeping a crew. Clarkson boarded *Brothers*, visited the house where Dean had lived in Bristol, and interviewed his landlord. Thomas Clarkson, *The History of the Rise, Progress, and Accomplishment of the Abolition of The African Slave Trade*, 2 vols. (London: 1808), 1:299–300, 2:474–75; hereafter referred to as Clarkson, *History*.

10. In 1783 Lord Mansfield reluctantly ruled in favor of the owners of the *Zong*, the case that became an "affair" when insurance companies refused to pay for the 133 or so men "lost" overboard. In truth, the men were not lost at sea but "thrown" overboard, many in chains, when Captain Collingwood feared the diminished value of his cargo and supplies because of disease not covered by insurance.

11. Clarkson, *History* 1:386, 389. See also Peter Marshall, *The Anti Slave Trade Movements in Bristol*, no. 37 (1968), and David Richardson, *The Bristol Slave Traders*, no. 65 (1985), in the Local History Pamphlet Series, ed. Peter Harris (Bristol: The Bristol Branch of the Historical Association).

12. The motto "Truth is Dangerous" was used for the political and antigovernment pamphlets Coleridge was reprinting that fall; quoted by Richard Holmes in *Coleridge: Early Visions* (New York: Viking, 1990), 105.

13. William Hazlitt, "My First Acquaintance with Poets," in *The Complete Works of William Hazlitt*, ed. P. P. Howe, 21 vols. (New York: AMS Press, 1967), 17:106–22; hereafter referred to as Hazlitt, CW.

14. The lines are from his poem "Lines written at Shurton Bars, near Bridgewater, September 1795, in Answer to a Letter from Bristol," ll. 41–42, Coleridge, CPW 1:96.

15. Robert Southey, *Letters from England*, ed. Jack Simmons (London: Cresset Press, 1951) no. 76, 482. The letters, composed between 1803 and 1807, when they were published, were written ostensibly by one Don Manuel Alvarez Espriella, a Spanish visitor to England,

but the editors of one or two periodicals sniffed out the ruse (xix); hereafter referred to as Southey, *Letters from England*.

16. Clarkson, *History* 1:293. See also *The Collected Letters of Samuel Taylor Coleridge*, ed. Earl Leslie Griggs, 6 vols. (Oxford: Clarendon Press, 1959), Letter to Poole, July 24, 1800, 1:608; hereafter referred to as Coleridge, CL.

17. He mentions the lectures in a letter to George Dyer, February 1795. Coleridge, CL 1:152. He delivered three that February. The "Moral and Political Lecture" was expanded to become the introductory address to the series, which he called *Conciones ad Populum* ("Addresses to the People") and which was published in December 1795.

18. Ibid.

19. Jane Austen, *Emma*, Vol.4, *The Illustrated Jane Austen*, ed. R. W. Chapman (New York: Oxford University Press, 1933), 300. Although there is no clear indication of the date of the action, Chapman speculates that the events in the book take place close to the date of composition, 1814, and that "Frank Churchill's design of foreign travel seems to assume a state of peace" (498).

20. Henry M. Buten, "Josiah Wedgwood and Benjamin Franklin," *National Philatelic Museum Bulletin* 3 (1951): 159. See also Herbert Aptheker, "Medallions in the Martin Jacobowitz Collection," *Negro History Bulletin* 33 (May 1970): 115–21.

21. The terms *Negro*, *black*, and *African* are used in accordance with usage at the time. See Eva Beatrice Dykes, *The Negro in English Romantic Thought* (Washington, D.C.: Associated Publishers, 1942). It is not clear, however, to what extent "black" also included gypsies and mixed bloods. *Creole* also was variously applied to native whites born on the islands as well as to those of mixed descent.

22. Southey, *Letters from England*, no. 65, 479. ". . . like the old Italiens, the Bristol merchants go on in the track of their fathers, and, succeeding to enormous fortunes, find the regular profit so great that they have no temptation to deviate from the beaten way" (480–81). Also Letters from Hannah More to Horace Walpole, June 1787 and

July 1790, in Hannah More, *Memoirs of the Life and Correspondence of Mrs. Hannah More*, ed. William Roberts, 2 vols. (New York: Harper & Bros., 1834), 1:267, 354. The sight of the capture was so disturbing to her, More writes, that had she known what was happening, she would have herself bought the girl in order to save her. Slave owners had many tricks up their sleeve, including the forced conversion of slaves to "indentured servants" before ships entered English ports.

23. Basil Cottle, Professor of English (ret.), University of Bristol, a direct descendant of Joseph Cottle (pers. com. 1988), notes with skepticism the practice of some Bristol tour guides in identifying metal circles in the streets of old Bristol as proof that gentlemen tethered their slaves there.

24. David Brion Davis, *The Problem of Slavery in the Age of Revolution: 1770–1823* (Ithaca: Cornell University Press, 1975), 117.

25. Byron, "The Island," Canto 4, stanza x, l. 251, ed. Jerome J. McGann, in. *Lord Byron: The Complete Poetical Works*, 7 vols. (Oxford: Clarendon Press, 1980–93), 7:69; hereafter referred to as Byron, CPW. In return for guns, tribal leaders would yield up more slaves. Southey noted that the guns sold to the Africans were often defective. *Letters from England*, no. 36, 198.

26. "London," l.8. William Blake, *Songs of Innocence and of Experience*, ed. Sir Geoffrey Keynes (Oxford: Oxford University Press, 1977), 150: "'The mind-forged manacles' of the second stanza show that in this poem Blake is writing of a mental state symbolized by the social injustices [the roots of industrial civilization], seen every day in London. It is a political poem."

27. A few stanzas in translation were included as a note to Book II of *Joan of Arc* (1796), Coleridge's joint dramatic venture with Southey; the note then became attached to lines in "Destiny of Nations," published in *Sibylline Leaves*, 1817. A few years later, the first four stanzas of the Ode were published by one "Olen" (A. Elton, Bart. also known as Sir Charles Abraham) in the *London Magazine* (October 1823), 356. Finally, the entire poem was translated by James

Dykes Campbell and printed in Appendix B of *The Complete Poetical and Dramatic Works of Samuel Taylor Coleridge* (London: Macmillan & Co., 1893) 476–77. The translation used here, fiercer than Elton's or Campbell's, is from an essay by Anthea Morrison in *An Infinite Complexity: Essays in Romanticism*, ed. J.R. Watson (Edinburgh: Edinburgh University, 1983), 145–60. Comments on style are from J. Roger Ebbatson. "Africa Delivered: Some 'Forgotten Scribblers' on the Slave Trade." *Ariel* 4 (October 1973): 3–18.

28. Nicholas Roe, *Wordsworth and Coleridge: The Radical Years* (Oxford: Oxford University Press, 1988), 5, quoted from B. Pollin and R. Burke, "John Thelwall's Marginalia in a Copy of Coleridge's Copy of *Biographia Literaria*," in *Bulletin of the New York Public Library* 74 (1970): 81. The same year as Coleridge won the medal for the Greek Ode, his friend Samuel Butler (1774–1839) won the Browne medal for a Latin ode on the same topic.

29. Letter to Clarkson, March 3, 1808. Coleridge, CL 2:78. The mentor was Richard Porson, whose belated announcement of the errors may have been prompted by Coleridge's political shifts. *The Watchman*, 116: n. 2.

30. The point about anti-French and anti-reformer bias is sardonically reinforced by Davis, *Problem*, 117.

31. George Whalley, "Bristol Library Borrowings of Southey and Coleridge, 1793–98." *The Library* 4 (September 1949): 115.

32. In February 1817, Southey's two-act drama *Wat Tyler* (1794) was published without permission and attacked as seditious. Years later Coleridge commented that there was nothing that would not have been praised forty years earlier in the public schools, "had it been written by a Lad in the first form as a *Poem*." Letter from Coleridge to T. G. Street, March 22, 1817, CL 4:713, letter from Coleridge to Clarkson, March 3, 1808, CL 3:78. I interpret Coleridge's remark as a defense of Southey, though I appreciate Reiman's interpretation (letter to the author) that the remark is intended as a belittling of Southey.

33. From "Lines written at Shurton Bars."

34. Wadström, *Observations*, viii.

35. John Gabriel Stedman, *Narrative of a Five Years' Expedition Against the Revolted Negroes of Surinam*, transcribed for the first time from the original 1790 manuscript, ed. Richard Price and Sally Price (Baltimore: Johns Hopkins University Press, 1988). Stedman had been sent to Dutch Surinam with instructions to quash the rebellion. The entries begin in 1778. The editors call the *Narrative* "one of the richest, most vivid accounts ever written of a flourishing slave society." Full of history, anthropology, and native lore, the story of Stedman's love for the 15-year old slave girl Joanna is particularly moving, set as it is among unemotional descriptions of torture and agriculture and extensive quotations from literature. Stedman refused to sign abolition petitions, however, and when he left for Holland, he handed over his personal slave to an English countess rather than set him free. See David Erdman, "Blake's Vision of Slavery," 1954 reprinted in *Blake: A Collection of Critical Essays*, ed. Northrop Frye (Englewood Cliffs, N.J.: Prentice Hall, 1966), 88–103.

36. The phrase is Sylvan Forester's, the Shelleyan hero of Thomas Love Peacock's *Melincourt* (1817) who is the founder of the Antisaccharine Society. As Mr. Forester tells Mr. Telegraph, whom he would dissuade from taking sugar with his tea, ". . . I never suffer an atom of West Indian produce to pass my threshold." It is worth noting that Forester is no fanatic: He would keep a small quantity of sugar for guests, though he himself believes that reform begins at home. "How can I seriously call myself an enemy to slavery, while I indulge in the luxuries that slavery acquires?" Thomas Love Peacock, *Melincourt*, Vol.2. *The Works of Thomas Love Peacock*, ed. H. F. B. Brett-Smith and C. E. Jones (London: Constable, 1934), chap. 5.

37. *Morning Chronicle*, September 4, 1819.

38. Coleridge would justifiably claim that he delivered (for him) a remarkable number of lectures—eleven, to Southey's twelve.

39. Hazlitt, CW 17:122. The conversation took place at Nether Stowey

shortly before Coleridge left for Germany in 1798. The talk Coleridge was scheduled to deliver the next day was a sermon for Dr. Toulmin of Taunton.

40. The description is taken from a letter from Dorothy to "a friend [Mary Hutchinson] who had left Racedown early in 1797." *The Letters of William and Dorothy Wordsworth: The Early Years*, ed. Chester L. Shaver (Oxford: Clarendon Press, 1967), 188n; hereafter referred to as Wordsworth, *Letters, Early Years*. Observations on Coleridge's "impassioned harangue" are from Joseph Cottle's *Reminiscences of Samuel Taylor Coleridge* (New York: Wiley & Putnam, 1847) 57.

41. Anonymous, the *Observer*, Part I: Being A Transient Glance at About FORTY YOUTHS of Bristol, Enumerating What are the Prominent Traits in their Characters, Whether They Be Worthy of Imitation, or Otherwise, interspersed with a few anecdotes (Bristol: 1795). Most of the youths described in *The Observer* are said to suffer typically from "puppyism," "libidinism," and "folly."

42. George Whalley, "Coleridge and Southey in Bristol, 1795," *Review of English Studies* 1 (1950): 330. The image of the ship driven between the Mariner and the sun is from "The Rime of the Ancient Mariner," fytte 3. McKusick indulges in similar speculations: "During his [Coleridge's] residence in Bristol . . . he may have observed at first hand some of the sickly survivors of these terrible voyages." James C. McKusick, " 'The Silent Sea': Coleridge, Lee Boo, and the Exploration of the South Pacific"(*The Wordsworth Circle* 24 (Spring 1983): 106.

43. Goethe's *The Sorrows of Young Werther*, 1774.

44. Noted by Patton, *The Watchman*, lxxv. Patton's heavily annotated mansucript is from a transcript of the Lecture made by E. H. Coleridge. The original, now lost, was partly in Coleridge's hand, partly in Southey's. Williams (1746–1826) was a self-taught genius and "keen opponent of slavery" who renounced property left to him by slave-holding brothers in Jamaica (DNB).

45. Coleridge, November 6, 1794. CL l:126.

46. Holmes, *Coleridge*, 108.
47. "Religious Musings" was first published as part of the collection. *Poems on Various Subjects*, April 15, 1796. The edition by E. H. Coleridge, relying on the 1834 text, shows some minor differences in this passage (Coleridge, CPW 1:108). Admirers of the poem no doubt recognized other passages Coleridge appropriated for *The Watchman* essays. Issue no. 2, March 9, 1796, took lines 260–357 from a passage in the poem now known as "The Present State of Society."
48. There were ten issues in all, from no. 1 on March 1, 1796, to no. 10 on May 13. *The Watchman* came out every eight days in order to avoid the weekly newspaper tax.
49. *Somerset v. Stewart*, June 1772, *Act of 12 Geo 3*, in Lofft, 1 98 *English Reports* 499.
50. Italics mine.
51. The Rev. Orville Dewey, *The Old World and the New*, 2 vols. (New York: Harper & Bros., 1836), 1: chap. 4, Journal entry, July 30, 1833.
52. Quoted by Patton, "On the Slave Trade," 139n. Coleridge and Southey included the passage in *Omniana or Horae Otiosiores*, ed. Robert Gittings (Carbondale, Ill.: Southern Illinois University Press, 1969). *Omniana*, an anonymous collection of 250 miscellaneous pieces, fifty of which were Coleridge's, the others Southey's, was published in two volumes in 1812, though the pieces were gathered mostly by 1806. Although Gittings notes that Coleridge's contribution was small and his items relatively brief, when they were serious and outspoken, they were wonderful. Gittings cites in particular the material against slavery (item no. 106).
53. Patton notes that David Erdman suggests the source of "the dream" was probably Daniel Isaac Eaton's *Politics for the People; or Hog's Wash* (no. 10, December 1793), itself a borrowing (*The Watchman*, 165: n. 1).
54. The Parliamentarian John Hampden (1594–1643) opposed King Charles I and Cromwell; William Tell, of course, is the legendary

thirteenth-century Swiss hero. In a notebook entry for February/ March 1802, Coleridge linked Clarkson with Toussaint and Bonaparte as subjects he was thinking of for a project—an epic, perhaps.

55. The line garbles the opening of words of Psalm 127: "Except the Lord build the house / They labour in vain that build it": "Except the Lord keep the city, / The Watchman waketh but in vain." See *Notebook* entry 122 g116, in *The Notebooks of Samuel Taylor Coleridge*, ed. Kathleen Coburn, 4 vols. (Oxford: Pantheon Books, 1957–90), 123. In 1799, the *Anti-Jacobin* parodied Coleridge the essayist and called him "the Bellman."

56. Noted by William L. James, "The Black Man in English Romantic Literature, 1772–1833," Ph.D. diss. (University of California at Los Angeles, 1977). The "Ode" was first published in the radical newspaper the *Cambridge Intelligencer*. Henry James Pye (1745–1813), Poet Laureate from 1790 to 1813, was the memorable butt of much Romantic satire.

57. Note to a 1797 variant, ll. 96ff., Stanza V, CPW 165.

58. The phrase is, of course, from Keats's "La Belle Dame Sans Merci," a poem suggestive in some ways of the influence of "The Rime of the Ancient Mariner." Unlike Wordsworth and Coleridge, Keats rejected the comforts of religion or philosophy.

CHAPTER 2

1. Joseph Cottle, reporting what he remembers Coleridge telling him, in *Early Recollections Chiefly Relating to the Late Samuel Taylor Coleridge*, 2 vols. (Longman, Rees, 1837), 1:319–20. After leaving Racedown, William and Dorothy stayed briefly at Nether Stowey before moving to Alfoxden on July 16, 1797, remaining there until June 25, 1798; in September they went to Bristol, Wales, and Germany. Although Coleridge says that Wordsworth "never troubled himself" about politics, he concedes in *Biographia Literaria* that both of them at the time were damned with "suspicion and obloquy."

Samuel Taylor Coleridge. *Biographia Literaria*, ed. J. Shawcross, 2 vols. (Oxford: Oxford University Press, 1954), 1:122 (chap. 10).

2. David Miall, "The Campaign to Acquire Coleridge Cottage," *Coleridge Bulletin* 1 (Summer 1988): 8; quoted from Edmund Gosse, *Illustrated London News*, September 24, 1892.

3. The term was affixed to him by friends because of his tendency to say anything that came into his head, Coleridge acknowledged with typical self-deprecating irony. As to Wordsworth's not talking much about politics, he certainly offered a different view to the Reverend Dewey many years later. Dewey records, "He [Wordsworth] remarked . . . that although he was known to the world only as a poet, he had given twelve hours thought to the condition and prospects of society, for one to poetry." Dewey 1:90.

4. In a letter to W.W. William Mathews dated May 23, 1794, Wordsworth declared himself to be "of that odious class of men called democrats" and pledged that the bond would "for ever continue." Wordsworth, *Letters, Early Years*, 119. The particular democrats he had in mind included Tooke and Thelwall.

5. *The Prelude*, Book 10, ll. 202ff., in *The Prelude, 1799, 1805, 1850*, eds. Jonathan Wordsworth, M.H. Abrams, and Stephen Gill. (New York: Norton, 1979); hereafter referred to as *The Prelude*, meaning the 1805 *Prelude*.

6. Letter from Azariah Pinney to Wordsworth, March 25, 1796; quoted by Bergan Evans and Hester Pinney, "Racedown and the Wordsworths," *Review of English Studies* 8 (January 1932): 13.

7. Letter from Dorothy to Mrs. John Marshall (née Jane Pollard), September 2, September 2 [and 3], 1795, Wordsworth, *Letters, Early Years*, 148.

8. The Pinneys had arrived on Nevis in 1764 and, with partners, bought estates on St. Vincent, St. Kitts, and St. Croix. Richard Pares, *A West India Fortune* (New York: Longmans, Green, 1950). The description of John Frederick is from Pares (166). Charles, a Tory and outspoken opponent of emancipation, received compensation from the Emancipation Act and continued to do business in the West Indies.

9. The crisis is never explained. *Mansfield Park* was composed between 1811 and 1813 and published in May or June 1814. Chapman (553) concludes that the date of the action is 1808.

10. Henry Nelson Coleridge, *Six Months in the West Indies*, 3d ed. (London: John Murray, 1832), 188–90. See chap. 7.

11. Coleridge and Wordsworth were the happy recipients of Tom Wedgwood's generous desire to aid young men of genius. A few years after Tom's visit, similar instructions were issued by Pinney in regard to a daughter-in-law.

12. Ill at the time with what Wordsworth diagnosed as gout that could cause manic behavior and "violence," Coleridge was without funds and in desperate need of a mild climate. Wordsworth wrote to Poole "solely on Coleridge's account" to see if something could not be quietly arranged by way of Josiah Wade of 5 Wine Street Bristol, "a most excellent and liberal man" who greatly valued Coleridge. Wordsworth, *Letters, Early Years*, 338–40. That Coleridge thought the Wordsworths would join him on Nevis seems to have been only wish-fulfillment.

13. Coleridge to Southey, July 25, 1801. CL 1:359–61. The phrase "poet and Philosopher in a mist" are from a letter to James Webbe Tobin, July 25, 1800. Perhaps Nevis loomed large in Coleridge's mind because of its apparent tranquility, for the letter begins, "I do loathe cities . . ." and goes on to extol the "heavenly climate" of Nevis, "the most lovely as well as the most healthy island in the W. Indies. . . ." The original plan may have been to go to Palermo and Constantinople.

14. Matthew Gregory Lewis, *Journal of a West India Proprietor* (1834; reprint, New York: Negro University Press, 1969), 115–16. Was it mere coincidence that Lewis's *Journal*, with its documented abuses, was not published until 1834, the year Emancipation took effect, although the manuscript had been completed in 1817? Statistics show that slaves died more than they propagated, due to disease, inadequate diet, and a brutal and exploitative labor regimen.

15. Michael Craton, "Jamaican Slavery," in *Race and Slavery in the*

Western Hemisphere, Quantitative Studies, eds. Stanley L. Engerman and Eugene D. Genovese (Princeton: Princeton University Press, 1975), 249.

16. Pares lists Lucas as Pinney's London factor. Six of the eight owners of the *Africa* were from Bristol (77, 122).

17. The name remained in the poem until 1815. In the Fenwick Notes (1842), Wordsworth indicates that he originally wrote the poem at Alfoxden in 1798 (having first composed it in his head some time earlier) without the first stanza, and that it was Coleridge who contributed, "A little child, dear brother Jem." Wordsworth said he found the allusion ludicrous but "enjoyed the joke of hitching-in our friend, James Tobin's name, who was familiarly called Jem."

18. Gustavus Vasa (or Vassa), 1745–97, was also known as Olaudah Equiano. Wordsworth to J.W. Tobin, March 6, 1798, *Letters, Early Years,* 210. The verse tragedy was by Henry Brooke (1703–81), originally published in 1739 and reprinted in 1796 and 1797.

19. Lewis, 173; Stedman, preface and poem, 549. Abolitionist verse was an essential part of Stedman's *Narrative.* Both Lewis and Stedman extend limited sympathy to some noble savages, while overall justifying exemplary harsh punishment for others. Not only did they hold that the Negro was inferior, they also argued on grounds of so-called humanity that the Negro was better off as a slave than as an indentured laborer.

20. Historians have noted that it was the Methodists and Evangelicals who were most likely to make converts because their ways seemed more readily accommodating to Africans. The point thus suggests general European ignorance of vaudun (voodoo), which was an effective modus operandi in the slave rebellions on St. Domingue.

21. The two-volume reference by David Rivers, *Literary Memoirs of Living Authors of Great Britain* (1798), lists 1112 living authors. Coleridge is included; Wordsworth is not. The Rivers volume is noted by Jack Stillinger in "Pictorialism and Matter-of-Factness in Coleridge's Poems of Somerset," *The Wordsworth Circle* 20 (Spring 1989): 66. In a letter to Wynn, September 22, 1797, Southey mentions a

"man, whose name is not known in the world—Wordsworth—who has written a great part of a tragedy, upon a very strange and unpleasant subject—but it is equal to any dramatic pieces [whic]h I have ever seen." *New Letters of Robert Southey*, ed. Kenneth Curry, 2 vols. (New York: Columbia University Press, 1965), 1:148–49; hereafter referred to as Southey, NL.

22. The Spy-Nosy anecdote and others are recorded in *Biographia Literaria*, chap. 10. Roe summarizes various West Country invasion plans, such as "Instructions Given by General Hoche [French] to Colonel Tate [an American ally] Previous to His Landing on the Coast of South Wales, in the Beginning of 1797" (255).

23. "And he went up into the mountain to pray, HIMSELF, ALONE." From Hazlitt, commenting on Coleridge's sermon of January 14, 1798, at Shrewsbury; quoted by Holmes, 178.

24. Davis calls Stephen the "most powerful intellect of the British abolition movement," *Problem*, 266.

25. Between 1794 and 1799, "Coleridge wrote lines against 'Afric's wrongs' into at least one poem every year." Carl Woodring *Politics in the Poetry of Coleridge* (Madison: University of Wisconsin Press, 1961), 59.

26. Roe, who summarizes these events, points to the recent success of Napoleon's Italian campaign as giving impetus to the French, and reason for the British to be alarmed.

27. Coleridge, CPW 1:256. "Fears of Solitude" was the title when extracts appeared in 1809 in *The Friend*. "The greatest temptation Coleridge has to fend off in "'Fears in Solitude,' as in the earlier 'Reflections on Having Left a Place of Retirement,' is that of 'political quietism.'" Peter Larkin, "'Fears in Solitude': Readings (from) the Dell," *The Wordsworth Circle* 22 (Winter 1991): 11–14.

28. Coleridge to Wordsworth, September 10, 1799. CL 1:527.

29. Birmingham was also known for coin forgery and counterfeiting. Southey, *Letters From England*, no. 36, 198. Southey scathingly called Birmingham the ultimate manufacturing hothouse, stinking of train oil and full of grimy mines that exploit the poor. "When

we look at gold, we do not think of the poor slaves who dug it from the caverns of the earth; but I shall never think of the wealth of England, without remembering that I have been in the mine" (197).

30. Coleridge, CL 1:193–94 (late March 1796).

31. From the essay "Modern Patriotism," *The Watchman* no. 3, 99.

32. *Lear* IV, i, 45; notes on entry 121G.115. The speech was given by Sir William Young in the House of Commons, March 19, 1796.

33. "In every cry of every Man, / In every Infant's cry of fear, / In every voice, in every ban, / The mind-forg'd manacles I hear" (ll. 5–8).

34. The 1842 Note. William Wordsworth, *The Borderers*. ed. Robert Osborn (Ithaca: Cornell University Press, 1982), 813.

35. From the 1800 "Preface." The OED gives this sense of "gaudy." Now obsolete, the meaning, still current at the start of the eighteenth century, was "not according to rule, out of order, without law."

36. Wordsworth to Fox, January 14, 1801. *Letters, Early Years*, 315. The letter was sent at Coleridge's suggestion, with complimentary copies of the second edition of *Lyrical Ballads*, which had just come out.

37. Southey, NL, to Tom Southey, August 22, 1805 1: 393. The ballad itself had been described in an earlier letter to Tom, when he was a naval officer stationed at Portsmouth.

38. In October 1798, reviewing *Lyrical Ballads* for the *Critical Review*, Southey said he did not "sufficiently understand 'The Ancient Mariner' to analyze it," and Wordsworth (who had contributed some details and knew its composition intimately) ungraciously blamed the poem for *Lyrical Ballads'* poor reception. Coleridge, CPW 1:186.

39. Hazlitt, "My First Acquaintance with Poets," 17:120. The third party along was one John Chester, a native of Nether Stowey. The date was 1798.

40. Newton (1725–1807) became a theological advisor of sorts to William Cowper. Newton's influence on Wordsworth can be seen, particularly, in *The Prelude* (Book 6, ll. 160–87). The average size of a slave ship kept decreasing over the years, a fact abolition opponents

would cite as evidence of their so-called humanity. But in truth the main reason for the decline was more efficient sailing. Regular trade ships such as the East Indiamen were much larger.

41. Cited by Coburn in a comment on *Notebook* item, 45G.37. Certainly reading the poem as contemporary criticism of trade and commerce would reinforce the idea that the sailor would have been relatively young—these were the men who went on voyages of exploration and "discovery."

42. Rushton became a good friend of Clarkson. *Poems* (West India Eclogues), xii.

43. Melville uses the image similarly in *Moby Dick*, when Ahab tells Starbuck, "When I think of this life I have led; the desolation of solitude it has been; . . . oh weariness! heaviness! Guinea-coast slavery of solitary command!"

44. *Table Talk*, 2 vols. ed. Carl Woodring, in *The Collected Work of Samuel Taylor Coleridge*, Bollingen Series LXXV (Princeton: Princeton University Press, 1990). Recorded 31 March 1832, 1: 272–73. Mrs. Barbauld (1743–1825) was a minor poet who impressed Coleridge in his earlier years (272, n. 6). Woodring adds that Henry Nelson Coleridge understood Coleridge to mean a distinction between "unencumbered imagination and inculcated moral" (273 n. 7); hereafter referred to as TT.

45. Henry Hutchinson (1769–1839), author of a somewhat strained humorous nine-canto verse narrative, *The Retrospect of a Retired Mariner*, led a typically stressful life at sea, including impressment and incarceration. Sara worried about him and at one time asked if he was on board the *Edgar*, whose captain had a reputation for flogging. Letter from Sara Hutchinson in Yorkshire to John Monkhouse in London, July 12, 1800, *Letters of Sara Hutchinson, 1800–1815*, ed. Kathleen Coburn (Toronto: University of Toronto Press, 1954) 3n.

46. Dorothy Wordsworth, the "Grasmere Journal," *The Journals of Dorothy Wordsworth*, ed. Ernest de Selincourt, 2 vols. (1952; reprint, Hamden, Conn.: Archon Books, 1970),1:124. The entry is for March 13, 1802. The sailor's name was Isaac Chapel. He also told

of having been in North America, where he traveled thirty days among Indians and was "well treated." Another source of slaving tales might well have been Edward Christian, brother of Fletcher Christian who sailed with Captain Bligh to the West Indies to bring back supplies of breadfruit trees for plantation slaves. The Christians were from the Lake Country, and Edward was intimately involved with William's and Dorothy's law suit against the earl of Lonsdale. Geoffrey Sanborn, "The Madness of Mutiny: Wordsworth, the *Bounty* and *The Borderers*. *The Wordsworth Circle* 23 (Winter 1992): 35–42.

47. The lines (422–23) were composed January 1798 and incorporated later in revised form into Book IV (ll. 363–504) of *The Prelude* and revised several times thereafter.

48. William Godwin, Essay V in the *Enquirer*, quoted by Shelley in a long note to "Queen Mab" and noted in *Shelley's Poetry and Prose*, eds. Donald H. Reiman and Sharon B. Powers (New York: Norton, 1977), 37n; hereafter referred to as Shelley, P&P. All references to the poetry are from this volume unless otherwise noted.

49. *Home in Grasmere*, ed. Beth Darlington (Ithaca: Cornell University Press, 1977), 103, ll. 778–79.

50. *Notebook* entries 44G.36 & 45G.37 (1796). The first, in Latin, is translated by Coburn. The possibility of "The Rime" being about the slave trade is discussed by J.R. Ebbatson, "Coleridge's Mariner and the Rights of Man," *Studies in Romanticism* 2 (Summer 1972): 171–206, and Christopher Rubenstein, in a paper, "A New Identity for the Mariner," given at the Second Coleridge Conference at Nether Stowey (August 1990).

51. Coleridge to Josiah Wedgwood, February 1799. CL 1:465–66.

52. *The Borderers*, 1842 version, 131, ll. 633–37.

CHAPTER 3

1. Blacks, though free, were still considered property on the tax rolls and so not counted in parish registers of the poor. Reviewing Clark-

son's *History* in 1808, Coleridge praises him for fighting "the legalized Banditti of Men-Stealers."

2. Hogarth, probably the most prolific painter and engraver of blacks in the eighteenth century, shows his connection to the slave trade by way of having had a "patron," says Dabydeen claiming the word means slave owner. David B. Dabydeen, *Hogarth's Blacks: Images of Blacks in Eighteenth-Centry English Art* (Athens, Ga.: University of Georgia Press, 1987); also David B. Dabydeen, ed., *The Black Presence in English Literature* (Manchester: Manchester University Press, 1985). The OED, however, indicates that this meaning of one who legally had the services of a manumitted slave in the days of Roman antiquity had long been obsolete by the eighteenth century.

3. *Sanditon*, by Jane Austen and Another Lady (Boston: Houghton Mifflin, 1975), was begun in January 1817. In March, Austen became too ill to continue (she died in July), and an Australian admirer undertook to finish the book in the Austen style. Sanditon is a small, fashionable bathing place by the sea in Sussex where a "rich West Indian from Surrey" is a desirable guest—no people spend more freely than the "West Injines." Austen certainly knew from family connections about West Indian estates, especially about plantations on Antigua and Dominica. In *Mansfield Park*, the selfish and worldly Crawfords, brother and sister, are described as small and dark—might they be mulattoes? (Reiman, unpersuaded, asks if they might be Welsh.) "Unfavorable circumstances" force Sir Thomas back from Antigua, by way of Liverpool (chaps 3 and 4). See Frank Gibbon, "The Antiguan Connection," *The Cambridge Quarterly* 11 (1982): 298–305.

4. Guilt might account for old Earnshaw's kindness in bringing "it" home. In the late eighteenth and early nineteenth century, gypsies were often described in the same negative terms as blacks. Christopher Heywood, in "Yorkshire Slavery in *Wuthering Heights*," *RES*, n.s. 38 (1987):184–98, traces slave-holding families by way of geographical designators in the Brontë novels, particularly *Wuthering Heights* and *Jane Eyre*, this last a favorite of Crabb Robinson.

Wuthering Heights was published in 1847, and a revised second edition in 1850. In "A Yorkshire Background for *Wuthering Heights*," Heywood expands his theme by way of studying the influence on Emily Brontë of the Reverend Thomas Dunham Whitaker's *Deannery of Craven*, with its description of the families and topography on which *Wuthering Heights* relies (*Modern Language Review* 88, 1993). Whitaker, Heywood observes, notes the involvement of the Clifford family of Skipton as Tudor founders and patrons of Atlantic navigation and slavery. Heywood also stresses Emily's satirization of the sugar-refining economic base of the plantation economy in Linton Heathcliff's "'sucking on like an innocent . . . at his stick of sugar candy.'" Heywood's broad theme is not that there were particular blacks to note as models but that there was indeed a black presence in this area and an awareness of its sigificance. Far from not knowing what she was writing about, Heywood asserts, the author deliberately drew on this awareness in order to establish the psychological terrain of her novel.

5. Quoted by Christopher Heywood, "A Yorkshire Background," 824.

6. William Cobbett refers to Whitehaven as "Lowther-town" in *Rural Rides*, ed. George Woodcock (1830, reprint, Hammondworth, England: 1967). Lowther (1736–1802), the son of a governor of Barbados and known throughout Cumberland and Westmorland as the "bad earl," was detested by many as "a madman too rich to be confined." As bad as he was, the Wordsworths' bête noire in the matter of their inheritance, so was the second earl of Lonsdale good. When he succeeded to the title in 1802, the Wordsworths could count on their inheritance.

7. Janet Nelson, a local historian (pers. com. 1988), writes of her extensive work tracing slave-trading families in the north of England, concentrating on the late eighteenth century.

In December 1804, in a letter to her good friend Catharine, married to Thomas Clarkson, Dorothy mentioned seeing Mary Elizabeth Bolton, the wife of John Bolton, who, it was said, was "a former slave-trader, of Storrs Hall, on Windermere." Wordsworth, *Letters, Early Years*, 515, n. 1.

8. The Lakes, Heywood notes (pers. com. 1990), "were the cockpit or cock's nest behind the Parliamentary battle leading to Emancipation, since Clarkson, Lowther, Cavendish, Bentinck, Wilberforce, Brougham, Carus and Sedgwick resided there or nearby."

9. Much of Bolton's trade was above reproach, "but there can be no doubt that he also traded in negro slaves." G. Bernard Wood, "A Negro Trail in the North of England," *Country Life Annual* (1967), 43.

10. Southey, *Letters from England*, no. 55, 338.

11. Dorothy Wordsworth, *Journals* 1:118. Reiman (pers. com.) calls my attention to the fact that Dorothy also papered the walls of Dove Cottage for warmth.

12. Quoted from Henry Adams, *The History of the United States of America During the Administrations of Thomas Jefferson* (New York: The Library of America, 1986), chap. xv: "Toussaint L'Ouverture," 266.

13. There was such an edict on July 2, 1802, but it is not clear whether the woman is from France or the West Indies.

14. Wordsworth's sonnets appeared under various bylines, however, and it is doubtful that he would have been well known as "Mortimer" or W.L.D. Hutchinson speculates that W.L.D. stands for "Wordsworth Literatati Dedicavit," while David Erdman (pers. com. 1990) waggishly declares that it does not mean "Wordsworth Loves Dorothy." "To Toussaint L'Ouverture" was published on February 2, 1803, "The Banished Negroes" on February 11.

15. From "England! the time is come when thou shouldst wean / Thy heart. . . ." Stuart's editorial announcement appeared January 20, 1803. *William Wordsworth's Poems in Two Volumes and Other Poems, 1800–1807*, ed. Jared Curtis (Ithaca: Cornell University Press, 1983), 170; hereafter referred to as *Poems, 2 Vols*.

16. Coleridge had himself posted to Malta for his health and was working as plenipotentiary for the Crown.

17. Wordsworth to Lady Beaumont, May 21, 1807. *The Letters of William and Dorothy Wordsworth: The Middle Years*, rev. ed., ed. Mary Moorman with Alan G. Hill. 2 vols. (Oxford: Clarendon Press, 1969–70), 2: 147; hereafter referred to as *Letters, Middle Years*, The series appeared in the 1807 volume. See *Poems, 2 vols.*, 161–62, 468.

18. Launched in February 1837 as a petition campaign by leaders of the working class who were still smarting from the middle-class Reform Bill of 1832, Chartism (The People's Charter, 1838–50) became increasingly violent. Centered in Lancashire and Yorkshire, the movement probably contained a number of blacks in its ranks, though they do not readily show up in illustrations or text references of the time.

19. A contrast might be drawn between the poet's desire in "Personal Talk" to have his little boat rock in its harbor and the Negro Woman's turbulent passage in September 1, 1802.

20. Milton's Satan was for the Romantic poets, particularly Blake, the archetypal ambiguous hero, impossible not to admire, impossible not to hate. The differences, however, between what *Paradise Lost* invites with its energetic Satanism, and what "Toussaint" dulls with its pallid symbolism, are the differences between Milton's "imaginative didactic propaganda" and Wordsworth's "failure of predigested form, thought, impetus or expresion to be imaginatively alive . . ." (James Thorpe III, pers. com. 1993).

21. Southey, letter to William Wynn. *NL* 1:254. Clarkson told Southey that Wynn's uncle was indeed involved in the slave trade.

22. Adams stresses the hatred Napoleon felt for the upstart who stood in his way of rebuilding the French colonial system in St. Domingue, France's most valuable commercial property in 1789. Adams, 259, 262, 373–84. In *The Black Jacobins* (first published in 1938) C.L.R. James analyzes Toussaint's complex personality as a driving force in and a reflection of the Haitian Revolution

23. *The Prelude* Book 7, ll. 701–707 was composed "almost certainly" in November 1804. "The mighty concourse" was added late (Norton ed., 519). In a note glossing the phrase "one vast mill," the editors cite Blake's meaning of "factory" as "dark satanic mills" (264).

24. The line is from Cowper's *Task*, Book II, l. 40. "Humanity" was composed in 1829, and though it recalls the Ancient Mariner's advice to the wedding guest by affirming that "All creatures and all objects, in degree / Are friends and patrons of humanity," its appropriation of the Mariner's words as a moral serves to undermine the subtle hellish truth of Coleridge's ballad.

25. *Notebooks* 1: August-September 1802, item 1232, 21.245.

26. The vote was 100 to 34 in the House of Lords, where Lord Grenville shepherded it through, and 283 to 16 in the House of Commons. To date, 519 petitions had been submitted.

27. It was introduced by Secretary of State Lord Howick, later the second Earl Grey. The quotation of the revised phrasing is taken from Davis, *Problems* (118), who points out that one of the most significant provisions of the law was not changed: that captured blacks had to be forfeited to the government and eventually freed. They could be enlisted in the armed forces, and they could be made apprentices, but they could not be sold.

28. Pares, 150; 152. Huggins was "the most notorious native of Nevis," Pares adds, a Creole (poor white), who started buying up estates from Pinney and Tobin as early as 1783. "But there was one thing against him, and John Pinney knew it quite well. Edward Huggins was considered to be cruel to his negroes."

29. Like Wordsworth, Clarkson had been a "sizar" (scholarship student) at St. Johns, Cambridge.

30. De Quincey, "Memorial Chronology." CW 14:307–8. De Quincey is tenacious on this point of righting the wrong to Clarkson, and is delighted finally that the "profligate contempt of justice" was finally overturned.

31. Coleridge reviewed Clarkson's *History* for the *Edinburgh Review* but became understandably furious when he saw that two paragraphs had been added, praising Wilberforce and criticizing Pitt—both of which, he fumed, contradicted his views.

32. In *Omniana*, no. 160, under the heading "Hint for a New Species of History." This is the same note in which Coleridge comments

on (and copies down) advertisements on Negro runaways. See chap. 7, n. 29.

33. "Psyche," ll. 3–4. CWP, 412.

34. In a note by E.H. Coleridge on Byron's "Hints from Horace" (1811), by way of the Personal Reminiscence of the late Miss Stuart, of 106 Harley Street. See also Henry Crabb Robinson, *Diary, Reminiscences, and Correspondence*, 2 vols. in 1, edited by Thomas Sadler (Boston: Houghton Mifflin, 1898), 1:270, entry for March 1810; hereafter referred to as HCR.

35. In *Omniana*, no. 141, 342.

36. John Wordsworth to Mary Hutchinson, April 11, 1801, *The Letters of John Wordsworth*, ed. Carl Ketcham (Ithaca: Cornell University Press, 1969), 116–17. John, whom Wordsworth referred to as "the silent poet," once wrote Coleridge's beloved Sara Hutchinson that he did not much care for "Tintern Abbey" or understand "The Ancient Mariner."

37. Letter to E. T. Hookham, June 6, 1809. *The Works of Thomas Love Peacock*, 10 vols. ed. H. F. B. Brett-Smith and C. E. Jones (London: Constable & Co. Ltd., 1934), 8:17. His immediate subject was the diverting of rivers into canals for the "damnable" purpose of commercial navigation.

CHAPTER 4

1. From Byron's "Darkness" (ll. 4–5), composed July 1816 at Diodati. Byron CPW 4:40.

2. Although books were expensive, in 1816 the Eastern Tales were still being devoured, especially *The Giaour* and *The Corsair* along with *Childe Harold* 1 & 2. *The Corsair* sold 10,000 copies on the first day of publication in 1814, 20,000 in one month. Leslie A. Marchand, *Byron: A Biography*, 3 vols. (New York: Knopf, 1957), 1: 433. As William St. Clair concludes from a model of "quantified analysis," though *The Corsair*, *The Giaour*, *The Bride*, and *Childe Harold* 1 and 2 were the big sellers, *Don Juan*, hitherto assumed not to have done well, comparatively, was in fact wildly successful because of

pirated editions. "Within a decade *Don Juan* had penetrated far deeper into the reading of the nation than any other modern book, with the possible exception of Tom Paine's *Rights of Man*, and new pirate editions were still being put on the market in the 1830s." "The Impact of Byron's Writings: An Evaluative Approach," in *Byron: Augustan and Romantic*, ed. Andrew Rutherford (New York: Macmillan, 1990), 18.

3. "The ravage of the reeking plain" is from *Childe Harold*, Canto 1, stanza lxxxviii in Byron, CPW 2; "splendid chains" is from *The Corsair*, Canto 1, stanza viii, in Byron, CPW 3; "the weak alone repent" is also from *The Corsair*, Canto 2, stanza x. *The Corsair* was composed sometime between December 1813 and February 1814, a period when the papers were reporting heavily on the Barbary pirates.

Though Shelley certainly made passive resistance his theme, he did not always hold his heroes to his views. In *The Revolt of Islam* Laon slays his enemies, though in self-defence.

4. The sense of the mulatto as a crafty antagonist emerges in accounts of the Haitian revolution and becomes central in tales such as Melville's *Benito Cereno*.

5. Charles Lamb, "Imperfect Sympathies," *The Works of Charles and Mary Lamb*, 2: Lucas. 7 vols. (New York: G.P. Putnam, 1903), 2: 62. Originally published in the *London Magazine*, August 1821, as "Jews, Quakers, Scotchmen, and Other Imperfect Sympathies" (Lucas, 349). Coleridge was well aware it was Kean who was one of the first to insist that Othello be played not as a black but as a tawny, lightened North African. See TT 1 (January 6, 1823), 25.

6. The DNB makes Smith out to be a vain self-promoter. His organization seems to have been largely "fictitious," with efforts "limited to correspondence" and collecting money.

7. *Don Juan*, Canto 4, lxxv. Letter to Francis Hodgson, from Athens, January 20, 1811. George Gordon, Lord Byron. *Byron's Letters and Journals*, ed. Leslie Marchand, 12 vols. (London: John Murray, 1982), 2: 36; hereafter referred to as L&J.

8. Gambia's most noble gesture is to make himself a slave in order to

free the captured Clifton, but it isn't enough. The Governor says that "tis not by the thunder of war, but by the still voice of conscience" that the liberty of mankind will be achieved. He places his hopes in Christian warriors, not rebellious blacks.

9. HCR, *Diary* 1:387, May 7 1818.
10. Peacock, *Melincourt* chap. 5.
11. *Don Juan*, Canto 4, cxv-xcvi.
12. *Don Juan*, Canto 5, vii. Though there is no evidence that these lines refer only to males, the fact that females stood apart suggests that this slave market was no different from others in its separation of women, men, and children, each category commanding a different price.
13. In an analysis of slave prices, in which he compares slaves to turnips (!), De Quincey describes the various responsibilities of slaves, from menial work to significant household business. "The Logic of Political Economy," CW 9:174-76.
14. Negroes had no such recorded history, of course, though Monk Lewis would write in his *Journal* that at least in the West Indies, as opposed to Africa, blacks now had the advantage of being exposed to English ideas.
15. The *Times*, July 7, 1816. Extract of a letter of July 4 from Spithead.
16. The *Times*, January 6, 1816.
17. The *Times*, July-October 1820. Malaria took a heavy toll on whites. In a review of Howard Temperley's book on the 1841-42 antislavery expedition to the Niger, *White Dreams, Black Africa* (Yale), John Spurling in the February 28, 1992, issue of TLS (32) remarks that "when Nigeria recovered its independence in 1960, after some sixty years of British rule, people suggested that its primary protector, the mosquito, should be emblazoned on the national flag."
18. There were earlier registry bills in Trinidad, ca. 1813, as Stanley Engerman observes (pers. com. 1993). A Registry Bill that did pass in 1819 fell woefully short of abolitionist demands.
19. Italics added. "Sonnet to Chillon," 1. 1. Byron, CPW 4:3. Of course, as Woodring points out, Byron's belief in freedom was never separate from his desire for fame. "Converting personal desire

into a vague political notion, he 'believed in' freedom" (*Politics in English Romantic Poetry*, 156). On the other hand, Woodring reminds readers of the truth of Leslie Marchand's observation that Byron reveals himself most fully in his verse, not his private letters.

20. A.S. Byatt, *Wordsworth and Coleridge in Their Time* (London: Thomas Nelson & Sons, 1970) 150. Both Shelley and Byron were obsessed with Napoleon, admiring and despising him. Byron began the "Ode to Napoleon Buonaparte" on April 9, the day of the "shameful abdication"; it was published on April 16, 1815, two months before Waterloo.

21. Cottle, *Early Recollections* 2:143–44. Pitt's speech in the House of Commons, on February 17, 1809, was "On the Continuance of the War with France" (see E.H. Coleridge on Byron's *The Age of Bronze*, 746, n. 2). Incidentally, Byron had written a rather curious comment in his *Journal* two years earlier: that he liked praise, despite the vanity of saying so, and that if he "could have had a speech against the *Slave Trade, in Africa*, and an Epitaph on a Dog, in *Europe* [i.e. in the *Morning Post*]" he'd be in heaven (L&J 3:236). Entry for December 10, 1813.

22. From *Omniana*, no. 160, 171.

23. Dated May 18. The *Times*, July 19, 1816. Craton points out the uniqueness of Jamaica in the British West Indies island chain, due to its unusual topography and early colonization, which established large, self-contained, and self-sustaining estates (252). The passage from Bryan Edwards's *History* (1793) is quoted by Craton, "Jamaican Slavery," 255, 257.

24. The *Times*, January 1, 1816. The dateline was Grenada, October 18, 1815. The barrister was George Whitfield, at one time the Attorney General of the colony. The torture devices he made his Negroes wear were "neck-tables." The references from Lewis's *Journal* are for the year 1816 (173). Lewis had two main estates, and Negroes make common appearances in his plays. He translated Kotzebue's "The Negro Slaves," for example, a dramatic and historical piece in three acts (London 1796), which Kotzebue had prefaced with a strong antislavery statement and dedicated to Wilberforce.

In truth abolitionist sentiment on the English stage was always mild, and never the main subject or theme of dramatizations. Reiman (pers. com.) calls my attention to the fact that Byron and Shelley persuaded Monk Lewis in 1816 to go to the West Indies to free his family's slaves. "The gesture caused Lewis's death." See also Michael Craton: ". . . an Englishman like Matthew 'Monk' Lewis, coming unexpectedly into a West Indian inheritance, would visit his property cursorily and briefly, bringing a gust of naïve idealism and *noblesse oblige*." Michael Craton, *Sinews of Empire: A Short History of British Slavery* (London: Temple Smith, 1974), 202.

25. Italics added. From the preface to *Laon and Cythna*, 1817. *The Complete Works of Percy Bysshe Shelley*, ed. Roger Ingpen and Walter E. Peck, 10 vols. (London: Ernest Benn, 1928), 1:241; hereafter referred to as Shelley, CW. The full title was *Laon and Cythna; or The Revolution of the Golden City: A Vision of the Nineteenth Century* (in the stanza of Spenser).

26. *Don Juan*, Canto 5, xxviii. Composition on Canto 5 began October 16, 1820, and by December, according to Marchand, there were 149 stanzas. L&J, 2:883.

27. *Childe Harold*, Canto 3, xci (and Byron's notes on this canto).

28. *Don Juan*, Canto 12, xx. Another reason for Byron's hostility may have been the fact that Wilberforce at one time challenged Hobhouse for the Westminster seat in the House of Commons.

29. *Don Juan*, Canto 10, lxvi–lxviii.

30. According to most accounts, Mungo Park was most likely murdered somewhere on the Niger River, between Timbuctoo and Boussa. There is no evidence that Byron went to non-Egyptian Africa, though he did intend to cross over while in Gibraltar, Marchand notes, but a contrary wind prevented the trip, and Byron left for Malta. Though no such trip was ever mentioned by Hobhouse, Marchand adds, it was a "strange statement" that Byron made to his mother on July 20, 1810: ". . . by the bye, I have now been in Asia, Africa, and the East of Europe. . . ." L&J 2:4 and note.

31. Byron to Francis Hodgson, September 3, 1811. L&J 12:89.

32. The Corn Laws of 1815, providing protective import tariffs for the wealthy landowners, were strengthened in 1822 and aggravated inflation. Woodring, *Politics in English Romantic Poetry*, 21, 207. Factory owners on the other hand opposed the Corn Laws since they raised the cost of labor.
33. *Don Juan*, Canto 12, lxxi.
34. *Don Juan*, Canto 14, lxxxii. Reiman (pers. com.) gives greater weight here than I to Byron's anger at Wilberforce as a leader of the Society for the Suppression of Vice. He notes that both Byron and Hazlitt "disliked" Wilberforce because of his support of censorship and the suppression of Sunday games, but I do not see these reasons particularly reflected in these cantos.
35. *Don Juan*, Canto 1, cxxxii.
36. Cobbett's rides, covering several counties in southern England, took place over a period from September 25, 1822 to October 26, 1826. "The Poor Man's Friend, or, A Defence of the Rights of Those, Who Do the Work and Fight the Battles." Addressed to the Working Classes of Preston, the series, which Cobbett undertook in 1826, never moved beyond four pamphlets.
37. From Dorothy to Catharine Clarkson, May 26, 1816, *Letters, Middle Years* 3:319. Despite Cobbett's concern to preserve cottage industry and village life, Dorothy disliked his rowdy radicalism, a not-unexpected attitude in one whose brother had recently written that the gods approve "the depth, and not the tumult of the soul" ("Laodamia," 1814–15).
38. "A Philosophical View of Reform," CW 7:19, was composed in the fall of 1819. In an eloquent paragraph, Shelley writes that the poet sounds the "depths of human nature" by penetrating the "spirit of the age." "Poets and philosophers are the unacknowledged legislators of the world" (20). The preface to *Laon and Cyntha* (December 1817), CW 1:239–40.

CHAPTER 5

1. Kentucky entered the union in 1792. At the time of the first Kentucky constitution, the vote to prohibit slavery in the territory was

15 for, 25 against, with clergymen and those without large land-holdings favoring Abolition. Returning to Louisville in May 1825, the Marquis de Lafayette, who had talked with Clarkson about the slave trade in 1814, noted now how much race relations had degenerated since the heady days of the American Revolution.

2. The first American edition of Clarkson's *Essay* was published in 1804 in Philadelphia. In 1816 it was reissued and promoted by the Rev. David Barrow, an indefatigable antislavery pamphleteer in Kentucky. James McPherson (pers. com. 1991) points out that the phrase "peculiar institution," from Latin *peculium*, meaning "private property," seems to have been a peculiar American usage. At the Constitutional Convention in 1787, South Carolina's Charles (Cotesworth) Pinckney argued that slaves were a form of property of particular interest to one region of the country," and that thus particular safeguards were needed in the Constitution to protect this property.

3. All of Birkbeck's volumes went into numerous editions. George read the third edition of the *Notes* and also Birkbeck's *Letters From Illinois*, published in 1818 by Taylor and Hessey, John Keats's publisher. The summer George arrived in western Kentucky, a Scottish immigrant in Louisville (one Kennedy) had just written to a cousin back home about the attractions of his newly adopted country: No king, no priests, no nobility, only "levelling democracy" and wilderness (Part of the George Keats Collection at the Filson Club Historical Society, Louisville, Ky.). Long before Birkbeck's *Notes* were published, however, America had been established in British minds as the new Jerusalem. By the end of the eighteenth century 2,000 emigrés, mostly Quakers, Unitarians, and like-minded dissenters, had already found their way into Kentucky and Pennsylvania. By the second decade of the nineteenth century, the number swelled in response to utopian calls like Birkbeck's, though the very year George and Georgiana left for America, rumblings were appearing in publications besides the *Quarterly* about the so-called better life at Birkbeck's "puffed up *paradise*." Charles E. Rob-

inson, "'Nymph of the downward smile and sidelong glance,': A Photograph of Georgiana Keats." *Collections*, University of Delaware Library Associates 2 (1987):34.

4. Birkbeck took the position that free Negroes would be more motivated to work than indolent and resentful slaves, but what worried him was the pitting of one group against the other in slave territory.

5. In *Letters from Illinois* (1818), a collection of responses to friends and acquaintances in England who had wanted to know what living in America was like, Birkbeck denounced slavery and ominously predicted the war to come. Only in the nineteenth century, with the rise of cotton (in Alabama and Mississippi) over the thriving tobacco (and rice) industry (in Virginia and Kentucky), did American slavery become as harsh as West Indian slavery. Engerman (pers. com.) points out that the westward movement encouraged the shift to larger plantation units for cotton in the deep South.

6. Letter to George, February 14, 1819. *The Letters of John Keats, 1814–1821*, ed. Hyder Edward Rollins, 2 vols. (Cambridge, Mass.: Harvard University Press, 1958), 2:60; hereafter referred to as *Letters*.

7. Georgiana's pregnancy might have caused them to move on sooner than intended, and financial setbacks might have made George reluctant to tell Keats about their change in plans.

8. To George and Georgiana, April 21, 1819 (part of the journal letter that spring). *Letters* 2:159, 159n. Keats had been reading the tenth edition (1803) of Robertson's *The History of America* (1777), but only the last two sections cover Virginia, and these only up to the seventeenth century.

9. "Ruth" was composed in Germany in 1799 and first published in 1800. Wordsworth said that he heard the tale from a wanderer in Somersetshire. *The Poetical Works of William Wordsworth*, 5 vols., eds. Ernest de Selincourt and Helen Darbishire (Oxford: Clarendon Press, 1952–59), 227–35. Lines quoted in order: 21–22, 118–120, 173, 153.

10. To George and Georgiana, October 14, 1818. *Letters*, 1:397. The Franklin he read was the popular scientist, obviously, not the cyn-

ical statesman. Rollins suggests that Keats is most likely repeating Bailey's remarks about "'the eagle-eyes of our Alfreds, our Sidneys, our Miltons. . . .'" (397n).

11. Ophia D. Smith, "The Family of Levi James and Its Alliances," *Bulletin of the Historical and Philosophical Society of Ohio* 8 (July 1950): 191–94. Part of the George Keats Collection.

12. The bill was passed on March 25, 1807, to take effect January 1, 1808, a period that left time for maneuvering. Section 2 forbids "master, factor, or owner" to "build, fit, equip, load, or to otherwise prepare any ship or vessel . . ." for slave trading, but what went on with "servants" or one's own property was another matter.

13. In at least two letters, Keats indicates that George had written something about the political and cultural life of Louisville. But long gaps in their correspondence, as well as the likelihood that several letters from George during this critical period have been lost, make the record sketchy.

14. "What Can I do to Drive Away" [To Fanny"], ll. 31–36. *The Poems of John Keats*. ed. Jack Stillinger (Cambridge, Mass.: Harvard University Press, 1978), 493; hereafter referred to as PW. Fanny showed the poem to Brown, who copied it in 1829. It was published in 1848. McGann stresses the biographical importance of the poem, saying that a careful reading "requires us to be aware of [Keats's] special feeling for his siblings, and especially for his brother George in America, who was on the verge of financial ruin" (46). The eighteenth-century myth of America as the New Jerusalem was certainly undergoing revision by the second decade of the nineteenth century.

15. Letter to George, August 1, 1816. *Letters* 1:105. Leigh Hunt, whose paternal lineage was West Indian, was ardent in his abolitionist sympathies, in both poetry and prose. In his *Autobiography* (1802), he wrote about his father, Isaac, who had come from Barbados, of his grandfather, who had been vicar there, and of his aunt Courthorpe who, on arriving in England, was dismayed to hear that her

black "servant" would be a free man on British soil. "It was frightening to hear her small mouth and little mincing tones assert the necessity not only of slaves, but robust, corporeal punishment to keep them to their duty . . . Having had slaves, she wondered how any body could object to so natural and lady-like an establishment." *The Autobiography of Leigh Hunt, With Reminiscences*, 2 vols. (New York: AMS Press, 1965), 1: 103–4.

16. Letter to Reynolds, May 3, 1818. *Letters* 1:281.

17. Letter to C.W. Dilke, September 22, 1819. *Letters* 2:180. Keats writes of reading the *Examiner* and newspaper accounts of the public meetings of "Reformer" Hunt (who had gone to jail with Cobbett in 1810).

18. Cobbett, *Rural Rides*, 118, 127, 261. Reiman (pers. com.) suggests that the rhetoric here is not so much anti-abolitionist as much as "it parallels Dickens's attack on Mrs. Jellyby in *Bleak House*, who cried over poor Africans and Asians, while treating badly her own children and her poor neighbors." Mrs. Pardiggle may also come to mind, she who forced her children to contribute to the Tockahoopo Indians. Still, Dickins's view is not the view of the anti-abolition forces who often accused abolitionists of engaging in distracting and irrelevant activities.

19. The *Times*, September 4, 1819. Charles Robinson points out (pers. com. 1991) that Keats no doubt preferred news from the *Chronicle*, a paper for which even Hazlitt retained some respect.

20. Entries for September 9, 1816. HCR 1:340, 330. Wordsworth and Coleridge had different reactions to the Corn Law of 1815, Wordsworth thinking it would help the poor, and Coleridge urging that it should be repealed.

21. Seymour Drescher, "Paradigms Tossed: Capitalism and the Political Sources of Abolition," in *British Capitalism and Caribbean Slavery*, eds. Barbara L. Solow and Stanley L. Engermann (Cambridge: Cambridge University Press, 1987), 207.

22. In the preface to *Account of the Regular Gradations in Man* (London: 1799, 144), White says he does not want to support "the pernicious

practice of enslaving mankind" nor encourage the sense of superiority of one people over another, but only to elucidate the history of mankind in an effort to establish the laws of nature. In an appendix, however, White presents selected passages from the work of Professor Soemmering's "Essay on the Comparative Anatomy of the Negro and European" (1785), which draws on Blumenbach (whom Coleridge read and commented on) and makes the kind of distinctions that would and certainly did aid and abet the enemies of the Negro.

23. Cottle, *Early Recollections* 2: 319. Cottle's poem is not without its sarcasm, directed at those who do not understand that English law "enslaves" workers. Looking back from the perspective of the *Quarterly Review*'s December 1836 article on the horrors of the factory system, Cottle can only imagine how much more horrible conditions were years earlier.

24. The quotations are from J.T. Ward, " Slavery in Yorkshire," *Bradford Textile Society Journal* (1960–61), 42; and from the *Leeds Mercury*, April 1832. Coleridge was deeply concerned about children working in the cotton factories and wrote to HCR, who was a lawyer, about prohibiting, limiting, or regulating such employment in the white-lead manufactory. HCR, 1:385, diary entry for May 3, 1813. He did not ask about laws enforcing Abolition or express interest in emancipation.

25. Robin Blackburn, *The Overthrow of Colonial Slavery, 1776–1848* (New York: Verso Publications, 1988) 146. Blackburn, in a personal communication to the author, writes that he has not "come across anything to suggest that white workers feared wage competition from free black workers." But J. Jean Hecht shows that particularly after 1783, when abandoned black seamen joined the royalist free blacks streaming in from America, the British working-class attitude toward Negroes was less kind than toward the emancipated and runaway blacks. J. Jean Hecht, "Continental and Colonial Servants in Eighteenth-Century England," *Smith College Studies in History* 40 (1954).

26. To George and Georgiana, September 21, 1819. *Letters*, 2:211. He joked about Winchester, noting "there is not one loom or any thing like manufacturing beyond bread & butter in the whole City."
27. Letter to George and Georgiana, September 17, 1819. *Letters* 2: 186.
28. The play opened May 13, 1819, and ran for several nights.
29. Brown believed that the manuscript had not even been opened. Joan Baum, *The Theatrical Compositions of the Major English Romantic Poets*, Salzburg: University of Salzburg Press, 1980, 230ff. *Otho* was first published in 1848, though Stillinger (PW, 656)) notes that some parts appeared earlier "as chapter epigraphs" in E.J. Trelawney's *Adventures of a Younger Son* (1831).
30. In *Otho*, the fanatic is Conrad, duke of Franconia, the evil genius of the play, who comes "bustling" on stage in the opening scene. Baum, 235.
31. Stanzas xiv-xvi (see below). "Isabella" was written some time between February and April 1818 (and completed by April 27, when Keats mentioned it in a letter to Reynolds). Conceived as part of a joint effort to rewrite a number of Boccaccio tales, the poem was given over entirely to Keats by Reynolds in October. Keats worked not from the Boccaccio itself but from the fifth edition (1684) of an English translation of 1620.

> With her two brothers this fair lady dwelt,
>   Enriched from ancestral merchandise,
> And for them many a weary hand did swelt
>   In torched mines and noisy factories,
> And many once proud-quiver'd loins did melt
>   In blood from stinging whip;—with hollow eyes
> Many all day in dazzling river stood,
> To take the rich-ored driftings of the flood.
>
> For them the Ceylon diver held his breath,
>   And went all naked to the hungry shark;
> For them his ears gush'd blood; for them in death

The seal on the cold ice with piteous bark
Lay full of darts; for them alone did seethe
A thousand men in troubles wide and dark:
Half-ignorant, they turn'd an easy wheel,
That set sharp racks at work, to pinch and peel.

Why were they proud? Because their marble founts
Gush'd with more pride than do a wretch's tears?—
Why were they proud? Because fair orange-mounts
Were of more soft ascent than lazar stairs?
Why were they proud? Because red-lin'd accounts
Were richer than the songs of Grecian years?
Why were they proud? again we ask aloud,
Why in the name of Glory were they proud?

The enslavement of Moors by Christians had been going on for hundreds of years, of course, as Reiman notes (pers. com.) excused, if not encouraged, by Papal discrimination between believers and nonbelievers.

32. Hardy's *Register of Shipping*, a contemporary chart, shows typical routes to India and China. Woodring notes the contemporary significance of Ceylon (*Politics in English Romantic Poetry*, 80).

33. An exception to poetry wielded in the cause of reform is the brief parody, written late, that Brown identified as a "mock extension" of *The Fairie Queene*, Book 5, ii, said to be written by one "Typographus" (see Stillinger, PW 484–85). The lines may be more significant than Brown thought, however, for in Book 5 of *The Fairie Queene*, Artegall slays Pollente, the tyrant who demands passage money and who also drowns his evil, greedy daughter, a kind of *belle dame sans merci*, whose name is "Munera."

34. Walter Jackson Bate, *John Keats* (Cambridge: Mass.: Harvard University Press, 1963), 468.

35. In the summer of 1790, when he was twelve years old, Hazlitt visited Liverpool with a friend as the guests of a Mrs. Tracey, a widow

from Jamaica, and stayed for five weeks. To his mother in July, he wrote of having met a Mr. Fisher, a very rich man, who obviously prompted the precocious Hazlitt to lofty thoughts: "The man who is a well-wisher to slavery, is always a slave himself; The King, who wishes to enslave all mankind, is a slave to ambition; The man who wishes to enslave all mankind for his King, is himself a slave to his King." From Ralph M. Wardle, *Hazlitt* (Lincoln: University of Nebraska Press, 1971), 30.

36. The "Letter" is in Hazlitt, CW 9: 13–59; it was written in August or September 1819 in response to an article in *Blackwood's Magazine*, August 1818, "Hazlitt Cross-Questioned," reputedly by Lockhart (249). In his essay "On Imitation," Hazlitt says, "to the genuine artist, truth, nature, beauty, are almost different names for the same thing," and in his essay letter to Gifford, he writes, "in seeking for truth, I sometimes found beauty." Bromwich cautions against jumping to conclusions based on repetitions of key words and phrases which may be mannerisms rather than evidence of systematic thought or coherent philosophy. David Bromwich, *Hazlitt, The Mind of a Critic* (New York: Oxford University Press, 1983), 379. Bromwich does note that Keats was one of the few readers, then, of Hazlitt's difficult 1805 "Essay on the Principles of Human Action."

37. This distinction between the urge to dominate and the desire to excel is made by Harry Levin, "Introduction to *Coriolanus*," in *William Shakespeare: The Complete Works* (The Penguin Text. rev.; Baltimore: Penguin, 1969), 1214.

38. Hazlitt, CW 7:7.

39. Hazlitt could be devilishly subtle, however, as when he wrote his publisher that Napoleon was better than the Bourbons and that a tyrant was better than tyranny (Bromwich, 54). But his larger point was that "tyrant and receptive victim are complementary elements of a single order of domination." Kevin Gilmartin, "'Victim of Argument, Slaves of Fact': Hunt, Hazlitt, Cobbett, and the Literature of Opposition," *The Wordsworth Circle* 21 (Summer 1990): 90.

40. Hazlitt has little to say about Blake, mentioning him in passing as an artist of the day who was a "profound mystic" (Hazlitt, CW 12:95). Keats nowhere gives evidence that he was familiar with Blake, though Amy Lowell feels he must have read the *Songs of Innocence*. Dilke, however, with whom Keats was living in Hampstead, was familiar with Blake and became a collector, though there is no evidence of just when he began to acquire volumes and of what.

41. From *The Spirit of the Age*, in Hazlitt, CW 11:148–49 (pub anon. 1825). Consistent always, Hazlitt had expressed similar views about Wilberforce several years earlier.

42. Though it might be said that Keats, too, was guilty of such subtle stereotyping in *The Fall of Hyperion* when he writes of the "sable" charm and dumb enchantment of dreams, it seems best to heed Bromwich's advice and not chase after words alone.

43. To George and Georgiana, January 23, 1818. *Letters* 1:214. The "King Lear" sonnet was composed in a burst of enthusiasm, Keats writes, on January 22, 1818.

44. "The condition upon which God hath given liberty to man is eternal vigilence; which condition if he break, servitude is at once the consequence of his crime and the punishment of his guilt" (Speech upon the Right of Election of the Lord Mayor of Dublin, July 10, 1790). The quotation was called to my attention by Reiman. *Bartlett's Familiar Quotations* indicates that the first part is also attributed to Thomas Jefferson (351:20). John Philpot Curran (1750–1817), lawyer, judge and statesman, was a friend of Godwin and Thomas Moore and a major orator of his time (DNB).

45. Moneta's charge to the poet in *The Fall of Hyperion*.

46. To George, March 19, 1819. *Letters* 2:80–81.

47. The ambiguous, and ambivalent, status of Moneta, goddess of memory, mother of the Muses, and Dea Moneta of the Roman mint, has been carefully analyzed by K.K. Ruthven, "Keats and Dea Moneta," *Studies in Romanticism* 15 (Summer 1976): 456. Moneta, it is suggested here, was Keats's acknowledgment of both the

"claims of poetry and those of cash necessity," views of the goddess that would have been familiar to Keats from his reading of Tooke's *Pantheon* and Burton's *Anatomy*.

48. To George, September 21, 1819. *Letters* 2:209.

49. To George, *Letters* 2:120, 184, 231.

50. To George and Georgiana, September 21, 1819. *Letters* 2:209. A year earlier, Keats had written to Benjamin Bailey that he thought he might be spending a year with George in America, but the remark probably owed more to a sense of missing George than to an intent to go to Kentucky.

51. Birkbeck, *Notes*, September 1817, 7.

52. Holmes, 90.

53. This is McGann's point, though he says that 1819 was a relatively good harvest year, an impression not supported by newspaper accounts or commentary in letters and periodicals. The *Times* states repeatedly that voluntarism can provide only temporary and inadequate relief for the homelessness, distress, and failure of government policy. McGann (drawing on Hartmann) is, however, wonderfully sensitive to the ways in which "To Autumn" suggests by artifice and silence that all was not well with Keats or the country. The very fact that the poem carries Keats away "to a charmed world far removed from the quotidian press of his money affairs and the dangerous political tensions of his society" is a myth, McGann asserts, and Keats knows it (58).

54. In *Redburn*, the narrator observes that blacks are no longer in evidence in what was once the world's largest slave-trading port. The only Negroes he sees in Liverpool are cooks and stewards who stroll the Mersey docks when their merchant ships are in port (194–95). How different from American seaport towns, he says, where Negroes "almost always form a considerable portion of the destitute."

55. To Dilke, March 4, 1820. *Letters* 2:272. Exile in America to avoid prosecution for sedition ironically reawakened Cobbett's patriotism. Since 1817, he had been living in North Hempstead, Long Island, but finding in the new land contrasts that only reminded him of better values in the old.

56. A letter from John Taylor to Joseph Severn, February 6, 1821, refers to a "letter from a Female Cousin [Mary Taylor] in Cincinnati" who has seen George and Georgiana in Louisville. *More Letters and Poems of the Keats Circle* 2 vols., 2d ed. Hyder Edward Rollins (Cambridge, Mass.: Harvard University Press, 1965), 111; hereafter referred to as *More Letters*.

57. From George to Keats, November 8, 1820. *Letters* 2:356; and in *The Keats Circle*, ed. Hyder Edward Rollins, 2 vols. (Cambridge, Mass.: Harvard University Press, 1948), 1:169; hereafter referred to as *Keats Circle*. In his letter to Keats, George states that his business partners were "the principal Iron founders in the western Country. I receive and pay all. They keep the engine in order, without expense to the Comp." George's businesses now included a steam gristmill, a sawmill, a timber business, and land speculation. George certainly was the "first citizen": He helped draft the city charter, served on the town council, was responsible for the first citizen's directory, promoted the first bridge across the Ohio River, and was active in numerous educational and cultural institutions. Robinson, "'Nymph,'" 37.

58. From George to C.W. Dilke, April 20, 1825. *Keats Circle* 1:289. The letter, several pages long, begins defensively, George well aware of the number of Keats's friends who have been critical toward him. As the letter moves on, George seems anxious to testify to his success, and to keep his distance from vulgar Americans: "We have a Philosophical Society here, not altogether uninformed, or unphilosophical, but certainly unpoetical . . ." (291).

59. From George to Valentin Llanos, July 10, 11, 1828. Llanos had become the husband of Fanny Keats on March 30, 1826. *More Letters* 1: 44–45.

60. Ibid. Reference to slaves employed in George's household can be found in obituary (December 1841) and auction notices (May 1842) in the *Louisville Daily Journal*. George used the phrase "servant hire" in the letter to Keats on November 8, 1820, when he wrote about unpaid bills (*Keats Circle* 1:168), and it is possible that this phrase

does refer to free blacks who may have worked for him in his mills or to servants in his household. But the fact, hardly surprising for the place and time, was that George did own slaves. "Free blacks being hired to work would not appear on the tax list" (James J. Holmberg, Archivist, Filson Club, in a personal communication to the author).

61. Although George did devote himself to establishing Keats's reputation in America, he did not particularly advance it with the best poetry. The "Ode to Apollo," for example, which he gave to the editor of the Louisville *Western Literary Messenger*, is a sentimental and predictable piece.

62. The remark was attributed to Keats by his friend and companion of his last days in Italy, the painter Joseph Severn (Bate, 670).

CHAPTER 6

1. Although this point is not proven, it rests on reported statements and on the known falling-off between Byron and Shelley at this time. Byron was always for Shelley "admirer, stimulus, rival, and underminer," as Nora Crook observes, and the relationship particularly after Byron moved to Pisa in November 1821 was "edgy." Nora Crook, *The "Charles the First" Draft Notebook*, The Bodleian Shelley Manuscripts (New York: Garland, 1991), 12:1.

2. Torbay had been the main anchorage of a Devon-based fleet for the blockage of Brest during the Napoleonic wars, but the fleet was blown off station. Walter Edwin Peck, *Shelley: His Life and Work*, 2 vols. (Boston: Houghton Mifflin, 1927), 2:280–81. "Torbay-rigged" might refer to a smallish boat with lots of sail, designed more for speed and maneuvers than for cruising. Building on some questionable and confusing reports at the time of Keats's death, James Rieger, in *The Mutiny Within: The Heresies of Percy Bysshe Shelley* (New York: George Braziller, 1967), suggests that Shelley's death was not accidental but the wished-for passive suicide of a gnostic who composed "imperfectly understood verse for a public he could not love" (222–23). In a letter to Bernard Barton, November 1822, Southey

pointed out the "dreadful fate" and irony of Shelley's death, like Harriet's, by drowning. NL 2:240.

3. To Gisborne. June 18, 1822, CW 10:404.

4. Shelley began working on *The Triumph of Life* in May or June 1822 and was still working on it in July, when Hunt arrived. Donald H. Reiman, *Shelley's "The Triumph of Life": A Critical Study*, University of Illinois Studies in Language and Literature, vol. 55 (Urbana, Illinois: University of Illinois, 1965) 250.

5. Reiman argues forcefully that "despair" is too strong for Shelley. Noting that Rousseau (of *Julie; ou La Nouvelle Héloise*) in *The Triumph of Life* presents the case against yielding to extremes of either optimism or despair, Reiman urges that a distinction be made between the "dark picture of human existence" in the poem, and hopelessness. *The Triumph*, Reiman contends, is no more grimly pessimistic than the nasty visions in *The Revolt of Islam* or "The Mask of Anarchy." *Shelley's "The Triumph of Life,"* 453.

6. In the preface to *Hellas*. Shelley, P&P, 406. *Hellas*, dedicated to Prince Mavrocordato, was begun in October 1821 to rouse support for the Greek fight for independence. Political slavery was man's own fault, Byron held in *Detached Thoughts*; if men "will" be slaves, then let them. Of course, unlike the enslaved Greek, the African Negro was in no position to "will" freedom.

7. Noted by Heywood in "A Yorkshire Background," 820.

8. This inequality was, of course, totally unforeseen and unintended by both Mary Wollstonecraft and Shelley, whose sympathies were for all victims of tyranny;

9. *Laon and Cythna*, 4:xxviii. Recast a few months later with a new title and without its incest motif, to accommodate a nervous publisher, *Laon and Cythna*, with some other changes, became *The Revolt of Islam*.

10. *The Revolt of Islam*, 4:xxiv, 1:xvi. Though dated 1818, it was actually published in December 1817, as Reiman points out. Shelley, P&P, xxx.

11. "America, A Prophecy," ll. 669–78. In the essay, "Logic of Political

Economy," De Quincey's point is that in America, slaves are viewed only in regard to their "praedial" uses, their ability to work the land like mere animals—a far cry from the much more various conditions of slavery in Roman times. CW 9:176.

12. "A Philosophical View of Reform," Shelley, CW 7:19. See also the notes to Lecture 9 in *The Philosophical Lectures of Samuel Taylor Coleridge*, ed. Kathleen Coburn (London: Routledge Kegan & Paul, 1949), 441. The remarks come from a Notebook entry made three days after the lecture. Coburn writes, "The large arcs of Coleridge's thinking [at this time] are nowhere better illustrated than in the analogy he draws between medieval and modern slavery at the end of Lecture IX" (introduction, 58). The lecture, reconstructed from notebook accounts and other sources, was delivered on February 22, 1819. As advertised, it was to be on the "Schoolmen [of The Middle Ages] and Scholastic Philosophy, with the opposite extremes, the Alchymists & Visionaries . . ." but Coburn is struck by the concluding passage on slavery, which was part of a harsh condemnation of commerce (Coburn, 285–88).

13. To John and Maria Gisborne, November 6, 1819. CW 10:121. An editorial note suggests that the line probably refers to the essay "A Philosophical View of Reform." This is a light-hearted letter from Shelley, though in retrospect it seems ominous in its playing out of the image of the sandy desert: "In all probability, I shall be overwhelmed by one of the tempestuous columns which are forever traversing with the speed of a storm and the confusion of a chaos that pathless wilderness."

14. Shelley had been studying Arabic with Thomas Medwin, recently returned from India. Michael Rossington, "Shelley and the Orient," *Keats-Shelley Review* (Autumn 1991): 25. A political post of some kind, Rossington suggests, would have "involved Shelley in furthering the commercial and moral designs of the British in India" (27).

15. From Leigh Hunt's preface to the edition of 1832. CW 3:227. Hunt adds that though Shelley's countrymen knew how "anxious" Shel-

ley was for the advancement of the common good, they "have yet to become acquainted with his anxiety in behalf of this particular means of it—Reform."

16. "The Mask of Anarchy," lxii; "To Sidmouth and Castlereagh: Similes for Two Political Characters of 1819," iii, iv. Sidmouth was Henry Addington, Home Secretary, identified most often by his detractors with fomenting worker discord by way of *agents provocateurs.* Castlereagh was Robert Stewart, oppressor of Ireland, war minister, and Tory leader in the House of Commons. On October 23, 1814, Hazlitt wrote, "However sturdy he may be in asserting our maritime rights he [Castlereagh] will, we imagine, go to sleep over those of humanity," and waking, find his pocket picked of his "African petitions, if indeed, he chuses to carry the credentials of his own disgrace about with him." Hazlitt, CW 7:84.

17. *The Prelude*, Book 7: ll. 701ff.

18. From, in order, Shelley's preface to *Hellas*, "A Philosohical View of Reform," and Byron's *The Age of Bronze*, CPW, 7:xiv.

19. *Prometheus Unbound*, II, iv.

20. David Brion Davis credits James Cropper (1773–1840) as the unofficial philosopher of the antislavery movement (*Problem*, 161). In 1822, Cropper organized the Liverpool division of the society and helped organize the national committee in London, where controversy developed over how best to influence Parliament and whether to advocate immediate or gradual emancipation. Cropper, a devout Quaker, worked in Liverpool for an American merchant and used the money he saved for the cause of emancipation.

21. De Quincey, "Notes on Gilfillin's Literary Potraits." CW 11:305.

22. Johnson's definition of "Grub-street" begins with a reference to writers of small histories, dictionaries, and temporary poems. Byron uses "Grub-street" in "English Bards and Scotch Reviewers" (1809).

23. "There are close parallel passages in the [1858] Lincoln and Douglas 'debates.' That the Americans were certainly unaware of the British gentlemen makes the point." James Thorpe III (pers. com.)

24. Had the duke been a King, however, he would have had to yield with a bow, such being the requirement that a monarch must bow to everyone, De Quincey pointed out.
25. Hazlitt in July 1823, from "Arguing in a Circle." CW 19:267–78. The latter half of the essay is an attack on the eloquent Burke for his glittering fallacies, but Hazlitt also gets to take some some shots at the "turn-coats" Southey and the other Lake poets (277).
26. TT, Appendix M, 2:361 (from Thomas Allsop's Report of Table Talk, 1820–1832, with John Sterling's Marginalia).
27. The reference to "canting Ludro" is in the letter to Hobhouse, January 25, 1819. Byron, L&J 6:96–97. The quotation "words—words alone" from *Troilus and Cressida* (Act V, sc. 3), appears in *Detached Thoughts*, no. 5, Byron, L&J 9:14, though, as Marchand notes in his identification of the *Troilus* reference, it is probable that an allusion to *Hamlet* was intended as well.
28. Byron, L&J 9:41.
29. Reiman (pers. com.) calls my attention to the fact that "one of Teresa Guiccioli's servants was a Negro who helped in her romance with Byron. Byron treated him and all his servants as fellow human beings."
30. Barrow's journey is mentioned in J. M. Coetzee, "A Betrayed People." Review of Noël Mostert's *Frontiers: The Epic of South Africa's Creation and the Tragedy of the Xhosa People*, in *The New York Review of Books*, January 14, 1993, 8–10. Sir John Barrow (1764–1848), Second Secretary of the Admiralty, was made a baronet in 1830 in recognition of his service to the Crown, particularly in the area of navigational science. A well-known writer on explorations, including China, which Dorothy Wordsworth read, he was a friend of John Murray and the author of 195 articles for the *Quarterly Review* (DNB). At one point in his career he was a tutor in mathematics to Lady Beaumont. By 1795, the Cape had become a controlling fortress on the passage to India. The Xhosa were fiercely independent and very different from the (West) African slaves the British were accustomed to reading about, Mostert notes. Their civilization was

indeed on the "frontier" between Cape Colony and the rest of South Africa. It is unlikely, however, that the average reader appreciated distinctions among African peoples. Moreover, the even more critical position the Cape was now assuming in British affairs would have encouraged aggressive missionary activities for purposes of imperial control.

31. Although a prefatory note indicates the main source of the tale as Joshua Pickersgill's novel *The Three Brothers* (1803), a Gothic romance, critics have shown that Byron heavily relied on several sources, particularly the Faust legend in its various transformations (Robinson, McGann). In none of the sources, however, is the devil explicitly said to be black.

32. In his analysis of the sources and meaning of the drama, particularly Act I ("by far the most imaginative and intense"), Charles Robinson argues how much the theme was owing not only to Byron's acknowledged sources, but to Shelley. Byron conceived the Stranger and Arnold as one, with the theme as a dramatization of "man's self-destruction whereby his immortal aspirations were annihilated by his own mortality" (196). Though *The Deformed Transformed* was written at the same time that Byron penned the "increasingly mellifluous" last cantos of *Don Juan*, Robinson points out, it is doubtful that Byron could have finished the drama, with its "bitter portrayal" of the failure to achieve love and transcend mortality, without yielding to "total cynicism." Charles E. Robinson, "The Devil as Doppelgänger in *The Deformed Transformed*: The Sources and Meaning of Byron's Unfinished Drama," *Bulletin of the New York Public Library* (March 1970): 171–202. The phrase "tyrannous hate" is Robinson's (200).

33. *The Deformed Transformed*, though barely into an opening chorus of Part Three, was published by John Hunt on February 20, 1824, while revolutionary movements were breaking out on the Continent, as E. H. Coleridge pointed out in his note on the drama. Coincidentally, on January 14, 1822, the Pisan circle had a self-styling satanic visitor in the person of the colorful E. J. Trelawny,

self-annointed "pirate and privateer" (in reality, a retired navy midshipman), who sailed into their lives with an American black speaking French and Italian, a reflection not so much of the Negro's accomplishment, as Trelawny's in acquiring him. According to Trelawny, however, the servant changed hands: "'In our voyage from Italy, Byron persuaded me to let him have my black servant, as, in the East, it is mark of dignity to have a negro in your establishment.'" (Trelawny, *Recollections*, 212; quoted by Marchand, *Byron, A Biography*, 3:1097.

34. Charles the First as a subject for a play had intrigued Godwin enough to recommend it to Mary for consideration (Baum, 213n).

35. *Charles the First*. There is some question about the placement of the song. Crook argues that Rossetti in 1870 was right to tack it on to Archy's speech, though it is not necessarily clear that the lines would have been in scene v (Crook, xlvii). The song has three four-line stanzas and shows no essential difference between manuscript and published versions.

36. Hazlitt, "On Paradox and Common-Place." CW 8:148. The Shelley who wrote *Prometheus* was to Hazlitt an evanescent flutter, a man without the "hard husk of nature and habit."

37. Cf. "O Slavery! thou frost of the world's prime, / Killing its flower and leaving its thorns bare!" (from the Chorus in *Hellas*, ll.676–77).

38. To Leigh Hunt, March 2, 1822. CW 10:362. The partial reference to *Lear* could suggest political events that were vitiating the noble ideas of *Prometheus Unbound*. Peck speculates that the "slight circumstance" was a cover for the increasing difficulty Shelley was having with Mary, particularly over Jane Williams, and while there is no reason to dispute the adverse influence of marital discord, an equally strong case can be made for the difficulty of the theme itself, which daily events were only complicating.

Crook, following Reiman (*Shelley's "Triumph of Life,"* 85), asserts that Shelley suffered increasingly from the failure of his work to win, and thus influence, the public (Crook, xxxii).

39. From "On this Day I Complete My Thirty-Sixth Year," stanza ii,

l. 7 (which McGann gives as "January 22nd 1824, Messalonghi"). CPW 7: 79. *The Island* was written as Byron was concluding the last cantos of *Don Juan.*

40. *Literary Gazette,* July 19, 1823. This is a review of *Don Juan,* Cantos 6,7,and 8, all three showing the "gloating brutality of a wretched debauchee" (451). Woodring emphasizes how *The Island* pays tribute to discipline, loyalty, authority, duty, and the need to subordinate the self to a leader. *Politics in English Romantic Poetry,* 222.

41. To James Montgomery in Sheffield, January 24, 182. *Letters, Later Years,* 248. Woodring points out that despite Wordsworth's growing movement toward order, he was, until 1825, still "a poet of the underdog." *Politics in English Romantic Poetry,* 146.

42. "Liberty," in particular ll. 15, 30–31, 68. PW 4:182. The fish had been a present from a Miss Jewsbury, to whom the poem is addressed, as Wordsworth explains in an accompanying note. "Humanity," intended to be a part of "Liberty," became a separate poem at the urging of Mary Wordsworth, who found the original plan unwieldy. As for poor Miss Jewsbury, she went to join her husband in India, where she died, and so the verse "Epistle" was never sent. Had it been, she might have seen the poems as gentle reproof for her cooping up natural creatures in unnatural surroundings.

43. The word "he" is also accented but is insignificant.

44. "Humanity," ll. 79–94. In noting subsequent changes both in the manuscript and published versions, de Selincourt, PW, shows that Wordsworth, though in a minor way, strengthened the antislavery sentiment, changing "still" protest to "should" and "yet that boast" (l. 83) to "proud boast!"

45. Dorothy to Catharine Clarkson, October 24, 1822. *The Letters of the Wordsworth Family,* ed. William Knight, 3 vols. (Boston: Ginn, 1907): 2:189–90. The Jonson lyric begins, "Queen and huntress chaste and fair." The parody consists of three verses of six lines each, with the tail lines: 1) "negro princess, ebon bright"; 2) "Negress excellently bright"; and 3) "sable princess, ebon bright."

46. Byatt notes "Wil*by*" in place of "Willy," but in any case, the point of the light mocking remains.
47. "On the Power of Sound" (1829), PW 2: 325.
48. Sara Hutchinson so wrote to Edward Quillinan, the husband of Doro Wordsworth, Wordsworth's daughter. *The Letters of Sara Hutchinson*, August 23, 1826 (323), and July 15, 1827 (349). Henry was the son of James ("The Colonel"), an older brother of Coleridge and the first editor of Coleridge's *Table Talk*. See Woodring, TT 1: lxivff. As Woodring indicates, the first edition was withdrawn because of anger at a reference to a family member.
49. William Hart Coleridge (1789–1849) was the son of Luke Coleridge. Southey, Letter to C.W. William Wynn, spring 1824, NL 2:265.
50. It was published anonymously in 1825 and 1826 and finally acknowledged in the third edition (1832). The quotation is from an editorial note by Thomas Sadler in Crabb Robinson's *Diary*, entry for January 10 and 22, 1824, 2:1–2. John Woolman's writings were published in Philadelphia, in 1775, in Dublin in 1794, and in London in 1824. Woolman, Crabb Robinson notes, was an illiterate tailor, a man of great modesty and love, who wrote in a simple style that might have attracted Wordsworth. It was the man, however, not the creed, that Robinson found totally admirable and "fascinating."
51. See TT 1:lxx–lxxi. In the *Notebooks*, Coleridge wrote that Henry took a position on slavery that erroneously implied the direct "politocratic power of the Gospel," meaning, perhaps, that Jesus was a moral activist. Jesus did not advocate "Abolition," Coleridge had reminded his brother, the Rev. George Coleridge, years earlier.
52. Henry Nelson Coleridge, 285–308.
53. Ibid., 194–95.
54. Quoted by Woodring in TT 1:311n. William F. Owen was the captain of HMS *Leven*.
55. TT 1: 310, July 21, 1833.
56. Wordsworth added this note to the poem, which was published in 1835.

57. The anecdote appears in a revised version of his autobiographical essay, years after Emancipation.
58. De Quincey, CW 1:19n.
59. Crabb Robinson, written in 1851, editorial note. HCR 1:336–37.

CHAPTER 7

1. It passed on July 31, 1833, four weeks after the death of Wilberforce. The last petition had come in with a reported 1,500,000 signatures. The act excluded India, Ceylon, St. Helena and the Crown colonies.

2. As used in the October 1833 issue of the *Westminster Review, negrophobia* appeared in a review of *Narrative of a Residence at the Court of London* by Richard Rush (envoy from the United States, 1817–1825), as part of a discussion of "Americanisms." Other listings in the OED show *negrophobiac* in 1867 and *negrophobist* in 1878, this last for H.M. Stanley, who used the word to refer to those who would attribute duplicity to a certain African tribe. *Negrophilism,* which seems always to have been used pejoratively to describe friends of the Negro, is cited for 1865, and *negrophilist* occurs as early as 1842. Various dictionaries of historical American usage confirm the pattern cited by the OED. In the 1820s the *Westminster Review* was one of the more influential journals against emancipation, along with the *Quarterly Review* and *Blackwoods. The Edinburgh Review* at this time took a stance for emancipation.

3. The well-known and immensely popular *Fraser's Magazine* was founded in 1830 by William Maginn. The "Discourse" appeared in the December 1849 issue and then in Carlyle's *Critical and Miscellaneous Essays,* 1872. Fred Kaplan, *Thomas Carlyle* (Ithaca: Cornell University Press, 1983), puts the piece in good perspective, noting how parts of the essay were exploited, particularly in the American South (371). Nonetheless, the facts remain that Carlyle, for a number of complex reasons, thought the Negro inferior and Emancipation a great mistake. Emancipationists were simply another another breed of the hypocritical "Sluggard-and-Scoundrel Protec-

tion Societies" he despised even more than he disliked West Indian Negroes.

4. Noted by Crabb Robinson, in an entry for February 1832. HCR 2:169.

5. Only the truths of the Gospel would matter, Coleridge held. Letter from Coleridge to Thomas Pringle (June 1833), who had been secretary of the Anti-Slavery Society since 1827. CL 6:940. The minister at the time was Earl Grey. In July 1834, the month Coleridge died, Viscount Melbourne became the new P.M.

6. Quoted by Rossington, 23.

7. TT, "On Negro Emancipation," June 8, 1833, TT, 1:385–86 [2:232]. "On the Rights of Negroes," June 15, 1833, TT, 1: 389–90 [2:233–34]. In vol. 2, Woodring presents items from a variant manuscript as Appendix H. So noted in brackets in subsequent notes.

8. The New York Public Library Rare Book Room contains letters from Toussaint, when he was commander-in-chief of St. Domingue.

9. Dewey, 92. Wordsworth saw nothing but "darkness, disorder, and misery in the immediate prospect," Dewey reports of him, seeing in Wordsworth a poet who had become argumentative, with little confidence in the people and no reason to take hope from the "unrestrained license of the multitude." In his record of conversations with Wordsworth, Dewey is clearly more interested in recording his own sentiments. He had written an impassioned speech on behalf of the Negro, pointing up differences in attitudes between the North and the South, and in effect predicting not only the Civil War but the inheritance of bitterness that would mark the heart of the Negro if attitudes were not to change. He urged his countrymen to unite in encouraging the government to turn over land, possibly one of the Californias, for the establishment of a separate Negro nation.

10. Quoted from Stephen Jay Gould, "The Moral State of Tahiti—and of Darwin," *Natural History* (October 1991) 12–19.

11. Southey, to C.W. William Wynn, June 3 and 4, 1833. NL 2:400.
12. Craton, "Jamaican Slavery," 272.
13. The Whig Reform Bill of 1832 was a movement for parliamentary reform, a reapportionment of seats by counties and boroughs to give greater power to those with smaller household qualifications. The bill was opposed by Tories who saw it as radical, and by militants, who felt it was inadequate.
14. TT, 1: 427, August 17, 1833 [2: 255, August 20, 1833].
15. The mob has no knowledge of the Constitution, imperfect as it may be and no sense of its history, Coleridge held. TT, 1:255, entry for November 20, 1831 (November 20, 1831 in 2:151). Woodring notes that Coleridge's reference to Ham is mistaken; that it was the son, Canaan, who was cursed in Genesis.
16. Crabb Robinson, entry for March 24, 1832. HCR 2:170.
17. TT, 1:386, June 15, 1833.
18. TT, 1:389–90, June 15, 1833 [2:233–34, June 17, 1833].
19. The colonies were: Bermuda, Bahamas, Jamaica, Honduras, the Virgin Islands, Antigua, Monserrat, Nevis, St. Christopher, Dominica, Barbados, Grenada, St. Vincent, Tobago, St. Lucia, Trinidad, British Guiana, Mauritius.
20. *Omniana*, 131. The heading is "The Vices of Slaves No Excuse for Slavery."
21. Crabb Robinson, July 25, 1834. HCR 2:194. In the 1840 letter to Benjamin Dockray Wordsworth mentioned, without explanation or evidence, that he had "mss verses of my own upon the subject [of emancipation]."
22. Reiman (pers. com.) makes the argument mainly for Shelley. In any case, the poets are too separate in time and different in their intentions and effects to warrant comparison. What they shared was their culture and a great faith in the powers of the poetic imagination.
23. Byatt, 68.
24. *The Prose Works of William Wordsworth*, edited by W. J. B. Owen and Jane Worthington Smyser, 2 vols. (Oxford: Clarendon Press,

1974), 3:231–74. The new volume was *Yarrow Revisited and Other Poems* 231. Crabb Robinson, entry for February 5, 1833. HCR 2:180. The Poor Law Act was passed in August 1834, but since it required periodic review, as Owen and Smyser point out, Wordsworth's remarks were timely. A modern-day reader is struck by the similarities between modern-day problems with welfare and Wordsworth's complaints over false humanitarianism and bureaucracy.

25. Part of a series composed during a recent tour with his son John and Crabb Robinson. "The Dunolly Eagle," (ll. 13–14). PW 4: 37. In the 1828 short lyric "A Morning Exercise," nature is shown to be magnificent, but also less than kind. One image in this poem is startling, as Wordsworth hears the cry of a "whip poor will" which fancy can turn into "the spirit of a toil-worn slave / Lashed out of life, not quiet in the grave (ll. 17–18)." PW, 2: 124.

26. To Dockray, April 25, 1840. *Letters of the Wordsworth Family* 3:200–2.

27. There were, of course, many sympathizers who declined commemorative invitations. On at least one occasion Clarkson was one of them, turning down an offer to contribute to the antislavery anthology, *The Bow in the Cloud*, 1834.

28. To Dockray, *Letters of the Wordsworth Family* 3:202. Wordsworth makes a historical brief for slavery, noting that it may not at all times and under all circumstances be deplored. In certain societies in the past, he notes, slavery protected the weak from the strong.

29. Simon Sebag Montefiore, "Blackness," *The New Republic* (February 8, 1993) 12. The piece is on mining villages threatened by announced closings. Many of the inhabitants, the author points out, are descendants of those who fought against the Boers in South Africa in 1902.

30. *Omniana*, no. 160, 170–71. It is impossible to say for certain when this was written. As Gittings makes clear in his introduction to the volume, *Omniana, or Horae Otiosiores*, published in 1812, was a reprinting (with some differences) of Aikens's *Athenaeum*, 1807–8, but

most of the pieces had been on hand since 1806, with Coleridge holding up the press. In 1836, Henry Nelson Coleridge reprinted Coleridge's contributions, with some corrections (*Remains*), and items added from the 1809–16 period (13).

List of Works Cited

Act of 12 Geo. 3, [May 14] 1772, K.B. *Somerset v. Stewart*. [The Mansfield Decision]. In Lofft, 1 98 *English Reporter* 499.

Act of 47 Geo. III, C.36 [March 25] 1807. An Act for the Abolition of the Slave Trade. In Sess. 1 1807 47 *Statutes at Large* 140.

Act of 3 & 4 Will. IV, C.73 [August 28] 1833. An Act for the Abolition of Slavery throughout the *British* Colonies; for promoting the Industry of the manumitted Slaves; and for compensating the Persons hitherto entitled to the Services of such Slaves. In 73 *Statutes at Large* 666.

Adams, Henry. *The History of the United States of America During the Administrations of Thomas Jefferson*. New York: The Library of America, 1986, 1:xv, "Toussaint L'Ouverture."

Aptheker, Herbert. "Anti-Slavery Medallions in the Martin Jacobowitz Collection." *Negro History Bulletin* 33 (May 1970): 115–21.

Austen, Jane. *Mansfield Park* (1814), Vol. 3 and *Emma* (1816), Vol. 4, *The Novels of Jane Austen*. Edited by R. W. Chapman. 6 vols. 3d ed. Oxford: Clarendon Press, 1932–54.

———. *Sanditon, by Jane Austen and Another Lady*. Boston: Houghton Mifflin, 1975.

Bate, Walter Jackson. *John Keats*. Cambridge, Mass.: Harvard University Press, 1963.

Baum, Joan. *The Theatrical Compositions of the Major English Romantic Poets*. Salzburg: University of Salzburg Press, 1980.

Birkbeck, Morris. *Letters from Illinois*. Philadelphia: 1818.

"Black Ivory, Britain's Infamous Slave Trade." *The British Empire*. London: BBC Time-Life Books no. 4 (1972): 85–112.

Blackburn, Robin. Letter to the author, August 15, 1988.

———. *The Overthrow of Colonial Slavery, 1776–1848*. New York: Verso Publications, 1988.

Blake, William. "London." In *Songs of Innocence and of Experience*. Edited by Sir Geoffrey Keynes. Oxford: Oxford University Press, 1977.

Blumenbach, Johann Friedrich. "Of the Negro." *On the Natural Varieties of Mankind*. 1775. Reprint. New York: Bergman Publishers, 1969: 305–12.

Bromwich, David. *Hazlitt, The Mind of a Critic*. New York: Oxford University Press, 1983.

Buten, Henry M. "Josiah Wedgwood and Benjamin Franklin." *National Philatelic Museum Bulletin* 3 (1951): 156–65.

Byatt, A. S. *Wordsworth and Coleridge in Their Time*. London: Thomas Nelson & Sons, 1970.

Byron, George Gordon, Noël Byron. *Byron's Letters and Journals*. Edited by Leslie A. Marchand. 12 vols. London: John Murray, 1973–82.

———. *Lord Byron: The Complete Poetical Works*. Edited by Jerome J. McGann. 7 vols. Oxford: Clarendon Press, 1980–93; vol. 6 (1991) is edited with Barry Weller.

———. *The Poetical Works of Lord Byron*. Edited by E.H. Coleridge. London: 1905. Reprint. John Murray, 1958.

[Carlyle, Thomas]. "Occasional Discourse on the Negro Question." *Fraser's Magazine* (December 1849), 670–79.

Checkland, S. G. "Economic Attitudes in Liverpool, 1793–1807." *The Economic History Review*, 2d ser., 5 (1952): 58–75.

Clarkson, Thomas. *An Essay on the Slavery and Commerce of the Human Species, particularly the African*. London: 1786.

———. *The History of the Rise, Progress, and Accomplishment of the Abolition of The African Slave Trade*. 2 vols. London: 1808.

Cobbett, William. *A Year's Residence in the United States of America* (1818–19). Reprint. Carbondale, Ill.: Southern Illinois University Press, 1964.

————. *Rural Rides* (1821–32). Edited by George Woodcock. Reprint. Hammondsworth: Penguin, 1967.

————. *Cobbett's [Weekly] Political Register.*

Coetzee, J. M. "A Betrayed People," review of *Frontiers: The Epic of South Africa's Creation and the Tragedy of the Xhosa People*, by Noël Mostert. *New York Review of Books*, January 14, 1993, 8–10.

Coleridge, Henry Nelson. *Six Months in the West Indies.* 3d ed. London: John Murray, 1832.

Coleridge, Samuel Taylor. *Biographia Literaria.* Edited by J. Shawcross. 2 vols. Oxford: Oxford University Press, 1954.

————. *Collected Letters of Samuel Taylor Coleridge.* Edited by Earl Leslie Griggs. 6 vols. Oxford: Clarendon Press, 1959.

————. *The Complete Poetical Works of Samuel Taylor Coleridge.* 2 vols. Edited by E. H. Coleridge. 1912 Reprint. Oxford: Clarendon Press, 1966.

————. *The Complete Poetical and Dramatic Works of Samuel Taylor Coleridge.* Edited by James Dykes Campbell. London: Macmillan & Co., 1903.

————. *The Notebooks of Samuel Taylor Coleridge.* Edited by Kathleen Coburn. vols. 1 & 2. New York: Pantheon Books, vols. 3 & 4. Princeton: Princeton University Press, 1957–1990.

————. *The Philosophical Lectures of Samuel Taylor Coleridge.* Edited by Kathleen Coburn. London: Routledge & Kegan Paul, 1949.

————. *Table Talk.* Edited by Carl Woodring. 2 vols. *The Collected Works of Samuel Taylor Coleridge*, Bollingen Series LXXV, Princeton: Princeton University Press, 1990.

————. *The Watchman.* Edited by Lewis Patton. *The Collected Works of Samuel Taylor Coleridge*, Bollingen Series LXXV. Princeton: Princeton University Press, 1970.

Cooper, Lane. *A Concordance to the Poems of William Wordsworth.* 1907. Reprint. New York: Russell & Russell, 1965.

Cottle, Basil. *Joseph Cottle of Bristol.* No. 64 in Local History Pamphlet Series, Bristol: Bristol Branch of the Historical Association, 1987.

————. *Robert Southey and Bristol.* No. 47 in Local History Pamphlet Series, Bristol: Bristol Branch of the Historical Association, 1979.

—————. Conversation with the author. Bristol, August 1988.

Cottle, Joseph. *Early Recollections Chiefly Relating to the Late Samuel Taylor Coleridge.* 2 vols. London: Longman, Rees, 1837.

—————. *Reminiscences of Samuel Taylor Coleridge.* New York: Wiley & Putnam, 1847.

Craton, Michael. "Jamaican Slavery." In *Race and Slavery in the Western Hemisphere: Quantitative Studies.* Edited by Stanley L. Engerman and Eugene D. Genovese. Princeton: Princeton University Press, 1975.

—————. *Sinews of Empire: A Short History of British Slavery.* London: Temple Smith, 1974.

Crook, Nora. *The "Charles the First" Draft Notebook.* The Bodleian Shelley Manuscripts, vol. 12. New York: Garland, 1991.

Cropper, James. *Letter addressed to the Liverpool Society for Promoting the Abolition of Slavery.* Liverpool, 1823.

Dabydeen, David B., ed. *The Black Presence in English Literature.* Manchester: Manchester University Press, 1985.

—————. *Hogarth's Blacks: Images of Blacks in Eighteenth-Century English Art.* Athens, Ga.: University of Georgia Press, 1987.

Davis, David Brion. *The Problem of Slavery in the Age of Revolution, 1770–1823.* Ithaca: Cornell University Press, 1975.

De Quincey, Thomas. *The Collected Writings of Thomas De Quincey.* 14 vols. 1853. Reprint. New and enlarged edition by David Masson. Edinburgh: Adam and Charles Black, 1889.

Dewey, Orville. *The Old World and the New. Journal of Reflections and Observations Made on a Tour in Europe.* 2 vols. New York: Harper & Bros., 1836.

Drescher, Seymour. "Paradigms Tossed: Capitalism and the Political Sources of Abolition." In *British Capitalism and Caribbean Slavery.* Edited by Barbara L. Solow and Stanley L. Engerman. Cambridge: Cambridge University Press, 1987.

Dykes, Eva Beatrice. *The Negro in English Romantic Thought.* Washington, D.C: Associated Publishers, 1942.

Ebbatson, J. Roger. "Africa Delivered: Some 'Forgotten Scribblers' on the Slave Trade." *Ariel* 4 (October 1973): 3–18.

————. "Coleridge's Ancient Mariner and the Rights of Man." *Studies in Romanticism* 2 (Summer 1972): 171–206.

Engerman, Stanley L. Letters to the author, April 10, 1993 & July 22, 1993.

Erdman, David. "Blake's Vision of Slavery," 1954. Reprint. *Blake: A Collection of Critical Essays*, ed. Northrup Frye. Englewood Cliffs, N.J.: Prentice Hall, 1966.

————. Telephone conversation with author, September 14, 1990.

Evans, Bergen, and Hester Pinney. "Racedown and the Wordsworths." *Review of English Studies* 8 (January 1932): 1–18.

Felix Farley's Bristol Journal.

Fryer, Peter. *Staying Power: The History of Black People in Britain.* London: Pluto Press, 1984.

Gibbon, Frank. "The Antiguan Connection." *The Cambridge Quarterly* 11 (1982): 298–305.

Gilmartin, Kevin. "'Victims of Argument, Slaves of Fact': Hunt, Hazlitt, Cobbett, and the Literature of Opposition." *The Wordsworth Circle* 21 (Summer 1990): 90–96.

Gould, Stephen Jay. "The Moral State of Tahiti—and of Darwin." *Natural History* (October 1991), 12–19.

Hazlitt, William. *The Complete Works of William Hazlitt.* Edited by P. P. Howe. 21 vols. New York: AMS Press, 1967.

Hecht, J. Jean. "Continental and Colonial Servants in Eighteenth-Century England." *Smith College Studies in History* 40 (1954).

Heinzelman, Kurt. "Self-Interest and the Politics of Composition in Keats's *Isabella.*" *ELH* 55 (1988): 159–193.

Heywood, Christopher. "A Yorkshire Background for *Wuthering Heights.*" *Modern Language Review* 88 (1993): 817–30.

————. Letter to the author, June 23, 1990.

————. "Yorkshire Slavery in *Wuthering Heights.*" *Review of English Studies*, n.s. 38 (May 1987): 184–198.

Holmes, Richard. *Coleridge: Early Visions.* New York: Viking, 1990.

Holmberg, James J. Letter to the author, June 14, 1991.

Hunt, Leigh. *The Autobiography of Leigh Hunt, With Reminiscences of Friends and Contemporaries.* 2 vols. New York: AMS Press, 1965.

Hutchinson, Sara. *The Letters of Sara Hutchinson, 1800–1835.* Edited by Kathleen Coburn. Toronto: University of Toronto Press, 1954.

James, William L. "The Black Man in English Romantic Literature, 1772–1833." Ph.D. diss. University of California at Los Angeles, 1977.

Johnson, Vera M., "Sidelights on the Liverpool Slave Trade: 1789–1807." *The Mariner's Mirror* 38 (1952): 276–293.

Jones, Stanley. "A Glimpse of George Keats in Philadelphia." *Keats-Shelley Memorial Bulletin* 28 (1977): 29–31.

Kaplan, Fred. *Thomas Carlyle.* Ithaca: Cornell University Press, 1983.

Keats, John. *The Keats Circle.* Edited by Hyder Edward Rollins. 2 vols. Cambridge, Mass.: Harvard University Press, 1948.

———. *The Letters of John Keats, 1814–1821.* Edited by Hyder Edward Rollins. 2 vols. Cambridge, Mass.: Harvard University Press, 1958.

———. *More Letters and Poems of the Keats Circle.* Edited by Hyder Edward Rollins. 2 vols. 2d ed. Cambridge, Mass.: Harvard University Press, 1965.

———. *The Poems of John Keats.* Edited by Jack Stillinger. Cambridge, Mass.: Harvard University Press, 1978.

Kirk, Naomi J. "George Keats." *Filson Historical Quarterly* (Louisville, Ky.) 8 (April 1934): 88–96.

———. "Memoir of George Keats." *The Poetical Works and Other Writings of John Keats.* Rev. ed. Edited by Maurice Buxton Forman. 8 vols. New York: Charles Scribner's Sons, 1938.

Klein, Herbert S. "The Atlantic Slave Trade and Its Impact on Africa and America." Paper presented at the Conference on Crosscurrents of Culture, 1492–1992. New York University, January 31, 1992.

———. "The English Slave Trade to Jamaica, 1782–1808." *The Economic History Review,* 2d ser. 31 (February 1978): 25–45.

Lamb, Charles. "Imperfect Sympathies." *The Works of Charles and Mary Lamb.* Edited by E. V. Lucas. 5 vols. New York: G. P. Putnam, 1903, 2:58–64

———. *The Letters of Charles Lamb;* to which are added those of his sister. Edited by E. V. Lucas. 3 vols. New York: AMS Press, 1968.

Larkin, Peter. "'Fears in Solitude': Readings (from) the Dell." *The Wordsworth Circle* 22 (Winter 1991): 11–14.

Lewis, Matthew Gregory, *Journal of a West India Proprietor.* 1834. Reprint. New York: Negro University Press, 1969.

The Leeds Mercury, April 1832.

Levin, Harry. "Introduction to *Coriolanus.*" In *William Shakespeare. The Complete Works.* Penguin Text, revised. Baltimore: Penguin, 1969.

Literary Gazette, July 19, 1823, 451.

Liverpool Saturday's Advertiser, November 24, 1810.

Macrae, Colin [of Demerara]. *Suggestion of a Plan for the Effectual Abolition of Slavery in all the British West India Colonies.* London: November 1830.

Marshall, Peter. *The Anti Slave Trade Movement in Bristol.* No. 37 in Local History Pamphlet Series, Bristol: Bristol Branch of the Historical Association, 1968.

Marchand, Leslie A. *Byron: A Biography.* 3 vols. New York: Knopf, 1957.

Martineau, Harriet. "View of Slavery and Emancipation." *Society in America.* New York: 1837.

McKusick, James C. "'That Silent Sea': Coleridge, Lee Boo, and the Exploration of the South Pacific." *The Wordsworth Circle* 24 (Spring 1993): 102–106.

McPherson, James M. Letter to the author, October 15, 1991.

Melville, Herman. *Redburn, His First Voyage.* 1849. Reprint. New York: Anchor Doubleday, 1957.

Miall, David. "The Campaign to Rescue Coleridge Cottage." *Coleridge Bulletin* 1 (Summer 1988): 8.

Montefiore, Simon Sebag. "Blackness." *The New Republic* 8 February 1993: 11–13.

Moorman, Mary. *William Wordsworth, A Biography.* 2 vols. Oxford: Clarendon Press, 1957.

More, Hannah. *Memoirs of the Life of Mrs. Hannah More.* Edited by William Roberts. 2 vols. New York: Harper & Bros., 1834.

The Morning Chronicle.

The Morning Post.

Morrison, Anthea. "Samuel Taylor Coleridge's Greek Prize Ode on the Slave Trade." In *An Infinite Complexity: Essays in Romanticism*. Edited by J. R. Watson. Edinburgh: Edinburgh University Press, 1983.

Morton, Thomas. *The Slave, A Musical Drama in Three Acts*. Produced at Theatre-Royale in London, 1818.

Nelson, Janet. Letter to the author, October 10, 1988.

Newton, John. *Journal of a Slave Trader, 1750–1754*. Edited by Bernard Martin and Mark Spurrell. London: Epworth Press, 1962.

The Observer; Being a Transient Glance at About Forty Youths of Bristol, 1795.

Pares, Richard. *A West India Fortune*. New York: Longmans, Green, 1950.

Peacock, Thomas Love. *The Works of Thomas Love Peacock*. Edited by H. F. B. Brett-Smith and C. E. Jones. 10 vols. London: Constable, 1934.

Peck, Walter Edwin. *Shelley: His Life and Work*. 2 vols. Boston: Houghton Mifflin, 1927.

Reiman, Donald H. Letter to author, September 25, 1993.

———. "Shelley as Agrarian Reactionary." In *Romantic Texts and Contexts*. Columbia: University of Missouri Press, 1987.

———. *Shelley's 'The Triumph of Life': A Critical Study*. Studies in Language and Literature. Vol. 55. Urbana, Illinois: University of Illinois, 1965.

Richardson, David. *The Bristol Slave Traders*. No. 65 in Local History Pamphlet Series, Bristol: Bristol Branch of the Historical Association, 1985.

Rieger, James. *The Mutiny Within: The Heresies of Percy Bysshe Shelley*. New York: George Braziller, 1967.

Robertson, William. *The History of America*. 3 vols. London, 1796.

Robinson, Charles E. "The Devil as Doppelgänger in *The Deformed Transformed*: The Sources and Meaning of Byron's Unfinished Drama." *Bulletin of the New York Public Library* (March 1970): 171–202.

———. Letter to the author, May 15, 1991.

———. "'Nymph of the downward smile, and sidelong glance': A Photograph of Georgiana Keats." *Collections*, University of Delaware Library Associates 2 (1987): 26–43.

Robinson, Henry Crabb. *Diary, Reminiscences, and Correspondence of Henry Crabb Robinson.* Edited by Thomas Sadler. (2 vols. in 1). Boston: Houghton Mifflin, 1898.

Roe, Nicholas. *Wordsworth and Coleridge: The Radical Years.* Oxford: Oxford University Press, 1988.

Rossington, Michael. "Shelley and the Orient." *Keats-Shelley Review* (Autumn 1991): 18–36.

Rubenstein, Christopher. "A New Identity for the Mariner." Paper presented at the Second Coleridge Conference. Nether Stowey, Cannington College, August 1990.

Rushton, Edward. *Poems and other writings to which is added "A Sketch of the Life of the Author."* 2d ed. London: 1824.

Ruthven, K.K. "Keats and Dea Moneta." *Studies in Romanticism* 15 (Summer 1976): 445–59.

St. Clair, William. "The Impact of Byron's Writings: An Evaluative Approach." In *Byron: Augustan and Romantic.* Edited by Andrew Rutherford. London: Macmillan, 1990.

Sanborn, Geoffrey. "The Madness of Mutiny: Wordsworth, the *Bounty* and *The Borderers.*" *The Wordsworth Circle* 23 (Winter 1992): 35–42.

Shelley, Percy Bysshe. *The Complete Works of Percy Bysshe Shelley.* Edited by Roger Ingpen and Walter E. Peck. 10 vols. London: Ernest Benn, 1928.

———. *Shelley's Poetry and Prose.* Edited by Donald H. Reiman and Sharon B. Powers. New York: Norton, 1977.

Smith, Ophia D. "The Family of Levi James and Its Alliances." *Bulletin of the Historical and Philosophical Society of Ohio* 8 (July 1950): 191–94.

Solow, Barbara L. and Stanley L. Engerman. "British Capitalism and Caribbean Slavery: The Legacy of Eric Williams: An Introduction." In *British Capitalism and Caribbean Slavery*, edited by Barbara L. Solow and Stanley L. Engerman. New York: Cambridge University Press, 1987.

Southey, Robert. *Letters from England.* Edited by Jack Simmons. 1807.
Reprint. London: Cresset Press, 1951.
———. *New Letters of Robert Southey.* Edited by Kenneth Curry. 2 vols.
New York: Columbia University Press, 1965.
———. *Omniana.* Edited by Robert Gittings. Carbondale, Ill.: Southern Illinois University Press, 1969.
Stedman, John Gabriel. *Narrative of a Five Years' Expedition Against the
Revolted Negroes of Surinam.* Transcribed for the first time from the
original 1790 manuscript. Edited by Richard Price and Sally Price.
Baltimore: Johns Hopkins University Press, 1988.
Stillinger, Jack. "Pictorialism and Matter-of-Factness in Coleridge's
Poems of Somerset." *The Wordsworth Circle* 20 (Spring 1989): 62–68.
Thorpe, James III. Letter to the author, April 20, 1993.
The Times (London).
Todd, F. M. "Aftermath." *Politics and the Poet: A Study of Wordsworth.*
London: Metheuen, 1957,
Vigier, François. *Change and Apathy: Liverpool and Manchester During the
Industrial Revolution.* Cambridge, Mass.: MIT Press, 1970.
Wadström, C. B. *Observations on the Slave Trade and a Description Of Some
Part of the Coast of Guinea.* London: 1789.
Walvin, James. *Slavery and the Slave Trade: A Short Illustrated History.*
London: Macmillan, 1983.
Ward, J. T. "Slavery in Yorkshire." *Bradford Textile Society Journal*
(1960–61), 42.
Wardle, Ralph M. *Hazlitt.* Lincoln: University of Nebraska Press,
1971.
The Westminster Review (October 1833), 374.
Whalley, George. "Bristol Library Borrowings of Southey and Coleridge, 1793–98." *The Library* 4 (September 1949): 114–32.
———. "Coleridge and Southey in Bristol, 1795." *Review of English
Studies* 1 (1950): 324–40.
White, Charles. *An Account of the Regular Gradations in Man and in Different Animals and Vegetables.* London: 1799.
Whiteley, Henry. *Three Months in Jamaica, in 1832.* The Anti Slavery
Society, no. 15, 1832.

Wood, G. Bernard. "A Negro Trail in the North of England." *Country Life Annual* (1967), 41–43.

Woodring, Carl. "On Liberty in the Poetry of Wordsworth." PMLA 70 (December 1955): 1033–48.

———. *Politics in English Romantic Poetry.* Cambridge, Mass.: Harvard University Press, 1970.

———. *Politics in the Poetry of Coleridge,* Madison: University of Wisconsin Press, 1961

Wordsworth, Dorothy. *The Journals of Dorothy Wordsworth, 1800–1803.* Edited by Ernest de Selincourt. 2 vols. Reprint. Hamden, Conn.: Archon Books, 1970.

Wordsworth, John. *The Letters of John Wordsworth.* Edited by Carl Ketcham. Ithaca: Cornell University Press, 1969.

Wordsworth, William. *The Borderers.* Edited by Robert Osborn. Ithaca: Cornell University Press, 1982.

———. *Home in Grasmere.* Edited by Beth Darlington Ithaca: Cornell University Press, 1977.

———. *The Letters of William and Dorothy Wordsworth: The Early Years.* 2d ed. Edited by Chester L. Shaver. Oxford: Clarendon Press, 1967.

———. *The Letters of William and Dorothy Wordsworth: The Middle Years.* 2 vols. Rev. Ed. Edited by Mary Moorman (with Alan G. Hill). Oxford: Clarendon Press, 1969–70.

———. *The Letters of William and Dorothy Wordsworth: The Later Years,* 3 vols. Rev. Ed. Edited by Alan G. Hill. Oxford: Clarendon Press, 1978–88.

———. *Letters of the Wordsworth Family.* 3 vols. Edited by William Knight. Boston: Ginn, 1907.

———. *The Poetical Works of William Wordsworth.* Edited by Ernest de Selincourt and Helen Darbishire. 5 vols. Oxford: Clarendon Press, 1952–59.

———. *The Prelude.* Edited by Jonathan Wordsworth, M. H. Abrams, and Stephen Gill. New York: Norton, 1979.

———. *The Prose Works of William Wordsworth.* Edited by W. J. B. Owen and Jane Worthington Smyser. 3 vols. Oxford: Clarendon Press, 1974.

————. *William Wordsworth's Poems in Two Volumes and Other Poems, 1800–1807*. Edited by Jared Curtis. Ithaca: Cornell University Press, 1983.

Index

Abolition Act: xii, 2, 3, 10, 32, 35, 55, 61, 62, 71, 84, 89, 93, 111, 160, 162

Abolition bill: 15, 72, 73, 74, 75, 112, 121, 124, 179, 211 n.12

Adams, Henry: 70

Africa. *See* Cape Town; Gold Coast; Guinea Coast; Sierra Leone; West Africa

Albion, The (Liverpool): 169

Alfoxden: 28, 37

America: 44, 60, 61, 78, 101, 102, 103, 104, 105, 106, 107, 108, 110, 119, 120, 129, 131, 132, 133, 134, 162, 177, 179, 209 n.3, 210 n.5

American Revolution: 7

Antigua: 32, 52

Audubon, John James: 105, 106, 129

Austen, Jane: and *Emma*, 6; and *Mansfield Park*, 31, 52, 198 n.3; and *Sandition*, 58, 198 n.3

Bakewell, Thomas: 129, 130

Barbados: 59, 90, 91, 93, 143, 145

Barbauld, Mrs.(Anna Letitia): 51, 123

Barrow, John: 146

Benezet, Anthony: 13

Bentley, Thomas: 7

Berwick Advertiser: 173

Birkbeck, Morris: 102, 103, 105, 107, 109, 113, 120, 124, 130, 131, 132

Birmingham: 43, 80, 131, 194 n.29

Black Boy Inn: 2

Blake, William: 9, 14, 15, 36, 45, 47, 50, 57, 120, 123, 139, 185 n.26

Bolton, John: 59, 200 n.9

Bonaparte (Buonaparte), Napoleon. *See* Napoleon

Bowyer, Robert: 77, 115

Bristol Corporation: 5

Brontë, Emily: 58, 198 n.4
Brothers (slave ship): 3, 183 n.9
Byron, Lord (George Gordon): and Wordsworth, 64; *Childe Harold's Pilgrimage*, 80, 88, 96; *The Corsair*, 81, 86, 89; *The Deformed Transformed*, 147; *Detached Thoughts*, 145, 146, 166; *Don Juan*, 40, 81, 84, 86, 87, 96–99, 124, 150, 151, 166; *Eastern Tales*, 80; *The Giaour*, 86, 88; *The Island*, 9, 150, 151; "Ode to Napoleon Buonaparte," 80; "The Prisoner of Chillon," 80, 153; "Sonnet to Chillon," 92

Cambridge Intelligencer: 12
Cape Town: 110, 111, 146, 147
Caribbean. *See* Barbados; Jamaica; West Indies
Carlyle, Thomas: 96, 162, 170
Clarkson, Thomas: 3, 4, 5, 10, 12, 13, 17, 34, 49, 52, 70, 74, 75–76, 84, 100, 102, 108, 120, 145, 155, 158, 161, 190 n.54
Cobbett, William: 71, 72, 98, 99, 100, 101, 103, 106, 109, 110, 112, 113, 124, 131, 132, 134, 158, 162, 166
Coleridge, Henry Nelson: 32, 156, 157, 158, 159, 171
Coleridge, Samuel Taylor: "The Aeolian Harp," 17; *The Ancient Mariner*, 12, 27, 42, 46, 47–51, 53, 54, 55, 76, 105, 118, 153, 168; and Bristol, 4, 5, 15, 19, 28, 38, 168, 188 n.42; and *The Watchman*, 19, 20, 21, 24, 25, 26, 35, 43, 55, 160; *Biographia Literaria*, xii, 39; "Fears in Solitude," 25, 38–40, 41, 42, 44–45, 66; "France, An Ode," 39, 40–41, 42, 43; *The Friend*, 42; "[Greek] Ode on the Slave Trade," 10–12, 68; "Kubla Khan," 26; Lecture on the Slave Trade, 9, 10, 15, 17–19, 20, 68; "Lines Written at Shurton Bar," 4; *Lyrical Ballads. See* Wordsworth; "A Moral and Political Lecture On the Present War," 5; *Notebook* entries, 43, 55, 72, 222 n.12; "Ode on the Departing Year," 27; *Omniana*, 52, 93, 189 n.52; on the Ministerial Plan, 163; on the Reform Bill, 167; "On the Slave Trade," xii, 5, 19, 21–25, 26, 38, 40, 68, 160; "Psyche," 76; "Reflections on Having Left a Place of Retirement," 18, 20, 39; "Religious Musings," 20–21, 24, 54
Coleridge, William Hart: 156, 157
Cooper, Thomas: 130
Corn Laws: 98

Cottle, Joseph: 8, 12, 48, 113, 190 n.1
Cowper, William: 71, 72, 174

Darwin, Charles: 165–66, 169
De Quincy, Thomas: 2, 3, 74, 87, 139, 143, 144, 160
Dewey, Orville: 165, 191 n.3
Dockray, Benjamin: 177, 178, 231 n.21, 232 n.28
Dominica: 10, 53, 59, 116
Dyer, George: 5

Edinburgh Evening Post: 174
Edinburgh Review: 77, 162
Edwards, Bryan: 93
Emancipation: xii, 3, 31, 59, 158, 159, 162, 163, 166, 168, 169, 171, 172, 173
Emerson, Ralph Waldo: 177
Examiner: 108

Felix Farley's Bristol Journal: 3, 73, 112, 174
Fox, Charles James: 46
Franklin, Benjamin: 105
Fraser's Magazine: 162, 174
French Revolution: 5, 13, 29, 39, 42, 45, 67, 92, 94, 134

Galton, Samuel: 8
Gentleman's Magazine: 89
George IV: 99
Gibbon, Edward: 83, 164

Gisborne, John: 136
Godwin, William: 21, 45, 53, 69, 148
Gold Coast: 8, 90
Guadaloupe: 62
Guinea cargo: 12, 114
Guinea Coast: 14, 26, 40, 47, 52, 88, 131. *See also* West Africa

Haiti (Hayti): 94, 141, 142, 155, 164. *See also* St. Domingue
Haitian Revolution: xii, 66, 70, 81, 134
Haydon, Benjamin: 128, 178, 179
Hazlitt, William: 16, 30, 38, 48, 62, 117, 120, 122, 137, 138, 143, 144, 145, 146, 148, 150, 215 n.35; on *Coriolanus*, 121, 122–23, 126, 127, 148; "Letter to Gifford," 121, 122, 125
Hunt, Henry: 100, 109, 115
Hunt, Leigh: 108, 120, 121, 136, 140, 141, 150, 211 n.15
Hutchinson, Henry: 52

Jacobin: 6, 8, 11, 29, 43, 92
Jamaica: 2, 10, 34, 53, 58, 64, 66, 73, 90, 93, 94, 114, 143, 164, 166, 167, 170, 171, 173, 206 n.23
James, C. L. R: xii, xiii
Jefferson, Thomas: 61, 69, 107
Johnson, Joseph: 14

Keats, George: 102, 103, 104,
106, 107, 108, 109, 110, 115,
117, 119, 122, 123, 126, 127,
128, 129, 130, 132, 133, 134,
219 n.60
Keats, John: and Fanny Brawne,
108, 115, 120, 126, 127; *The
Champion*, 115; *The Fall of Hy-
perion*, 26, 126, 127, 128, 135;
Endymion, 103, 121; *Hyperion*,
119, 120, 128; "Isabella," 117–
19; "La Belle Dame Sans
Merci," 148, 190 n.58;
"Lamia," 125; "On Sitting
Down to Read King Lear
Once Again," 124–25; *Otho the
Great*, 115, 116, 117; "Sleep
and Poetry," 119; "To Au-
tumn," 107, 119, 131, 218
n.53; "To Fanny," 107; "To
My Brother George," 108
Keats, Tom: 102
Kendal Mercury: 174
Kentucky. *See* Louisville
Kingston Mercantile Advertiser: 180

Lamb, Charles: 76, 78, 81, 157
Lancaster: 58, 59, 177
Leeds Mercury: 114
Leyland, Thomas: 2
Lewis, Matthew Gregory
(Monk): 34, 39, 95, 192 n.14,
205 n.14, 206 n.24
Liberal, The: 136, 144

Literary Gazette: 151
*Liverpool Chronicle and General Ad-
vertiser:* 174
Liverpool Gore General Advertiser:
172
Liverpool Saturday Advertiser: 77
London Magazine: 148
London Times. See Times (London)
L'Ouverture, Toussaint. *See*
Toussaint L'Ouverture
Louisville: 102, 129, 130, 132,
134

Manchester: 41, 80, 111, 112,
113, 134, 140
Mansfield Decision: 23, 44, 72,
110, 183 n.10
Mavrocordato, Prince Alexander:
138, 221 n.6
Melville, Herman: 2, 196 n.43,
204 n.4, 218 n.54
Middle Passage: 3, 4, 14, 40, 47,
50, 65, 159, 160, 181, 181 n.3
Montgomery, James: 152
More, Hannah: 7, 44, 184 n.22
"Morgannwg" (Edward Wil-
liams): 18
Morning Chronicle: 15, 110
Morning Post: 13, 42, 43, 60, 62,
65, 169. *See also* Stuart, Daniel
Morton, Thomas: 85, 204 n.8

Napoleon: 8, 61, 62, 63, 66, 67,
70, 72, 78, 92, 121, 124

Index

Nevis: 31, 32, 33, 73, 192 n.13
Newton, John: 48–49, 195 n.40

Observer (Bristol): 16
Othello: 81, 104, 147

Pantisocracy: 13, 17, 33, 52
Park, Mungo: 97, 207 n.30
Peacock, Thomas Love: 78, 86, 187 n.36
Peterloo: 112, 114, 131, 139, 140, 179. *See also* Manchester
Pinney, Azariah: 29, 30, 31, 35
Pinney, Charles: 31
Pinney, John Frederick: 30, 31, 35
Pinney, John Pretor: 29, 30, 31, 32, 33, 34, 35, 73–74, 93, 191 n.8 & 11, 202 n.28
Pitt, William (prime minister): 37, 92, 124, 202 n.31
Poole, Thomas: 5, 25, 30, 33

Quarterly Review: 103

Racedown Lodge: 28, 29, 30, 31, 33, 35, 52
Reform Bill: 167
Reign of Terror. *See* French Revolution
Robertson, William: 104
Robinson, Henry Crabb: 85, 100, 112, 157, 161, 176, 179
Roscoe, William: 2, 182 n.5

Rushton, Edward: 3, 51, 182 n.8

St. Domingue (St. Domingo) xii, 11, 26, 36, 61, 62, 66, 67, 69, 70, 95, 106, 138. *See also* Haiti
St. Kitts: 2
St. Vincent: 172
Scott, Walter: 59, 80, 134, 173
Shelley, Percy Bysshe: *Adonais*, 134; *Alastor*, 177; "A Philosophical View of Reform," 101, 140; *The Cenci*, 118, 139, 148; *Charles the First*, 137, 148–50; *Hellas*, 137; "Hymn to Intellectual Beauty," 82; "Julian and Maddalo," 138; *Laon and Cythna*, 101, 139; "The Mask of Anarchy," 131, 140, 141; "Ozymandias," 140; *Prometheus Unbound*, 119, 126, 137, 142, 150; "To Sidmouth and Castlereagh," 140–41, 223 n.16; *The Triumph of Life*, 137, 148, 149, 150
Sierra Leone: 89, 90, 116
Slave trade. *See* West Indian trade; West Indies
Slavers: 2, 16, 21
Smith, Adam: 23, 71
Smith, William Sidney: 83, 204 n.6
South Africa. *See* Cape Town
Southey, Robert: and alarmism, 100; and Bristol, 7, 12; and

Southey, Robert *(continued)*
Emancipation, 163; as Laureate, 166; in Birmingham, 43; *Letters from England*, 60, 71; "The Sailor Who Had Served in the Slave Trade," 12, 17, 48–53, 54; *Wat Tyler*, 13, 186 n.32
Southey, Tom: 47, 52
Stedman, Captain J. G: 14–15, 17, 36, 43, 86, 187 n.35, 193 n.19
Stephen, James: 2, 40
Stuart, Daniel: 42, 62, 76. *See also Morning Post*

Thelwall, John: 11
Times (London): 12, 21, 41, 43, 67, 83, 84, 89, 90, 91, 94, 111, 116, 142, 169, 170, 171
Tobago: 172
Tobin, James Webbe: 35
Toussaint L'Ouverture: xi, xii, xiii, 26, 61, 68, 69, 70, 81, 82, 141, 153, 177. *See also* Wordsworth, William
Traffick, *See* West Indies, Middle Passage
Tyne Mercury; or Northumberland, Durham, and Cumberland Gazette: 173

Vasa (Vassa), Gustavus: 36
Voodoo: xii, 11, 193 n.20

Wade, Josiah: 92
Wadström, C. B: 14, 22
Walpole, Horace: 7, 44
Watchman, The. See Coleridge, Samuel Taylor
Wedgwood, Josiah: 6
Wedgwood medallion: 6, 7, 114
Wedgwood, Tom: 192 n.11
Wellington, Duke of: 97, 169
West Africa: 7. *See also* Guinea Coast
West Indian lobby: 21, 34, 44
West Indian trade: and rum, 2, 95; and sugar, 1, 14, 15, 19, 144
West Indies: 1, 7, 8, 33, 39, 44, 47, 52, 53, 55, 59, 61, 66, 67, 95, 109, 110, 111, 112, 131, 134, 139, 142, 147, 156, 158, 165, 170, 178, 179, 197 n.46. *See also* Barbados; Dominica; Guadaloupe; Jamaica; Nevis; St. Domingue; St. Kitts; St. Vincent; Tobago
Westminster Review: 162, 170
Westmorland Gazette and Kendal Advertiser: 170
White, Charles: 113
Whiteley, Henry: 171
Wilberforce, William: 2, 12, 21, 23, 40, 74, 86, 89, 91, 96, 97, 98, 99, 100, 109, 124, 132, 145, 156, 161
William IV: 172

Williams, Edward: 136

Wollstonecraft, Mary: 138

Wordsworth, Dorothy: 6, 28, 30, 31, 52, 60, 61, 92, 100, 155, 199 n.736

Wordsworth, John: 52, 78, 203 n.36

Wordsworth, William: "The Armenian Lady's Love," 160; "The Banished Negro," *see* "September 1, 1802"; "Blest Statesman," 175; *The Borderers*, 45, 51, 56, 69; "The Brothers," 45; "The Discharged Soldier," 53; "The Dunolly Eagle," 176; "Humanity," 71, 153–55, 176, 202 n.24; "Liberty," 152, 153, 176; *Lyrical Ballads*, 37, 42, 45, 46, 47, 53, 54, 62, 69, 76, 113, 154, 176, 195 n.38; "Michael," 46; "The Intimations Ode," 148; "On the Power of Sound," 156; "Queen and Huntress Chaste and Fair," 155–56; "Personal Talk," 66; Preface to *Lyrical Ballads*, 45, 46, 68, 76; *The Prelude*, 9, 45, 48, 60, 65, 70, 71, 121, 141, 155; *The Recluse*, 42, 54; "Resolution and Independence," 69, 177; "Ruth," 104–05; "September 1, 1802," 60–61, 62, 63–66, 67, 68, 72, 155, 175; "To Thomas Clarkson," 74–75; "To Toussaint L'Ouverture," xi, 61, 63, 67–71, 72, 164, 175; "We Are Seven," 35